KU-608-965

PUBLIC SPEAKING

W. SUSSEX INSTITUTE
OF
HIGHER EDUCATION
LIBRARY

GARY T. HUNT

California State University
at Los Angeles

Prentice-Hall, Inc.
Englewood Cliffs, New Jersey

To Marilyn

Library of Congress Cataloging in Publication Data

Hunt, Gary T
    Public speaking.
    Bibliography: p. 33, 141, 201, 305
    Includes index.
    1. Public speaking.   I. Title.
PN4121.H863   808.5'1   80–21508
ISBN 0–13–738807–1

© 1981 by Prentice-Hall, Inc.
Englewood Cliffs, New Jersey

All rights reserved.
No part of this book may be reproduced
in any form or by any means
without permission in writing from the publisher.

Printed in the United States of America.

10 9 8 7 6 5 4 3 2 1

Prentice-Hall International, Inc., *London*
Prentice-Hall of Australia, Pty. Ltd., *Sydney*
Prentice-Hall of Canada, Ltd., *Toronto*
Prentice-Hall of India Private Limited, *New Delhi*
Prentice-Hall of Japan, Inc., *Tokyo*
Prentice-Hall of Southeast Asia (Pte.) Ltd., *Singapore*
Whitehall Books Limited, *Wellington, New Zealand*

Art director: Florence Dara Silverman
Book design: William Gray
Cover art: Bill Longacre
Cover design: A Good Thing, Inc.
Drawings: Herman Costa
Photo research: Anita Duncan

PREFACE

Public Speaking is a newcomer to a field already crowded with textbooks, some of which are widely used and respected. If I have ventured to add to their number, it is because I think that *Public Speaking* is a type of textbook that has not previously been available to beginning speech students. This book treats public speaking as a communication skill that is valuable in itself, to be sure, but has even more value as a help in every student's career after college, no matter what field he or she may enter. The book is thus practical and career oriented. Theory is not ignored, but the emphasis is consistently on the practice of good public speaking—on learning skills to be used effectively in a variety of social situations and jobs. The book uses professional speeches and hypothetical work-related examples to demonstrate to students that public speaking is a communication tool essential to success in most jobs.

Each chapter begins with a list of Tips for Speakers, a selection of dos and don'ts as a guide to mastering an aspect of public speaking. The chapters themselves are easy to read and generously illustrated with examples, sample speeches, and drawings. Each includes a summary and exercises. Many have complete sample speeches.

The book is divided into four sections. Part One, "Orientation," seeks to familiarize the student with the topic of public speaking. It includes the Introduction and a chapter on listening.

Parts Two and Three discuss the basic elements that make up all effective public speaking. Part Two, "Speech Variables," concentrates on how to prepare a successful speech. It begins with Chapter 3 on audience analysis, which emphasizes the need for a speaker to know as much about an audience as he or she can ascertain. Chapter 4 guides students in choosing and researching a topic and includes a section on how to use a library. Chapter 5 shows students several ways to outline and organize their speeches. Chapter 6 discusses the need for a sound and logical presentation and demonstrates the kinds of logical errors that they should avoid as speakers. Chapter 7 teaches students how to prepare effective introductions and conclusions to their speeches. Chapter 8 discusses the use and usefulness of various types of visual supplements to speeches.

Part Three, "Speaker Variables," shifts the emphasis from the content of the speech to the contribution of the speaker to effective public speaking. It begins with Chapter 9, which shows the need for a speaker to convince an audience of his or her expertise and reliability. Chapter 10 discusses the importance of language in public speaking and demonstrates how to use it effectively. Chapter 11 concentrates on speech delivery and includes both verbal and nonverbal techniques.

In Part Four, "Types of Speeches," the basic elements of good speaking discussed in the first eleven chapters are applied to speaking situations. Chapter 12 analyzes informative speaking—what makes a successful informative speech and how to prepare one. Chapters 13 and 14 are devoted to persuasive speaking. Persuasion in American society is discussed; and students are taught how to put together an effective persuasive speech and to analyze the ethics of a given persuasive situation. Since most people have to give an address on a special occasion at some point, Chapter 15 includes discussions and examples of introductory speeches, eulogies, dedications, and similar addresses. The last chapter, "Speaking and Careers," seeks to orient the student to the post-classroom uses of public speaking.

Since concepts discussed in all of the chapters are related to one another, there is cross-referencing to enable students and professors to refer backward or forward as discussions intermesh. As a further help to teaching the course, a combined Teacher's Manual and Test Item File has been prepared.

Acknowledgments   This book has benefited from the reviews and comments of many of my colleagues in the field. I would like to thank Glenn Harwood, William Wiethoff, Nancy Arnett, Allen Weitzel, B. Bruce Wagener, Richard L. Johannesen, Douglas Freeman, Bernard Brommel, Wil A. Linkugel, Liz Jordan-Huenberg, Marilyn Cristiano, Hazel Heiman, Randy Lake, Bruce Gronbeck, Dennis Bormann, Richard Katula, Martha Haun, and Caroline Drummond. At Prentice-Hall, I would like to thank first my editors John Busch, who originated this project, and Gerald Lombardi, who saw it through; Anne Pietropinto, its production editor; Florence Silverman, its art director; and Ray Keating, the book maufacturing buyer. I would also like to give special thanks to Herman Costa, who drew the cartoons, and to Kevin Mulligan, Howard Cohn, Stephen Policoff, and Hugh McGough for their talent and hard work. And finally, I would like to acknowledge the very special contribution of Marilyn Deubler, to whom this book is dedicated.

CONTENTS

ORIENTATION

PART 1

INTRODUCTION

Tips for Speakers

To achieve effective communication as a speaker, you must:

1. Pay attention to audience feedback.
2. Be flexible in your presentation.
3. Be tuned to the audience's level of understanding of a topic.
4. Speak on the same attitudinal wave length as your audience.

THE STUDY OF PUBLIC SPEAKING

Public speaking has been written about and studied for nearly 3,000 years. Some of you may already be familiar with the subject, but most students encounter it for the first time in this course. We are going to be looking at most phases of public speaking from the initial planning to the final presentation of the speech. As we cover these topics, you should develop a sensitivity and understanding for the subject. At the end, you should be a much better public speaker. Moreover, you will have acquired a useful skill. A good student should question the relevancy of any course that he or she takes. Why should it be included in a student's academic program? Here we will try to answer that question for public speaking by considering it from both a historical and contemporary perspective.

Historical Perspective: Rhetoric

Since as early as 1000 B.C., scholars, teachers, and philosophers have been concerned about how people speak in public. Both the Greek and the Roman philosophers studied oratory and developed theories about effective speaking. Plato wrote extensively about what he called rhetoric, but it was Aristotle (381–324 B.C.) who wrote the first full-blown treatise on the subject.[1] To Aristotle, there were five important elements in public speaking: (1) the basic ideas (invention) that are talked about in the speech; (2) the style or language that the speaker uses; (3) the arrangement or organization of the speaker's ideas; (4) how the speaker delivers his or her speech; and (5) the speaker's ability to speak from memory. Aristotle can thus be considered the father of the study of public speaking. Even today, speech departments offer classes in what is called *classical rhetoric* where his ideas on public speaking are still studied.

Romans such as Cicero (106–43 B.C.) and Quintilian (35–96 A.D.) also wrote about rhetoric. Their focus was on the orators who were speaking in Rome during their lifetimes. Many of the ideas taught today, including some discussed in this book, can be traced directly to these Roman writers. For example, one of the chapters in this book deals with credibility, the listener's perception of the speaker. Credibility in public speaking was written about extensively by Cicero long before modern scholars began to examine the concept.

Rhetoric was also extensively studied in seventeenth- and eighteenth-century England. The three most influential rhetoricians during this period were George Campbell, Richard Whately, and Hugh

---

[1] *The Rhetoric of Aristotle,* trans. by Lane Cooper (Englewood Cliffs, N.J.: Prentice-Hall, 1960).

New York Public Library

CICERO, ancient Rome's foremost orator, was born on January 3, 106 B.C. Cicero did not come from a powerful family. But his unique skills as a speaker in the law courts and public assemblies earned him great respect. He was elected to office, entered the Senate, and became Consul of Rome in 63 B.C. As a defender of the conservative Roman constitution, Cicero was executed when Marc Antony and Augustus seized power in 43 B.C. Fifty-seven of Cicero's speeches have survived. Many are considered masterpieces of oratory. For centuries, speakers and writers have used Cicero's orations as models and standards for their own works.

Blair. Each emphasized a particular aspect of public speaking: Campbell the worthiness of the speaker's idea; Whately, the speaker's arguments; and Blair the speaker's language or style. Each of these elements, of course, is important. And each is also discussed in this book.

Throughout the nineteenth century, the subject of rhetoric was an important part of the curriculum in elementary and secondary schools in both Britain and the United States. Many of the intellectuals of the period were trained in speech making. Oratory was an important skill for politicians and a popular form of entertainment. Large crowds listened for hours to famous speakers.

A Contemporary View: Public Speaking as Communication

Communication involves receiving as well as sending messages.

By the turn of the century, however, the public had begun to change. Speaking well in public was still useful and important for many careers; but the long, flowery speeches of the past were no longer admired. In the twentieth century, the focus of study has shifted from the art of oratory to the study of communication. This view does not regard public speaking as a form of public entertainment or as an art to be practiced for its own sake. Instead, it is studied as a useful tool for communication among people. As such, it is both relevant and valuable. For in learning to be a skilled public speaker, you are in fact becoming a more skilled public communicator.

Communication, to paraphrase Mark Twain, is something that everybody talks about but nobody does anything about. People blame "lack of communication" for a wide variety of social and personal ills, so much so that it has become a modern cliché. Yet communication is a concept vital to public speaking. Let us first look at what communication is and then at how good communication should govern public speaking.

Communication: What Is It?   We can define communication as the process of people sending and receiving information. This is a simple definition, but each of the terms in it is in fact quite complex.

Process.   By process in this context we mean that communication goes on all around us all the time. We cannot really "stop" communication to examine it. For example, when two people interact verbally, they listen and they talk. But they are also stimulated by events going on all around them that are not part of the actual conversation. There is "more to" a verbal exchange than just what the two people say to each other. They are influenced by what has been said, what they see, their memory, their past. This multidimensional process makes communication dynamic. It is ongoing. It never stops. Thus communication is said to be a process.

People.   Communication is essentially among people. It involves persons talking and listening. Since people are imperfect, they are also imperfect communicators. They have problems and handicaps that make communication less than precise. If communication worked well all of the time, we would always be completely able to understand everything that anyone tells us. But obviously we do not. We are able to "get," or abstract, only a fraction of someone else's ideas. Sometimes, we are unable to understand the other person at all. When this happens, communication is said to have broken down.

Sending and Receiving.   When we communicate, we send information. When we communicate orally, we send this information primarily, but not solely, by listening with our ears to what someone says. We also receive information by watching the actions and behaviors of others. As we shall see in Chapter 11, a person has a verbal message—what he or she says—and a nonverbal message—his or her physical actions. Most of the time the verbal message supports the nonverbal one. But, occasionally the verbal and nonverbal will be in conflict.

Information.   This is what is sent. Sometimes called the message, it is what the communicator wants to tell the listener. In public speaking the message is the speech.

Communication: A Model.   To help you understand how the process of communication works, let us examine the model at the top of the next page. This model shows how the speaker and his or her audience are linked together through feedback. The speaker sends a message (the speech) to the listeners. The listeners receive the message and react to it. This reaction (feedback) in turn becomes a mes-

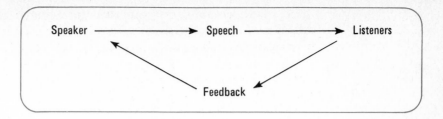

sage sent by the listeners to the speaker. The speaker, in his or her turn, reacts to the feedback, using it to help shape the speech. A good speaker will adapt and refine his or her speech when that speech is obviously missing the audience. When it is obvious that the speech is "getting through," the speaker will keep on in the same fashion.

As the model indicates, the speaker and the audience have a reciprocal relationship. The speaker depends on the audience to listen and to try to understand his or her message. The audience depends on the speaker to adjust that message, so that they can best understand it.

The Importance of Communicating with an Audience. Far too often public speakers forget that they are expected to *communicate* with their audiences. To help us understand why communication in public speaking is so important, think for a moment about the difference between talking at the audience and communicating with them:

Talking at the Audience	*Communication*
1. Is speaker-centered	1. Is audience-centered
2. Is quick	2. Takes time
3. Requires little effort	3. Is difficult to achieve
4. Requires a tremendous amount of energy from the audience	4. Requires a tremendous amount of energy from the speaker
5. Is static	5. Is dynamic
6. Creates little mutual understanding between speaker and audience	6. Creates much mutual understanding between speaker and audience
7. May frustrate the audience	7. May frustrate the speaker
8. Is unlikely to produce a strong bond between the speaker and audience	8. Is likely to produce a strong bond between the speaker and the audience

Communication has the potential for producing a successful interaction between the speaker and audience. There are a few rules that a speaker should follow to achieve effective communication.

1. The speaker must pay attention to audience feedback to the speech.

2. The speaker's goal must be to make the audience understand his or her message.

3. The speaker must be willing to adjust and to be flexible in his or her presentation of the message.

4. The speaker must put the interests of the audience before his or her own.

These four rules are difficult for most speakers. Most of us like to talk. When we talk, we are the center of attention. Unfortunately, if we talk without giving any thought to our listener, we are probably not communicating. Public speakers often fall into this trap. The important thing to remember is that the speaker must do everything in his or her power to communicate with the audience rather than just talk at them.

Miscommunication. There are a number of common mistakes that interfere with communication. Let us look at three.

Speaking Over the Audience. This happens when the speaker talks above the level of understanding of his or her audience. It occurs most often when experts forget that their audiences are less knowledgable about a particular subject than they themselves are.

Talking Down to the Audience. This error is less common. It occurs when speakers condescend to their audience. Most often it is

One of the surest ways for speakers to bore an audience is to talk over their heads.

the result of the speaker underestimating an audience's intelligence or understanding of a topic.

Speaking on a Different Attitudinal Wave Length. Speakers have to recognize that the audience's attitudes will influence their reception of a particular speech. For example, if you are a political radical and a speaker advocates conservative, right-wing politics, your political convictions will act as a barrier to your focusing on the speaker's message. To some extent, you must be on the same general attitudinal wave length as your audience for your message to be effectively received.

There are, of course, many other examples of miscommunication not covered here. These three are cited as examples of some of the difficulties of communicating with an audience. Later in the book, we shall be discussing in depth these and other examples of communication problems faced by speakers.

SETTINGS FOR PUBLIC SPEAKING

Many new students of public speaking are amazed at the number of opportunities there are to use the skills it teaches. Let us look briefly at four settings of public speaking.

Classrooms. All teachers are public speakers. This means that since your first days in kindergarten, you have encountered numerous speakers. Some have been good, others probably less so. Lecturing is just another term for public speaking.

Sermons. At church or synagogue, the clergy often preach sermons. The sermon is a time-honored form of public speaking. Billy Graham and the late Archbishop Fulton Sheen became famous and influential because of their skill at this type of public speaking.

Politics. Public speaking is a part of almost all political campaigns. Moreover, legislative bodies rely on public speaking to conduct business. This has been true since the ancient Greek city-states.

Sales Pitches. You may not think of the sales pitch as a speech, but it is. Good salespeople almost by definition have to be effective speakers. They also have to master the background skills to speaking, such as audience analysis, if they are to succeed at their jobs.

Again these settings are only given as examples. We shall discuss many others throughout the book. Chapter 16 was written precisely to show how speaking skills can be valuable in a variety of careers.

Summary

Public speaking goes back to the ancient Greeks and Romans. Aristotle identified five important elements in a speech: (1) the basic ideas; (2) the style or language; (3) the organization; (4) the delivery; and (5) the speaker's ability to speak from memory. The Romans added the concept of speaker credibility. These ideas are still studied in what is called classical rhetoric.

Public speaking continued to be an important field of study in succeeding eras. Today it is treated as a branch of communication and is used in many settings—classrooms, businesses, churches, political forums. Communication is the process of people sending and receiving information. In public speaking, this means that the speaker and the audience must interact. There are four rules for achieving this: (1) the speaker must pay attention to audience feedback; (2) the speaker must work to make the audience understand the message; (3) the speaker must be flexible in his or her presentation; (4) the speaker must put the interests of the audience before his or her own.

Exercises

1. Develop a two-minute minipresentation on the general category of "communication barriers." Discuss what a communication barrier is, suggest some examples, and provide some ways to improve communication.
2. Try to think of an example of what you consider to be one-way and of what you consider two-way communication. Using your two examples, tell how they are different from each other.
3. In addition to the four presented in the textbook, identify four other settings where public speaking is used. Would you consider these to be the most common settings?
4. In class, discuss the topic "Good Public Speakers in Contemporary America." As you discuss the topic, make sure that each person considered is analyzed in terms of his or her:
   a. style
   b. audience
   c. issues
   d. delivery
   e. credibility

LISTENING

Tips for Speakers

1. When listening, use all of the senses to gain information.
2. To listen most efficiently, be alert but relaxed.
3. To avoid distraction, concentrate on the main ideas within a speech.
4. Besides the content, listen for the speaker's attitude toward his or her message.
5. Refrain from evaluation until you fully understand the speaker's ideas.
6. Nevertheless, be sure that the speaker has established credibility and documented his or her claims.

From birth, we are made aware of the power of communication. A baby soon discovers that crying brings results. After that, the child learns as many sounds as possible that stand for things he or she wants. Children learn to make these sounds by listening to their parents and imitating what they say. The transition from a baby's first gurgle to reciting a speech from Shakespeare is chiefly the result of good listening.

LISTENING IS THE PRIMARY COMMUNICATION ACTIVITY

We listen much more than we speak.

Human communication consists primarily of *speaking*, in which we send messages, and *listening*, in which we receive them. Although this book deals primarily with speaking, we must recognize that we listen much more often than we speak. More than 70 percent of our waking hours are spent in verbal communication. And more of that time is spent listening than speaking.

Since we listen more often than talk, listening must be considered the primary communication activity. We listen to the radio when we get up in the morning; we listen to companions and overhear strangers; in class, we listen to professors and classmates. Outside of school, we listen to friends and relatives; to records, radios, and television. More than one-half of our communicating time is spent listening; and yet, listening is a skill that very few of us have mastered. Good listening can help to make even mediocre public speaking effective. Speaking skills and listening skills are not very different—they both involve developing a communication consciousness.

In an experiment, a group of college students were asked to listen to a 10-minute lecture. Immediately afterwards, the students were tested on how much they remembered. The students were able to remember only 50 percent of what was said. Two weeks later, they were able to remember only 25 percent.[1]

Nonetheless, most of what a person learns comes from listening. Whether it is in the classroom, on the athletic field, or on the job, we must listen to understand what is going on. We must force ourselves to be "other centered," a situation most people dislike because we all enjoy being the center of attention. But to understand what is said to us, we must focus on the person who is saying it.

There is an ancient Zen puzzle: If a tree falls and there is no one there to hear it hit the ground, is there a noise? Perhaps not. But

[1] Ralph G. Nichols, "Do We Know How to Listen? Practical Helps in a Modern Age," *The Speech Teacher*, 10, no. 2 (March, 1961), pp. 119–120.

certainly for communication to occur, someone has to listen. There is a mutual dependence between the speaker and the person spoken to. The listener has to understand the speaker's message; the speaker must pay attention to audience feedback.

Feedback is the messages that listeners send to speakers. We touched on feedback briefly in the first chapter and shall discuss it in more detail later in this chapter. Feedback enables speakers to measure the effect of their messages on the listeners. Thus, speakers can adapt their speeches in order to communicate more effectively. Frequently, the communication cycle is interrupted at exactly this point. Most often, this breakdown is the fault of the speaker, who is unable to respond to the feedback sent by his or her audience.

However, the breakdown can also result from the audience's failure to be an active receiver. Listening is hard work. Most people are passive listeners. They tend not to make the needed effort when listening becomes difficult. As a result, they miss the rewards that come from true communication, which requires listeners to become actively involved.

Why People Listen

People listen for many reasons: to learn, to be amused, to be polite, to earn money, to gain an advantage, to relieve boredom, to compare opinions, to increase understanding, to be nosey, to be liked. Sometimes people listen out of fear, or in self-defense. In general, people listen most closely to things that have some bearing on their own lives. For example, we may pay little attention to news of an airline crash in Europe. But if a friend were on that plane, we would pay very close attention to the newscaster's report.

We listen to messages that support our own attitudes and beliefs. For example, people who believe that the United States is in constant danger of being attacked by its enemies listen carefully to reports of military installations in Cuba and anti-American sentiment in Asia and Africa.

People also tend to listen to the unexpected. "Dog bites man" is not news. But it is an old journalistic cliché that "Man bites dog" will capture public attention and sell newspapers.

Four Basic Listening Functions. By paying attention to—by hearing and grasping—the many spoken words that surround us, we can benefit from active participation in the listening process. Of the several important listening functions, four are basic:

1. *Listening to gain work-related information.* Although many companies provide job manuals for their employees, much of what we

learn about a job comes from listening. Good listeners can process what they hear and apply it to the task at hand.

2. *Listening to be more effective in interpersonal relationships.* Interpersonal relationships are impossible without communication. Information is passed back and forth from person to person, from friend to friend. As the pattern of interaction becomes more definite, a bond is formed between the speaker and the listener. The more easily we can form these bonds, the better we shall be at making friends and relating to business associates.

3. *Listening to gather data to make sound decisions.* Most of our knowledge comes from listening. Before we make a decision, we should listen to what other people have to say. Advice is invaluable when having to make up one's mind.

4. *Listening to respond appropriately to what we hear.* When someone says something to us, we answer. How appropriately we answer, however, depends on how well we listened.

Listening in Public Speaking

Listening is especially significant in public speaking. In fact, critical listening is as important as effective speaking. On a national scale, it is as important for the nation to listen to what the president has to say as it is for the president to inform the people of what is going on. In a classroom, an excellent lecture is pointless if the students pay no attention to it. The member of any audience who does not listen deprives him or herself of whatever benefits he or she might have gained from listening to what was being said.

This is probably your first college-level speech course. You will be listening to many speeches in this class—many more than you yourself will be giving. Much of what you learn should come from listening to your classmates. Listening to what they say and watching how they say it can teach you both the factual content of their speeches and their techniques of organizing and giving a speech.

THE LISTENING PROCESS

There are several ways to define the listening process. It can be regarded simply as the receiving of sounds, or as the method for obtaining information and meaning from every part of the speaking experience. To get the most out of listening, you must use all of the relevant senses to gain information.

What do we mean by "all of the senses?" To begin with, it should come as no surprise to learn that the ears are not the only instruments

We listen with all of our senses.

that send data to the brain. The eyes, the nose, the mouth, and the sense of touch also transmit the information that helps us to understand. To grasp a speaker's message, we must use all of our faculties to obtain information. By using these faculties, listening becomes a total activity.

The Ears.   Most people are surprised to learn that only a quarter of the information we receive is processed through our ears. Our ears transmit words and other sounds. Since, as we shall see in Chapters 10 and 11, one word can mean different things to different people and sounds may be meaningless, sole reliance on our ears for listening increases the possibility of not understanding the speaker's message. We must, therefore, pay very close attention to what is being said. Not only must we hear the words being used, we must also understand the message being given.

Later in the chapter we will discuss the distinction between hearing and listening. At this point, it is essential to remember that listening means getting and understanding the message. It is no easy task. Imagine, for example, that you were required to attend a meeting of highly trained technicians. They might easily use words you would not understand. Although you could hear what they were saying, you would have difficulty understanding it because you would be unable to attach meaning to their vocabulary.

The Eyes.   About 60 percent of our useful information comes through what we see. When we "listen with our eyes," we attempt to understand the transmitter's meanings about the concept or idea being discussed. In a conversation and in public speaking, we listen to the speaker's words and carefully watch his or her physical behavior. The use of our eyes helps us to understand what we hear with our ears. Through observation, we pick up both verbal and nonverbal cues that enable us to understand the open and hidden meanings the speaker attaches to the information being transmitted. It is, therefore, important for us to see and study the person speaking.

The speaker's precise meaning can never be communicated directly. Meanings are in people, not in words; they are internal. The meaning of a concept such as justice or democracy, for example, will vary according to each person's experience, frame of reference, and attitude toward the subject at any given moment. A receiver will never relate completely to a speaker's meaning. In communication, we try to understand another person's meanings as best we can. As we shall see in Chapter 11, one way to do this is to look for consistency between the verbal and nonverbal messages. This consistency helps us relate to the message. Inconsistency, on the other hand, makes it difficult to grasp. For example, a speaker delivering a funeral oration with smirks and broad grins would badly confuse the audience. His or her words might express grief, but the visual message would suggest amusement. The speaker's *meaning* would be a puzzle.

Listening with our eyes enables us to focus on the other person and on his or her ideas. Visual contact increases the active involvement the receiver has with the transmitter and makes the communication more efficient.

Hearing and seeing are the primary techniques for listening to public speaking. The other senses—touch, taste, and smell—can also be useful in special situations, where products are demonstrated, for example. It is the active involvement of all our senses that enables us to listen effectively.

Getting Information

Getting information is what listening is all about. Almost all the information we pick up is gathered through our listening behavior. How it gets there and what happens to it once it has arrived is the function of three related characteristics: perception, intelligence, and thinking.

Perception.   The physiological and psychological process of abstracting relevant details from data is called perception. Since each of us abstracts different details from the same data, each of us also perceives things differently from anyone else.

Intelligence.   The second characteristic, intelligence, is the measure of our cognitive ability. People seem to develop listening skills separately from intelligence. Yet, there is some connection between intelligence and listening. Common sense tells us that more intelligent people should be better listeners, if only because they will find it easier to relate new data to what they already know. By contrast, people who have trouble understanding words will also have problems understanding the complete message.

Thinking.   In listening, thinking is essentially a matter of labeling and identification, of mental grouping. Once we have received the message, we think about it. We search our memories for any additional information that can be used to help us understand the new data. Then, we store the information in our memories for later use.

Feedback

All of these processes occur in handling the messages and information that are received when people communicate. Inherent in any

Feedback is essential to effective communication.

form of human communication is the "give and take" of ideas. In public speaking, the speaker "gives" a message that the audience "takes." For this communication to occur, the speaker must know how to transmit information and the audience must know how to receive it. At the same time, as we pointed out earlier, the audience is also giving information to the speaker in the form of feedback. Effective public speaking requires the speaker to receive or "take in" this feedback, grasp its meaning, and use it in his or her speech. Let's consider a few examples of feedback at work:

1. A minister is preaching an especially inspiring sermon. During it, she repeatedly asks the congregation for a show of hands to signify their religious recommitment. The show of hands is the feedback which tells the preacher that the congregation is receiving her message and is affected by it.

2. It's half-time and the high school football team is losing 13–0. In the locker room, the coach tells his players the story of a former student at the school who had a promising career as a halfback until he was injured in one of the games and had to quit football forever. When he graduated from high school he told the coach, "When things get rough out on the field, tell the boys to go out there and win one for me!" The speech might be effective in moving the players to tears. But it might also emotionally drain the players so that in the second half they would be unable to perform well. In that case, the feedback they send to the coach is twofold. The tears show that they understand what the coach has said; but their poor performance in the second half also tells the coach that he needs to be more careful in the myths he uses to inspire his players to win.

3. A local war hero is addressing a crowd at the annual Fourth of July celebration on "What It Means to Be an American." The speaker surveys the audience for some kind of response. There is only prolonged silence. This, too, is feedback, but it may not be easy for the speaker to interpret. The audience may have completely missed the point, and the silence may indicate misunderstanding. Or perhaps the audience is awestruck by the brilliant oratory; or hostile to the speaker's ideas about patriotism. Silence is difficult to understand. The speaker must look for additional cues.

Hearing and Listening

Hearing. Hearing, unlike listening, is a totally physiological process in which sound waves make our eardrums vibrate. This vibration is carried by tiny bones in the middle ear to the inner ear, or cochlea, where the vibrations are translated into nerve impulses and are carried to the brain. The brain then identifies these nerve impulses as sounds. This process is completely automatic. It requires no effort. Indeed, without earplugs of some sort we cannot stop it even if we would.

There are, however, obstacles to effective hearing. The sound source may be too far away from the receiver. The volume of the sound may not be loud enough for the receiver to hear. There may be other noises which distract the receiver's attention from the sounds he or she is trying to pick up.

Suppose you are in a classroom where a student is giving a speech. Outside, workers are building a new library. The construction noise prevents you from hearing what the student speaker is saying. Unless you can clearly hear what is being said, you will find it exceedingly difficult to get the speaker's message.

There are occasions in which the hearing problem rests with the receiver, not with the source of sound. It is estimated that approximately 10 percent of any adult audience, including college students, have some difficulty hearing. If you have difficulty hearing, you should seek professional assistance. Modern technology can test hearing acuity via a painless and quite inexpensive exam. Although we can hear without listening, it is impossible to listen without being able to hear. Poor hearing definitely limits our listening effectiveness.

Listening.   Hearing alone does not enable a person to listen to or to understand a message. There is no element of interpretation in hearing. Once the process of interpreting begins, listening occurs. First, the ear analyzes speech sounds and organizes them into recognizable patterns. Next, the listener interprets the patterns, and finally, he or she is ready to begin the seven levels of listening:[2]

1. *Isolation.* At this level, the listener notes the individual aspects of the spoken word and isolates particular sounds, ideas, facts, organizations, and other stimuli.

2. *Identification.* Once the particular stimuli have been recognized, a meaning, or identity, is given to each of the independent items.

3. *Integration.* We integrate what we hear with the other information already stored in our brains. For this reason, our general knowledge is important at this level of listening. For listening to occur, we must already have some background or understanding of the particular subject area of the message. If we have no material to retrieve that can be used to integrate the new information, listening is difficult.

[2] Seth Fessenden, *Listening* 75 (Indianapolis: Bobbs-Merrill, 1975).

4. *Inspection.* At this level, the new information that we have received is contrasted and compared with whatever information we already have on that particular subject. This process is easiest when new information supports our preconceptions. If, however, the new information contradicts our previous ideas about something, then we must find out which piece of information is closer to the truth.

5. *Interpretation.* At this point, we actively evaluate what we hear and where it came from. We begin to object and approve, to recognize and to weigh the information and its sources.

6. *Interpolation.* Since no message carries meaning in and of itself, it is our responsibility to provide supporting data and ideas from our own background in order to fill in the details of the message we hear.

7. *Introspection.* By reflecting on and examining new information, we attempt to personalize that information, applying it to our own situation.

These seven steps do not represent the entire range of listening activity, but they do provide a method for studying listening behavior. They are also a guide to the problems that sometimes arise in the listening process. After reviewing them, it should be clear that good listening is not just passive hearing but an *activity* that requires the participation of the listener.

Five Factors that Affect Listening

Listening requires both physical and mental effort on the part of the listener. It is a psychological process that involves the listener's personality, his or her motivation, role in society, attitude toward the subject, and situation in life. These five aspects of the listener strongly influence how well he or she listens. The reasons for this are obvious:

1. *Attitude.* We tend to listen more carefully to topics with which we agree than to those with which we disagree. We tend to tune out those things that throw us off balance or cause us to question our position on a given subject.

2. *Motivation.* Much of listening involves our own value system. When we can get something out of it, we are more likely to listen. "What's in it for me?" is a valid question. Unless we are assured of some reward, there is little chance that we will work to listen to something when we'd rather daydream or take a nap.

3. *Personality.* Who we are also influences our listening behavior. If we consider ourselves cooperative, thoughtful, and analytical, we will probably be better listeners than if we think of ourselves as lazy, argumentative, and self-centered.

4. *Life Situation.* Our physical environment also plays an important role in listening. It is much easier to listen to someone speaking in a quiet college classroom than in the repair hangar at a busy airport.

5. *Role in Society.* Our willingness to listen can also be influenced by our role in society. As students, we are expected to listen more carefully than if we were part-time janitors in a local factory. Similarly, professionals, such as psychologists, counselors, and physicians, are paid to listen. One would expect them to have developed a good listening technique.

Listening Improvement

Although, speakers must initiate good communication, receivers have to listen. If listening breaks down, the chief fault is with the listener. This does not mean that speakers do not have to make their presentations clear, lively, stimulating, specific, well prepared, and well paced. But assuming that a speaker is making an effort to be heard and understood, it is the responsibility of the listener to receive the communicator's message. Listening requires us to concentrate very hard on what is being said. Unlike reading, in which we can go back over a passage several times if need be in order to understand it, listening has no built-in rewind switch. Unless we are using a tape recorder, we cannot play back what the speaker has said. Therefore, we must listen well to the message as it is being presented. Unfortunately, most of us are poor listeners. After we have listened to someone speak for a few seconds, we let our minds wander onto topics of more interest to ourselves. We think about what we're going to do when the speaker is finished or what we're going to eat that night for dinner. We seem to dwell on anything other than what the speaker is discussing.

It is not difficult to spot the listeners and the nonlisteners in an audience. The good listener is usually alert, relaxed, but not droopy. His or her eyes are generally focused on the speaker. At times, the good listener may react by nodding in agreement or disapproval of what the speaker has said.

In marked contrast is the listless slouch of nonlisteners. Their hands and elbows can barely support their heads. Their eyelids half close. They contemplate the size of the knot in their shoelaces. Another example of the poor listener is someone who constantly nods in agreement with every word the speaker makes. Listeners of this type are so involved in making a good impression that they fail to get the message. They only react to the words.

Whereas the whole audience may hear the sounds that come from

There are good and bad listeners.

HOW TO IMPROVE YOUR LISTENING SKILLS
1. Develop a desire to listen.
2. Build good listening habits.
3. Pay attention.
4. Delay evaluation.
5. Listen for ideas and content.
6. Capitalize on thought speed.
7. Use spare time wisely.

the speaker, only the good listener actively turns those sounds into understandable structures and ideas. The transition from a poor listener to a good listener is not as hopeless as it may seem. Most people are not aware that one can learn to be a good listener. All that is necessary is to exert some effort and to follow a few simple rules.

Seven Rules for Listening Improvement.

Develop a Desire to Listen. The first step in improving your listening ability is to create within yourself a desire to listen. The problem here, of course, is that most people would much rather talk than listen. How often have you been asked a question by someone who didn't wait for your reply?

"How are you today?"

"Oh, I'm feeling pret—"

"Well, you look great. How's school?"

At other times, we become so conscious of our own upcoming responses and so anxious not to say something foolish that we are busy preparing what we are going to say next while we are being spoken to.

In developing a desire to listen, it's important to remember that listening is a very attractive and profitable skill to have mastered. Responsive, interested listeners are rare. Yet there is no easier way to learn than by listening; no easier way to make a friend than by listening to what people want to say. Again, we return to incentives: "What's in it for me?" You can answer that question yourself by evaluating the rewards of being a good listener in any given situation. If listening is important to keep a friend, to pass an exam, to find out directions, or to be invited out, then it is certainly worth your time and energy to learn how to listen well.

Build Good Listening Habits.   It is not enough to want to listen. We also have to build good listening habits. The way to begin is to *listen with all your senses.* As we mentioned earlier, good listening involves the active cooperation of our ears and eyes and sometimes of our nose, mouth, and sense of touch as well. All our senses must work together for us to listen effectively.

Pay Attention.   This is the key element. By staying alert, you will get both the speaker's verbal and nonverbal messages. A speaker's words tell only part of the story. In order to understand the full meaning of a speaker's message, we must look for the nonverbal signs—both conscious and unconscious—that round out, that complete, and that give dimension to what the speaker is trying to communicate. Keep in mind that communication is a mutual process. Unless you are willing to commit yourself to the speaker, there will be no communication.

Delay Evaluation.   Give the speaker the time to say what he or she has to say. Evaluation after understanding leads to good listening. We should never evaluate until after we have understood the speaker's position. This is particularly important in critical listening, a subject we will discuss in more detail later in the chapter.

Most people have mental or emotional blocks about some subject which prevents them from perceiving and understanding certain information. Certain words such as "mother-in-law," "pervert," "income tax," "evolution," "liberal," "racist," "abortion," "CIA," "big business," "policeman," are like built-in explosives for some people, who feel threatened by what these words evoke. As soon as some listeners hear these or similar red-flag words, they immediately turn their minds off, blocking whatever else the speaker may say. The best defense against this behavior is to recognize the tendency in ourselves and to guard against it. By proper planning, we can learn to keep an open mind even when a speaker slips a few shockers into his or her message. By keeping our listening mechanism open and active, we may learn something that takes the sting out of these "red-flag" words in the future. Once again, it is a question of incentive and our own best interests. Closing oneself off to new ideas and experiences can be an expression of fear that prevents us from growing. We cannot help evaluating or judging what we are exposed to. A good listener, however, refrains from evaluation until he or she has fully understood the speaker's ideas.

Listen for Ideas and Content.   Listening for ideas and content means not being distracted by the speaker's delivery. How often have you heard people say: "Oh, politics is just a popularity contest. As long as the candidate is attractive and speaks well, no one cares about the issues." That may be true. Given people's listening habits, it should be no surprise to learn that most people never get beyond how a speaker looks or sounds. They never really listen to what he or she is saying. In good listening, however, we must focus on ideas. In many ways, this is the heart of good listening: identifying the speaker's main idea. We must keep our own ideas in the background and that includes ideas about the subject under discussion as well as our thoughts on how pleasant the speaker's voice is and how nicely he or she is dressed.

By concentrating on the main ideas within a speech, you can avoid the distractions that plague the poor listener. Uncomfortable seats, stuffy rooms, neighbors who sniffle and cough throughout the speech will all fade into the background if you actively focus on what the speaker is saying.

In focusing on a speaker's main points or ideas, it is also necessary to cut through the surrounding maze of supporting material and qualifiers, additional information that is used to illustrate the central argument. Too often, listeners become bogged down with the supporting material and miss the main idea completely—in other words they don't see the forest for the trees.

An emphasis on focus and concentration does not rule out the need to be aware of the subsidiary cues a speaker imparts. On the contrary, we cannot receive a total picture, or understanding, of a speaker's message without being sensitive to and aware of the roll of an eye, gestures, and so forth. A good listener responds to the mannerisms that pertain to what is being said and is not distracted by those that are totally coincidental to the communication situation.

Capitalize on Thought Speed.   When listening, it pays to capitalize on thought speed. Thinking is a much faster process than talking—four or five times faster. We can assume, therefore, that an audience has plenty of time in which to anticipate what the speaker is going to say, to summarize what the speaker has said, to question the speaker's evidence, and to listen between the lines.[3] By listening for the key ideas in a speech, we can separate important from unimportant information. And by listening actively with all of our senses, we can absorb all of the speaker's meaning. Sensitivity to tone of voice, facial expression, and bodily action is as important as an awareness of the words themselves. By close observation of both verbal and nonverbal cues, a good listener can measure a speaker's sincerity,

[3] Ralph G. Nichols, *The Speech Teacher* 10, no. 2, pp. 118–124.

depth of conviction, and true understanding of his or her material. It is this total understanding of a speaker's message that is the goal of a good listener.

Use Spare Time Wisely. There are two ways a listener can use spare time efficiently. One is constantly to summarize what you hear, using your own words and following the speaker as he or she goes along. The second is to anticipate the speaker. If he or she has identified a problem, try to solve it before the speaker does. Using your spare time in this way keeps your mind active, keeps you focused on the major ideas of the speech, and assists in the process of critical thinking which occurs after the speaker has stated his or her case.

Merely acquiring information is not enough, however, and does not complete the listening process. Once information has been internalized, it must then be understood and evaluated.

Good Listening Behavior.

1. *When you are interested in a particular message or speech, show it.* Too many people are afraid or unwilling to react. If you are involved, show it. This helps to motivate the speaker and, more importantly, it keeps the flow of information moving. Give cues of interest as they become appropriate.

2. *When a speaker is not coming through, show that also.* There is a line of distinction here. One does not expect listeners to hiss or throw eggs when speakers fail to make themselves understood. But it is important to demonstrate to the speaker through eye contact and facial expression that his or her message is being lost. This should cause the speaker to change course to insure that the message reaches its intended destination.

3. *Good manners require 100 percent involvement in the public speaking situation.* Be and look as interested as possible. Perhaps the biggest offenders of this rule are politicians, particularly members of Congress and state legislatures. It is often disconcerting to visit these bodies during a debate and see the legislators reading newspapers, drinking coffee, chatting with friends and looking quite bored with what is being said. This behavior is traditional, but that does not make it admirable. The basis of good manners suggests that we at least *look* as if we want to listen to another person when he or she is talking. In the public speaking class this is very important. Since everyone will have to speak, we should treat others as we expect to be treated. This means that when someone else is speaking, we should want to be interested. Again, this acts as a regulator. Our attention tells the speaker that we are interested and involved.

4. *When further involvement is called for, show it.* Often speakers will solicit involvement from their listeners by asking rhetorical questions, by offering written information, or by requesting questions at the end of the presentation. These are opportunities for involvement. Asking a question, for example, helps the speaker. If the speaker calls for a show of hands, raise yours. If literature is offered, and it can help you understand the speaker's point of view, take it. This type of behavior may sound artificial, but it can make public speaking much more enjoyable for both speaker and listener.

TWO TYPES OF LISTENING BEHAVIOR

Although there are several reasons why people listen, there are only two types of listening behavior, factual and empathic. Each of these is especially important in public speaking.

Factual Listening

The first type of listening behavior is called *factual listening.* Proper mastery of the techniques of factual listening lets us grasp facts, concepts, and information. The human mind can only process so many facts at a time. Since we are constantly exposed to new and varied material, we must depend on our brains to sort through and organize all of this input. Our minds are computers that sift the material and make it coherent. When we use our minds in this way, we are practicing factual listening, also known as listening for recall. We do much of this kind of listening in a public speaking situation. As we listen, we are trying to get the speaker's essential ideas.

Focusing on the Other Person's Message.   Factual listening is the act of focusing on another's message so as to abstract relevant factual data and information in order to comprehend the speaker's point. All of the techniques for improving listening skills which we have discussed apply to factual listening. Whether we listen for pleasure, to gain information, or to make judgments, we use factual listening to select the speaker's main ideas and to understand the essence of his or her message. For example:

1. You are watching a television commercial. The actress giving the sales pitch is extolling the virtues of her brand over the competition. She explains its good points—the usual sales hype. But somewhere in the middle of this routine she says: "Research has proven that my brand is as effective as brand X, and yet costs a dollar less." A good

listener will pick out this one relevant point in the message: "This brand is as effective and is one dollar cheaper."

2. The first day of your new job, your supervisor provides you with a wide variety of facts which you will have to master. Some of these facts are also in the company manual, but most of the day-to-day information is only available through an oral exchange with the supervisor. In that exchange, she tells you about everything from job description to where the supply room is. To function effectively, you must process the oral information immediately.

Getting the Facts. Remember that factual listening means "getting the facts." The listening improvement skills provided earlier in this chapter will also help you here. There are, however, four specific skills that are especially useful in factual listening:

1. *We must involve ourselves totally in the communication situation.* Besides paying attention, this means relating the speaker's major ideas to our own experience. We must determine why the information the speaker presents is important to us and why we want to make it a permanent part of our store of knowledge.

2. *We must master the art of successful note taking.* This does not mean writing down every word the speaker says. A good note taker writes down the key points in a speech and sufficient details to refresh his or her memory when the notes are reviewed.

3. *We must look for and analyze the speaker's supporting materials.* Speakers usually highlight their main points with examples and illustrations. These materials may support the speaker's claim, or they may provide other ways of looking at the same idea. A responsive listener will look at these examples with an inquisitive eye.

4. *We must look for the speaker's overall structure and organizational pattern.* There are several standard ways of arranging information in a speech—chronological, spatial, cause-effect, and problem-solution, to mention only a few. If we can identify which of the arrangements a speaker is using, we can anticipate how the speech will develop. We can then follow it more easily and should be able to remember the main points of the argument more accurately.

Factual listening is a skill with infinite applications for any communication situation. For example, all journalists, from Walter Cronkite to cub reporters, use factual listening in their daily routines. To report the truth of a story, they must get the facts. Similarly, sales clerks, even though they may have years of experience on the job, have to listen and understand what the customer wants before they can present their product and make a sale.

In a public speaking situation, factual listening is equally important. Whether the speakers are congressional candidates or college professors, we as the audience must be able to find the facts and central ideas within their argument. Otherwise, it is pointless for them to be speaking or for us to be listening.

Empathic Listening

The second type of listening behavior is called *empathic listening*. Empathic listening helps us to understand the speaker's psychological and emotional attitude and how that influences his or her speech. This type of listening behavior can also be called "active listening" or "listening for understanding." Every message contains two parts: the content or factual material and the speaker's feeling or attitude toward that content. By listening for understanding, a person can grasp both parts of the message. A good consumer of public speaking will practice empathic listening when he or she tries to identify with the speaker's primary message.

Watching for Nonverbal Cues.   As we discussed in the section on improving listening skills, there are several techniques with which a good listener can get both parts of the speaker's message. One way is to watch for nonverbal cues. (See Chapter 11.)

Putting Yourself in the Other Person's Position.   At the core of an effective empathic listening technique is the ability to put yourself in the other person's position. This is not easily done. For one thing, each of us listens from a unique perspective. We often listen only to what is important to us or only to those things with which we agree. Good empathic listening demands that we put ourselves in the speaker's position. It demands that we try to think of why a speaker would say just what he or she did say. It demands that we think of examples to support the speaker's position, whether we share that point of view or not. We can then receive the message as the speaker intended it to be received. This is extremely difficult because our own ideas and values will often be opposed to what has been said to us. But we have to try. Only then can we fairly agree to disagree, question, or accept what we have heard.

Concentrating on the Message Rather than the Delivery.   A third technique for correct empathic listening is to concentrate on the speaker's message rather than his or her delivery. This technique was discussed earlier, but needs repeating here. As listeners, we often find ourselves concerned with how someone says something—the person's delivery—rather than with what he or she is actually saying. To be a good listener, we must focus on the message. This means almost completely separating the speaker's message from his or her method of presentation. There are several ways we can do this:

1. *Take mental notes of the main points.* This involves getting the crucial ideas by restating them yourself to make certain you know what the speaker has said.

2. *Think of additional ways to support the speaker's points.* Here the listener cognitively attempts to raise points which are relevant within the situation. Thinking of illustrations and examples while the speaker is talking is a tremendous aid to comprehension.

3. *Look for ways the speaker has organized or structured his or her presentation.* This involves looking beyond the immediate format of a speech or presentation to find the deeper foundation or arrangement used by the speaker. This is of particular importance to empathic listening. To accomplish this effectively, the listener must restate the important parts of the presentation in his or her own words, using different styles and approaches.

CRITICAL LISTENING

Understanding is at the core of good listening. But it is not enough simply to understand another position. Good listening demands that we actually react to it. The timing of the reaction is crucial. We can analyze and evaluate only after we have fully understood the other person. Thus, we should withhold evaluation until we are very sure that we recognize the speaker's position. Of course, we must eventually evaluate and assume a critical perspective about the speaker's message. We should never accept what someone else has told us without giving the matter a great deal of thought.

Listening as a Critic

At the final stage of the listening process we begin to listen as a critic. In a sense, listeners are the consumers of a speech and they should become consumer-oriented. If we criticize first, we never fully understand, and our judgments are based on incomplete information. But once we have a foundation, we are ready to evaluate and should criticize. Let's consider some typical situations where critical listening is required.

Political Speeches. Because ours is a democracy, we must be critical of candidates and officials if we wish to exercise our rights of

BENITO MUSSOLINI, "Il Duce" (the leader), was born in 1883 and became dictator of Italy in 1922. Like Hitler, Mussolini used public speaking as an instrument of power. Mussolini was a fiery, confident speaker who could easily control a crowd. His speeches, often delivered from the balcony of his official residence, the Palazzo Venegia, were major public events during his 23 years in power.

UPI

citizenship. We might think twice about supporting candidates who woo voters with unrealistic campaign promises or who obscure issues with foggy rhetoric.

Sales Speeches.   We get sales pitches on television, radio, and in person. People want to sell us every possible product and service. For our own good, we should listen carefully. For example, suppose an automobile mechanic tells us that our car needs massive repairs when we thought that only minor work was necessary. The situation is so bad, he advises us, that "I wouldn't want my family riding around in a car with this problem." This is a simple emotional appeal. Although the claim may be accurate, we need to be wary of the mechanic's sales pitch.

Philosophical Speeches.   We live in a society that offers self-help cures of all kinds. Speakers offering answers, panaceas, and philosophies are heard all the time. In Los Angeles, for example, travelers arriving at the international airport must deal with members of the Hare Krishna Society who approach every passenger with a persuasive solicitation for funds. We are a semicaptive audience for all types of philosophical appeals. Good listening requires that we be aware of these situations and be ready to analyze them critically.

The need to listen critically is apparent in all phases of life. We need to evaluate critically messages we receive in our place of employment, our religious life, and even in our leisure time, where we are hit by appeals generated through mass media.

Four Important Concepts in Critical Listening

Critical listening is possible only after a listener has fully understood a speaker's message. Before we can analyze, we must understand. There are four important concepts in critical listening that apply to public speaking.

1. *Make sure that a speaker has fully supported and documented any claim that he or she may make.* The unsupported claim is a problem in many public speaking situations. Unsubstantiated, any speaker's claims are open to question. When the speaker begins to provide the listener with reasons, however, his or her case becomes more believable. Documentation is the speaker's responsibility. A speaker who presents a case shabbily, without documentation, limits his or her potential audience acceptance. As listeners, we must require all public speakers to support and document their arguments. We all have ideas and our freedom of speech allows us to broadcast them. But as listeners, we need to distinguish carefully between the ideas of those speakers who have thought out what they have to say and those speakers who have not. This is done through requiring good support and documentation from the speaker.

2. *We should expect speakers from particular constituencies to represent those constituencies when they speak.* It is very unusual for a speaker to be completely objective. Instead, people speak to advocate certain causes, products, and programs. This is a simple fact of life, especially in a pluralistic and democratic society like ours. For example, when the local school-board member appears before the PTA to "explain" a recent board decision, we may safely assume that he or she has a bias in favor of the board decision; it is also probable that he or she will run for another term. On another level, when Mobil dispatches speakers to local service clubs to talk about the factual aspects of the energy crisis, these speakers are expected to represent Mobil's self-interests. The critical listener in both of these situations

will recognize this and will weigh the speaker's biases when evaluating this material, rather than simply—and naively—accepting their statements as factual. The key is simply to expect the speaker to have a particular position to represent.

3. *We should expect the speaker to demonstrate his or her credibility on a particular topic.* This concerns the question of whether one is qualified to speak on a subject. A speaker's credentials should insure that he or she has the expertise that a given field requires. In the popular media, we often see eminent people speaking on topics far removed from their area of expertise. For example, Linus Pauling, the Nobel Prize-winning physicist, has long been advocating the use of Vitamin C as a cure for the common cold. Members of the medical community point out that Pauling has no training whatsoever in medicine and that he advocates an untested cure. Famous actors and athletes commonly endorse products ranging from shaving cream to automobiles. It happens constantly, and we need to question the qualifications of all these advocates. As public speakers ourselves, we have a responsibility to establish our own qualifications. For example, if we are going to talk about something that we have been doing for years, we should establish the fact of our experience for our listeners. Similarly, if we have been studying a particular topic for only a few weeks, we need to tell our listeners that we are novices on the subject. It is very important for both the listener and the speaker to establish the speaker's level of competence. (See Chapter 9.)

4. *Insist that the speaker move from generalities to specifics.* Many speakers fall into the trap of discussing their particular topic only in general terms. Consider the following advice to a potential customer:

> *You should buy this kitchen range made by Company X because it is the best on the market, no doubt about it. The range will meet all of your needs, whatever they are, and you will remember today as the day you made the best purchase of your life.*

For the sake of demonstration, this example is a bit extreme, but it is not untypical of a hard sales pitch. As listeners, we should require the speaker to cite and document very specifically each claim he or she makes. If the claim cannot be specifically substantiated, then as critical listeners we should be suspicious.

As we begin to practice some of these concepts in critical listening, we will emerge as better consumers of communication, less likely to be swayed by speakers who employ unethical or questionable tactics.

Summary

Listening is the primary communication activity. People listen much more than they talk. They listen (1) to gain work-related information; (2) to be more effective in interpersonal relationships; (3) to make sound decisions; (4) and to respond appropriately to what they hear. Listening uses all of the senses. Sixty percent of our information comes from what we see; only 25 percent from what we hear. Feedback is the messages that listeners send to speakers. Since good communication is a shared exchange, feedback is essential for communication to occur. Hearing is the physiological process of receiving sounds. Listening is the mental process of interpreting them. There are seven levels of listening: isolation, identification, integration, inspection, interpretation, interpolation, and introspection. Good listening is an active process that requires concentration and effort.

Factual listening is the act of focusing on the message. Empathic listening is listening to understand the speaker's psychological and emotional attitude. Critical listening is the act of judging or evaluating the speaker's message. As critical listeners we make sure that speakers have fully documented their arguments, identified their position, established their credibility, and been able to move from generalities to specifics in discussing their arguments.

Exercises

1. What do you consider to be the primary responsibilities of the listener in a public speech? Make a list of five duties that a good listener should accomplish. The list should not include those responsibilities mentioned in this chapter.
2. Write a brief position paper entitled "Me As a Listener." Analyze your strengths and weaknesses as a listener in light of this chapter. What might you do to improve your listener behavior?
3. As a speaker what can you do to help the listener accomplish his or her task? Identify five speaking techniques that may help the listener.
4. From your experience, give an example of the following:
    a. early evaluation
    b. focusing on the speaker rather than on his or her ideas
    c. not staying ahead of the speaker.

PART I: SUGGESTIONS FOR FURTHER READING

Aristotle. *The Rhetoric*, trans. by Lane Cooper. Englewood Cliffs, N.J.: Prentice-Hall, 1960.

Barker, L. *Listening Behavior*. Englewood Cliffs, N.J.: Prentice-Hall, 1971.

Blair, Hugh. *Lectures on Rhetoric and Belles Lettres*, 2 volumes, ed. by Hugh Harding. Carbondale, Ill.: Southern Illinois University Press, 1965.

Campbell, George. *The Philosophy of Rhetoric*, ed. by Lloyd Bitzer. Carbondale, Ill.: Southern Illinois University Press, 1963.

Civikly, J. *Messages: A Reader in Human Communication*, 2nd ed. New York: Harper and Row, 1978.

Dominick, B. *The Art of Listening*. Springfield, Ill.: Charles C. Thomas, 1958.

Johnson, W. *Your Most Enchanted Listener*. New York: Harper and Row, 1958.

Miller, G., and M. Steinberg. *Between People*. Chicago: SRA, 1975.

Mortensen, C. D. *Communication: The Study of Human Interaction*. New York: McGraw-Hill, 1972.

Nichols, R., and L. Stevens. *Are You Listening?* New York: McGraw-Hill, 1957.

Schramm, W. *Men, Messages, and Media: A Look at Human Communication*. New York: Harper and Row, 1973.

Soreno, K., and C. D. Mortensen, eds. *Foundations of Human Communication Theory*. New York: Harper and Row, 1970.

Swanson, D., and J. Delia. *The Nature of Human Communication*. Palo Alto, Cal.: SRA, 1976.

Watzlawick, P. J. Beavin, and D. Jackson. *Pragamatics of Human Communication*. New York: Norton, 1967.

Whately, Richard. *Elements of Rhetoric*, ed. Douglas Ehninger. Carbondale, Ill.: Southern Illinois University Press, 1963.

Speech Variables

PART II

ANALZYING THE AUDIENCE

Tips for Speakers

1. Learn as much as you can before your speech about your listeners' backgrounds, beliefs, and attitudes.
2. Work to achieve true communication with your audience by responding to audience feedback.
3. Try to determine the unique "personality" of your audience in any speaking situation.
4. Audience analysis should take place before, during, and after a speech.
5. Continually revise your speech as new information about the audience becomes available.
6. Be ready for surprise responses from your audiences, no matter how thorough your analysis has been.

THE AUDIENCE

Understanding the audience is the backbone of successful communication. No part of public speaking affects our chances of being understood and believed by our listeners more than does competent audience analysis. Before we begin to speak—or even to plan a speech—we should know as much as possible about who will be listening to us: their backgrounds, their beliefs, their social positions, their knowledge about and involvement with our topic. Many speeches are attempts to influence—for example, to vote for a school bond issue, to buy a car, or to give up smoking. Before we try to persuade an audience, before we even begin to speak, we should make certain that the audience is both willing to listen to what we have to say and able to understand it.

Moreover, speakers should continue to analyze their audiences during the speech itself. When we speak to an audience we must note how our listeners respond, and we must, if necessary, adapt or alter our presentation to make it more effective. A speech is not merely a performance by a speaker but an act of communication. To succeed, the speaker can not simply send a message to the audience. He or she must also be sensitive to the audience's reponse to that message.

Too often, speakers fail to pay attention to their audiences. Although the day of the public speaker as entertainer is past, the self-centered speaker who concentrates exclusively on his or her delivery is still common. The effective speaker, however, is always alert to whether the audience understands the presentation and is prepared to adapt a speech to their needs and character. This approach assumes considerable give and take between speaker and listeners. It is during this exchange that an important part of audience analysis occurs.

Types of Audiences

Before examining in detail how to analyze an audience, let us outline the kinds of audiences we as speakers are likely to encounter. Every audience, whether large or small, is important. Each has its own characteristics, and each type should be understood by the public speaking student. Whether in school or at work, we all eventually find ourselves speaking to many kinds and sizes of audiences. Some are so small and familiar that no analysis seems necessary; some, so large and unknowable that any try at analyzing them seems futile. In each instance, however, analysis will help us to focus our message, to anticipate the audience's response, and to react to it.

It is difficult for a speaker to get a clear picture of the makeup of a mass audience.

Dyadic. This is the smallest possible communication "group," consisting of one speaker and one listener. In a "dyad" the speaker and listener almost always exchange roles, usually often. Neither speaker will ordinarily talk for very long without being interrupted. As a result, we may not consider dialogue (what we say in dyadic groups) as public speaking at all. But many of our most important verbal exchanges are one-to-one conversations. For example, an interview for a job or college admission is usually limited to two persons: the candidate and the interviewer. What the applicant says to the interviewer may greatly affect whether he or she gets the job or is admitted to the school. At the same time, what the interviewer says may influence how the candidate feels about the prospective employer or school. If the interviewer fails to make the firm or college attractive enough, a strong candidate may look elsewhere.

It is on a personal level, however, with family or friends, that we most often talk in dyadic groups. Examples are innumerable: children and parents, brothers and sisters, classmates, friends, lovers. Although each of these speakers knows the other member of the dyad extremely well, some audience analysis is still important. Someone who wants to borrow money from a friend, for example, should try to determine that friend's financial state, feelings about lending money, and general mood, before making the request. When members of the dyad know each other less well—for example, when a student talks to a professor about a late assignment, or a surgeon consults a patient about an operation—audience analysis is even more important. What is the professor's attitude toward late papers? Is the patient able to face the implications of the operation?

Small Group. The small group is common both in formal and informal circumstances. As in dyads, speakers and listeners in small groups will often exchange roles. In an informal setting, a group of acquaintances may talk over drinks or dinner. Someone in such a gathering may only want to make a good impression on the others. At another time, however, he or she may try to persuade the group to eat in a Chinese restaurant or to see a movie. In all these cases, analyzing the audience would help the speaker succeed.

In small formal groups, effective speaking is even more important. The attorney who can convince a jury will win the case. The worker who can explain to a supervisor his or her plan for reducing absenteeism is more likely to be promoted than someone who fails to illustrate his or her points clearly. Knowing about the views of other members of the group helps a speaker to have the maximum effect upon them.

One-to-Many. This is what we envision when we think of making a speech, and it is probably the most common formal setting for public speaking. This text focuses on the one-to-many situation, in which a single speaker meets with many listeners. The audience may make comments or ask questions, but this is usually after the speech, which is often quite long. Before talking to this type of audience, therefore, we should know as much as possible about the important characteristics of its members. Analyzing an audience helps us prepare a speech that the greatest possible number of listeners can understand and believe.

Mass. When a speaker's audience is large enough to fill a football stadium or so diffuse that it listens chiefly over radio or television, it is called a mass audience. Few of us are likely ever to address a mass audience, but most of us are occasionally part of one. An example of mass communication would be the president's State of the Union message to Congress, broadcast over national radio and television. Other examples include the speeches given to huge crowds at political or religious rallies or the commencement addresses held in the stadiums of large state universities. It is difficult to analyze an audience of this size. A speaker can never know exactly who is listening, what their beliefs, backgrounds, and levels of education are, or how they feel about the subject of the speech. Often something important may be known about the overwhelming majority of the audience—their political or religious beliefs, economic status, or nationality—but even this generalization will not be true of every member of the audience. The speaker, then, is forced to rely on very general information and to treat the audience with very little sense of who they are as individuals.

Student Audiences

Whatever the size or makeup of an audience, the speaker or speakers must make themselves understood. The more complex an audience is, the less the speaker can know about it and the more difficult becomes the task of directing a speech to it. But unless our listeners do understand what we say, we cannot hope to inform or persuade them. Let us consider how this applies to the two main kinds of audiences most frequently encountered by students of public speaking.

Classroom. Public speaking students often have to make classroom presentations. In most cases, the "audience" is the class and is already known to the speaker. At times, however, the instructor may assign a group of students to "role play," that is, to act as if they were another group for the sake of a particular speech or series of speeches: a legislature, a jury, potential buyers, the members of a union local, or whatever. When this happens, the speaker must analyze the audience from a different point of view, gather information about it before preparing the speech, and keep that special audience in mind through each stage of the planning process. As we shall see, every important step in preparing a speech will be affected by the makeup of the audience it is intended for.

Real-Life.   Sometimes, public speaking students will address actual groups within the college community, clubs or campus political groups, for instance. Every audience of this kind will have its own character. To address the student-union board, for example, a speaker should know such things as who was on it, what it did, what issues and problems it was considering. Although speaking to the members of an actual organization resembles speaking to classmates who are role playing, the need for analyzing the audience of a real organization is much greater and more complex.

AUDIENCE-CENTERED COMMUNICATION

Communication should be a bridge between speaker and listeners.

There is no such thing as one-way communication. Even a completely silent audience will send nonverbal messages to the speaker. A speaker who ignores the character of an audience cannot communicate effectively. A speaker on the lecture circuit may deliver the same speech on, say, energy use, to every audience, regardless of whether they are well educated, directly affected by energy shortages, or completely unacquainted with the problem. Such a speaker may stumble now and then on an audience for whom the speech works, but most of his or her listeners will be bored, puzzled, and annoyed.

Communication is the act of bridging the distance between speaker and listeners, so that in some way a dialogue occurs. "One-way communication" blocks even the first step toward such an exchange. As we saw earlier, mass audiences can be so complex that no speaker could ever know much about them. But when the president speaks to the nation about the energy crisis, for example, he knows that he cannot be overly technical and that not everyone listening is as well read or informed about the issues as he is. Instead, he must talk about energy matters on a level that everyone can relate to: rising gasoline prices, the profits of the oil companies, the cost of heating homes and of running machines. Only a scientist can grasp the complications of extracting a gallon of oil from shale, but everyone worries about paying more for fuel.

Speakers too often adopt a "take it or leave it" attitude. They forget that they are like stage performers who flop if they do not reach their audience. A theology professor invited to deliver a guest sermon at a small-town church may choose to speak on God-is-dead theology. But the congregation is probably more concerned about whether their children will join cults or have abortions than about theories which scarcely touch their daily lives.

Public Speaking as Two-Way Communication

As we saw in the last chapter, the listener is not merely a passive receiver but an active sharer in the communication process. The listener responds, verbally or otherwise, to the speaker. Communication occurs only when he or she understands what the speaker is saying. When a doctor tells us the results of an examination, for example, we want to know not just the medical term for our condition, but its nature and causes and how and why we are to be treated for it. We expect to be able to ask questions and to receive clear, full answers. In other words, the speaker in two-way communication assumes the listener's active participation. The principal elements of two-way communication may be expressed as follows:

1. *The speaker feels a responsibility for the listener's understanding.* No matter how big an audience, there is a degree of reciprocity between speaker and listeners. The primary responsibility for successful communication lies with the speaker, but both parties must cooperate. If the audience fails to understand what has been said, the failure usually stems from the speaker's not having found the proper level of understanding for this audience. The speaker will need to analyze further the audience and its interest in and understanding of the subject. But the first step toward thorough audience analysis and successful communication occurs when the speaker acknowledges his or her responsibility to make the audience understand what is being said. This cannot be overemphasized.

2. *The speaker responds to listener feedback to the speech.* It is audience feedback that tells a speaker whether the audience analysis has succeeded and whether he or she is reaching the listeners. Feedback can be spoken or unspoken. It begins almost as soon as a speaker sees an audience, and the speaker must pay close attention to what it reveals about the audience and the speech. No prior audience analysis can ever be more than tentative, because it has to be tested during the speech itself. When a speaker discovers that a speech needs to be revised for a particular audience, he or she must revise it.

What would happen, for example, if a speaker misjudged a prospective audience beforehand? Suppose that in college you had done a project on solar energy and as a result were invited by your old high school science teacher to discuss the project with the school science club. When you were in school, the science club's members had all been eager young future scientists. You assume that the current members will have at least some knowledge of solar energy, and you plan your presentation accordingly. When you arrive, however, you find that these students know nothing at all about solar energy. The science advisor tells you that all ninth graders are required to join either the science or home economics club. These students have chosen science as the lesser of two evils. Fortunately, you find this out before beginning your speech. Since your audience knows nothing about your topic and is not overly interested in science, you can adapt your talk to their level of interest and information. Audience analysis and a quick reaction to what you have learned can save the speech.

3. *The speaker works for a dialogue with the listeners.* In public speaking, a genuine communication exchange is extremely difficult to effect. This two-way "give and take" is common only in dyadic situations, where both parties alternate as speaker and listener. But in a larger group, the roles of speaker and listener become fixed and inflexible. One person—the speaker—does all the talking. The rest become an audience whose function is to listen. Under these circumstances, communication exchange becomes more difficult.

The effective speaker must be aware of his or her impact on an audience. Prior audience analysis and planning prepares the speaker for a set of expected results. Audience feedback lets the speaker monitor the effect of a speech. When the speaker discovers a weakness that should be remedied, he or she can change tactics promptly. An inattentive or unprepared speaker, on the other hand, always risks losing the audience. The speaker who succeeds in achieving a communication exchange is actually talking *with* the audience rather than to them. Audience and speaker are having a dialogue.

4. *The primary goal of the speech is the audience's understanding, not the speaker's enhancement.* In the nineteenth century, the focus of public speaking was on the speaker and the speech. A speech was an exercise in oratory. The audience came to admire the speaker's talents, not to improve their own knowledge or understanding. But in two-way communication the emphasis is on the listener. Every decision in planning and organizing a speech should be governed by the needs of the intended audience. If the audience will learn nothing or remain unaffected by a speech, that speech should not be given. In this context, audience analysis becomes extremely important. It is the audience's needs and ability to learn about the subject that gives more shape to the speech than either the subject itself or the speaker's opinions about it.

Public Speaking as Dynamic Interaction

Audience analysis is difficult because every audience is unique, every occasion fluid and unpredictable. A speaker must be dynamic; that is, he or she must be able to respond to change. Although a speaker may know a lot about a particular group, their response to a given speech is always more or less uncertain. Members of an audience may share some characteristics—for example, they may all be residents of Columbus, Ohio, college graduates, and registered Republicans—but they will differ individually from one another and collectively from other similar groups. Individually, some may be well off, others poor; some native Ohioans, others migrants from other states or immigrants from abroad; some black, some members of religious minorities, and so on.

Collectively, of two groups of educated Republicans in Columbus, Ohio, one may have had its delegates chosen to represent the area's Republicans at the state convention, while the other may have been passed over; or one group may have stable leadership, while the other is divided and quarrelsome.

Where the meeting is to be held and when, current political, social, or economic conditions, even the weather, are further factors that can influence an audience. As a speaker, you should not overlook special circumstances such as these, even when you have also considered what seem to be more important factors. Taking note of these changing and unpredictable conditions is difficult but essential if you want to give an effective speech.

The speaker, therefore, can never consider his or her audience analysis complete. Factors affecting audience attitude may change even during the speech, and the speaker will have to adapt to the new conditions. The process of continually adjusting a speech can be so frustrating that many public speakers wonder whether it is worth the trouble. Why bother to gear a speech to a specific audience when a ready-made speech might work as well? But whenever a speaker uses a generalized speech, he or she sets the trap of talking at the audience. The speech that is written without a specific audience in mind will rarely strike the listeners as addressed to them. An audience that is convinced that the speaker is not truly attempting to speak to them may not bother to listen.

AUDIENCE ATTITUDES AND CHARACTERISTICS

Who makes up audiences? The answer, of course, is people. This is obvious, but it complicates the task of the audience analyst. We have already discussed how unpredictable audiences can be, and this is in part because people as individuals are so complex. Each of us is a bundle of beliefs and attitudes that is difficult to classify. Some parts of our personality and thinking may be sensible and consistent while others are harder to understand, especially for an outsider. We may regard the family as the most important and valuable social unit, yet have stormy relations with our relatives. We may be conservative in our tastes and beliefs, yet be unable to control the itch to gamble.

The speaker seeking to predict the reactions to a speech must assume that there is a mass of unknown and unknowable information about the audience which cannot be discovered in advance, but which may nonetheless affect audience response to the speech. The point is that while analysis can never be conclusive, it still reveals much about an audience. When done skillfully and consistently it helps a speaker make a more effective speech.

Audience Attitudes

One important influence on a listener's response to a speech is his or her set of attitudes. Attitude is the feeling we have about things we know or believe. We know, for example, that we live in the United States of America and in the twentieth century. We may believe that the United States guarantees greater human rights to its citizens than most other nations. We may believe that this century has seen the greatest advances in science and technology in history. Our attitudes toward these facts and beliefs might be that we are lucky to be living in this country and that this century is a time of unprecedented excitement and possibility. Attitudes are harder to defend than either factual knowledge or beliefs. But we will often cling as stubbornly to our attitudes as we will to the most objective data. As a result, attitudes go far toward determining our responses to a speaker's claims and the likelihood of our being persuaded by them.

Sources of Attitudes. Although we derive our attitudes from many sources, for many people the most important source is the family. Our outlook almost always bears a strong resemblance to that of our family. From birth, our parents and relatives have educated and influenced us. We may absorb this influence without knowing it, or freely and as a matter of choice. Our political beliefs and voting patterns, our religious faith and practice, and our social attitudes often resemble those of our parents. These beliefs and habits will rarely, it is true, be mere carbon copies of those of our parents. We grow up at a different time and are exposed to influences with which our parents were not familiar. But even if we are not aware of it, their influence and example nevertheless powerfully shape our attitudes toward those beliefs and habits.

Besides our families, other important sources of attitudes include our religious training, friends, social and economic status, schooling, the roles we play (for example, child, student, employee), and our ambitions and occupational or career choices. The way we live and perhaps especially the work we do help to shape our attitudes, and those attitudes in turn help us to interpret our experiences. Thus, our attitudes may be said to be *functional;* that is, they are used in day-to-day living.

Types of Attitudes.　Audiences are likely to have attitudes about most topics. Each attitude will be either static or dynamic. A static attitude is well defined and resists change; a dynamic attitude might change, given the right motivation. As speakers we should try to learn not only what attitudes the audience hold but also how likely they are to keep or change them, that is, whether the attitudes are static or dynamic. (For a discussion of certain attitudes that affect most audiences, see Chapter 13.)

We should not assume, however, that dynamic attitudes will be relatively easy to change and static attitudes impossible, or at least difficult. Although generally speaking a person's dynamic attitudes are those he or she is still evaluating or will evaluate if prompted, not every listener will respond by considering the changes that the speaker urges. Many of our static attitudes, on the other hand, are habits that exist because we take them for granted. In such cases, a listener might well change attitudes if the issue is put in a new light. For example, someone who had always thought that income taxes were an essential source of revenue for the federal government might think again when a speaker outlines other means of producing revenue or offers examples of governments that do not tax incomes.

Specific Audience Attitudes

Both static and dynamic attitudes can be general feelings that an audience may hold without reference to a particular situation. Just as important are those attitudes the audience holds toward the ideas we propose and toward us as speakers or persons. These factors bear directly on the tactics we should use to give a speech and on its chances of reaching a particular audience. Let's consider specific attitudes in some detail.

Attitudes toward Your Ideas.　Every group of listeners will have some feelings about your ideas before you present them. These feelings can be expressed in one of the following ways: The audience will agree with you; the audience will disagree with you; or the audience will be neutral or indifferent.[1] Since each of the three main conditions has different implications for the speaker, we shall discuss each one in turn.

Audience Agreement.   This is highly desirable for a speaker. It occurs when the speaker analyzes the audience and finds that they already endorse what he or she has to say. In this case, the speaker's goal is to reinforce the positive attitudes that already exist. It is not necessary to introduce the proposal, since the audience already knows about it. If the speaker were to treat the audience as if they knew nothing about the proposal or did not already support it, he or she might well alienate them and lose that support.

Sometimes, the speaker can go beyond reinforcing positive attitudes. Suppose the speaker wants to drum up support for a new medical center. Since the listeners all support the idea, the speaker may try to encourage them to announce their support and to work openly for it, for example, by helping with a publicity campaign or by raising funds. The speaker should try to encourage those who are already actively involved to maintain or increase their commitment.[2] (For further discussion of reinforcement in persuasive speaking, see Chapter 14.)

Audience Disagreement.   At times, most speakers have to face a hostile audience, one that is already opposed to their ideas. Audience analysis should insure that this comes as no surprise. The speaker's task is to overcome as much of the listeners' resistance as possible. It is unrealistic to hope to convert many of these hostile listeners entirely after one speech. The speaker can try, however, to reduce outspoken and private opposition and to move the audience toward neutrality or indecision on the issue. The speaker must plan the speech thoroughly, make arguments from the ground up, acknowledge the opponent's point of view, and present his or her own argument as strongly as possible.

To return to our example of the proposed medical center: Suppose the audience opposes a new center as too expensive and not needed, given the medical services that already exist in the area. The speaker could therefore stress the economical aspects of building the center or show that it would not, as feared, cost too much. The speaker could also point out those medical services that are not currently provided in the area and show how the new center would fill those needs. This

[1] Robert T. Oliver, *The Psychology of Persuasive Speech,* 2nd ed. (New York: Longman's, Green, 1957), p. 85.

[2] Robert N. Simons, *Persuasion Understanding, Practice and Analysis* (Reading, Pa.: Addison-Wesley, 1976), p. 99.

argument might make few immediate converts, but it could make opponents reconsider their position.

Insufficient Information. If the proposal is new or unusual, the audience may not know enough before the speech to make a sound judgment. To win the listeners' support, the speaker needs to provide that information. He or she must proceed at a pace appropriate to the audience's level of understanding. It may not be possible, for example, both to inform and to persuade in the same talk. In that case, the speaker should be content to inform, since listeners can seldom be persuaded about something before they know about it. Many speakers, with a kind of "they'll think what I tell them to think" arrogance, overlook this.

An audience that was undecided about the medical center would need to know what it would offer, how it would improve existing services, and how much it would cost. The listeners might also want to know whether there were alternatives to the proposals under discussion and why this one was preferred.

Attitudes toward You. The audience's reaction to the speaker is as important for the success or failure of the speech as is their reaction to the speaker's ideas. If they have heard the speaker before, they may already have opinions about his or her credibility, talents, and general appeal. An audience is much more likely to believe a speaker it likes than one it dislikes. By analyzing the audience, a speaker can determine its feelings, if any, toward him or herself and should take those feelings into account when planning the speech. (See Chapter 9.)

Audience Characteristics

Information about individual members of an audience can be extremely useful in helping the speaker gauge the effect of his or her speech. This information can be gathered before, during, or even after a speech. It includes data about individual personalities, demographic information, the constituencies members of the audience represent, and their roles as members of the audience. Before a speech, this information helps the speaker to decide how to aim or slant the speech for maximum effect. During the speech, it constitutes much of what we earlier called feedback and lets the speaker know whether the speech is making the impression that he or she intended it to make. Often, as we have emphasized, a smart speaker will be able to adjust a speech even while it is in progress in order to increase its effectiveness. After the speech has been delivered, the information helps the speaker to evaluate its success or failure.

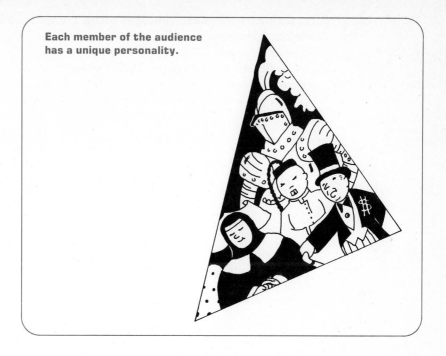

Each member of the audience has a unique personality.

Personality.   Each person has a unique personality, a basic fact too often ignored by those who address a large gathering. Moreover, when individuals join to form an audience, then that audience also has its own unique personality. Very often, the situation in which a group comes together will contribute to—or sometimes even determine—the group personality. For example, a college football team listening to the coach before a crucial game will have a personality quite different from the same group of athletes relaxing in the student lounge or struggling with a chemistry experiment. A speaker should gather as much information as possible about both the individual and the collective personalities of every audience.

Demographics.   Demographics are data about the composition of a population. They include facts about age, sex, race, religion, nationality, education, political beliefs, and social and economic circumstances. The thoughtful speaker will always pay close attention to these elements when planning a speech and will look for what is unusual in an audience to provide clues about how it may best be approached, informed, and/or persuaded. To know that an entire audience is very young would be extremely useful to a speaker preparing a talk on sex education, for example. Someone about to give a pro–birth-control speech would be helped immeasurably to learn that the audience included a very high proportion of unwed mothers or of Roman Catholics. A speaker who is discussing income tax would want to know how much money members of the audience make, what jobs they hold, and how many tax lawyers or accountants are among them. These are just a few examples of how demographic information can be useful to a speaker.

Constituencies.   The causes, principles, and groups that members of an audience *represent* are their *constituencies*. A constituency may be either explicit or implicit. A group of Scout leaders attending a convention, parents and teachers at a PTA meeting, or a group of state governors at a regional conference all represent explicit constituencies. Each individual stands not only for the organization of which he or she is a member but also for that organization's principles and ideals.

An implicit constituency may be more difficult to discern. Nevertheless such groups exist. When an audience forms, implicity or explicity, into one or more constituencies, the speaker cannot overlook the impact this may have on audience response. A single senior citizen might not think of himself or herself as standing for the interests or problems of all older people, but an auditorium full of the aged would almost automatically perceive themselves as such a constituency. An intelligent speaker will acknowledge this and prepare for a concerted response from the group about any topic that affected the interests of the aged.

Roles.   Almost without thinking, people slip in and out of roles easily and frequently. When we attend classes, we are students, but when we head for our after-school or summer jobs, we become workers. To our parents, we are sons and daughters, to our children, fathers and mothers. Day in and day out, we play a wide variety of roles. This is also true when we are in an audience. Opponents of forced busing at a protest meeting play the role of aggrieved citizens. Later that same evening, they may become card players or diners. The next morning, they become workers or students. When a public speaker prepares a speech, he or she should consider the range of roles that the audience plays at various times. The speaker should emphasize the specific role or roles the audience will play while listening to the speech. This will depend, of course, not only on who is in the audience but also on what the speech is about.

The unique characteristics of each audience—including personality, demographics, the constituencies the audience represent, and the roles played individually and collectively by its members—offer valuable clues about how an audience is likely to respond to a speech. The wise public speaker will therefore consider these elements during the planning process. The accompanying Audience Analysis Worksheet will help you to organize your information-gathering in this phase.

ANALYZING THE AUDIENCE AND PREPARING A SPEECH

Let us consider how a speaker would go about preparing a speech based on thorough audience analysis.

1. *The speaker must determine who will be in the audience.* Who will hear the speech? The speaker must answer this question before beginning to gather data and prepare the speech itself. If the speaker has not encountered this particular audience before, this step becomes more important. The answer will come from two sources: documents and other people. By studying whatever written material exists on the prospective audience, by talking to people who know about it, and especially, if possible, to members of the audience itself, the speaker should be able to learn the following: how large the audience will be, its age range, the proportion of males to females, its physical and mental state, its level of education, the occupations and experience of its members, and how well acquainted it is likely to be with the speaker's topic.

The speaker should, of course, talk to anyone who is likely to have useful information about the audience. He or she should also read as

AUDIENCE ANALYSIS WORKSHEET

Demographic Characteristics
Age: Economic Status:
Educational Level: Political Status:
Occupational Type: Other Influences:

General Audience Attitudes
What are their political orientations?
What are their social orientations?
Where do they get their information?
What constituencies do they serve?

Specific Audience Attitudes toward Proposal
What do they think of your proposal?
Sources of their attitudes?
What attitudes can be changed?
What strategies may work?

Specific Audience Attitutes toward Communicator
What do they think of you?
What are your strengths (with listeners)?
What are your weaknesses (with listeners)?
Possible sources of credibility?

much as possible about the prospective listeners. Sometimes the audience will be drawn from the membership of an organization that has a constitution, by-laws or other official documents or records. At other times, there might be an article about it in a local or campus newspaper. When the audience is the members of a class, the speaker is likely to have personal access to the entire audience. Word of mouth can therefore be effective for gathering information.

2. *The speaker must gather "data" about the audience.* Once the speaker knows who will make up an audience, he or she must learn about their attitudes and characteristics. These features have been discussed earlier in this chapter. Once again, the speaker should use whatever is available from both written and live sources. With this information, the speaker can form "hunches," that is, make assumptions, about how the audience would be likely to react to various circumstances and proposals.

3. *The speaker must write out a "position paper" explaining how he or she thinks the audience will react to the speech.* The position paper need not be formal or overly long, but it should reflect what the speaker has learned from the data. The paper should include the audience's general and specific attitudes. These will still only be "best guesses," but they are the most reliable information the speaker has. It is understood that more information will be sought and that the position paper will be revised as preparation for the speech continues.

4. *Based on the information in the position paper, the speaker should make the basic outline of the speech.* After all possible useful information about the audience has been amassed and the position paper written, the speaker can go on to the outline. Every decision about content, organization, tone, etc., should be made with the response of the audience in mind. It cannot be overemphasized that the successful speech is one that evokes the desired response from the audience.

5. *As more information becomes available, the speaker should continually review the outline and revise the speech.* Flexibility is the key to the planning process. The speaker must continually adjust the outline and make all possible improvements in the speech—even while delivering it! The planning was based on educated guesses about the information the speaker gathered. Whenever the speaker finds a way to improve the likely effectiveness of the speech, he or she should make the recommended changes. No speech is ever completely successful, but a sharp eye and quick mind can bring every speech closer to that ideal.

A wise speaker hunts for information about an audience.

Summary

Understanding the audience is crucial to successful communication. A successful speech is one that evokes the desired response from the audience. Audience analysis is an attempt by the speaker to find out as much about the audience as possible so that he or she can give the speech in a manner that gets that response. A generalized speech will seldom move or convince an audience. Audience analysis should be conducted before, during, and after a speech.

When planning a speech, a speaker should (1) determine who will be in the audience; (2) gather as much demographic data about the audience as possible; (3) write out a position paper explaining how he or she thinks the audience will react; (4) make a basic outline of the speech based on the position paper; (5) continually review the outline and revise the speech as new information about the audience becomes available.

Speakers must take into account the attitudes or predispositions held by the audience. These fall into three categories: general attitudes, attitudes about the content of the speech, and attitudes about the speaker. The speaker must adjust the speech to allow for each of these, to take advantage of those that are positive and to offset those that are negative. Audience analysis can never be more than a ''best guess'' about the audience's reaction. It is a valuable tool, but the speaker must always be ready for surprises.

Exercises

1. From what you know about your classmates, write a brief ''position paper'' about them as a potential audience. Be sure to take into consideration factors such as:
   a. age
   b. ethnic background
   c. social position
   d. economic position
   e. social behavior
   f. attitudes
   g. sex breakdown

2. What might you say about the following audiences:
   a. Young Republicans
   b. senior citizens at the St. Paul Presbyterian Church
   c. Society of White House News Correspondents
   d. UCLA basketball team
   e. Executive Committee of the National Organization for Women (NOW)

3. How would you approach each audience to talk about the topic "The Need to Contribute to the National March of Dimes Campaign"?
4. In class, briefly discuss "student political attitudes" on your campus. What generalizations can you make about them? Why? What additional information would you need before you would be willing to talk with an audience, made up of students at your school, about a political topic?

Choosing and Researching a Topic

Tips for Speakers

1. When selecting a topic, choose a subject you are familiar with, interested in, or feel strongly about.
2. A good topic communicates new information to your audience and is relevant to their interests.
3. In order to research your topics efficiently, become thoroughly familiar with the library's facilities.
4. Take accurate notes so that you can transmit correctly facts, quotes, and sources in your speeches.
5. One of the most successful research tools is a well-conducted personal interview.
6. The value of a topic can be judged by what your audience will get in return for listening.

TOPIC SELECTION: A FIRST STEP

Selecting a topic is the first step in developing a speech. As we shall see, careful consideration in choosing the subject of a speech can be your best insurance against problems later on. An impulsive choice can easily cause problems for every stage of planning and developing a speech presentation.

A Problem for Beginning Speakers

Selecting a topic is often a problem for the novice speaker. To begin with, he or she may be unsure of the audience. What do they expect to hear? What might they enjoy? What subject will hold their attention? Some students also lack confidence in their own skills. They worry that their speaking abilities are inadequate or that they simply don't know enough about a topic, particularly one that is controversial or complex. Many inexperienced speakers also mistakenly undervalue their personal experiences and interests as sources of worthwhile speech topics. In their preoccupation with the search for a "safe" but interesting subject they often overlook the fund of information that they already possess.

Experienced speakers, on the other hand, can draw from a larger pool of potential speech topics. They know their ability to evaluate their audiences and they choose their topic accordingly. Research for other speeches may, indeed, have made them very knowledgeable about certain topics. Finally, they know their own skills. Past successes and failures have taught them which subjects they are best equipped to speak about.

Confidence and Getting Started Right

Confidence in public speaking is essential. Confident speakers generally have more success than those who are not at ease. Unfortunately, many public speakers experience at least some degree of stage fright. Stage fright is the apprehension felt when speaking to an audience. This fear is normal. Some degree of fear will make us try harder and take the speaking situation more seriously. You should expect to be nervous when you begin to prepare a public speech, even as early as the topic selection phase.

As long as this apprehension is moderate, it can actually help you to try harder. It is only excessive fear that can paralyze a speaker, and this is rare. For most of us, therefore, stage fright is not an insurmountable problem. As you become more experienced, stage fright will be automatically reduced. Controlling each phase of the speaking situation will help you gain confidence. A good topic is the first step in gaining this control.

Later, in the chapter on speaker credibility, we shall discuss ways to help you reduce stage fright. These techniques should help you relax as you prepare, think about, and, finally, deliver your speech. But, for now, do not let your confidence be damaged by the first appearance of stage fright. You should expect it. But you should also expect it *not* to be a major problem.

The Importance of a Careful Choice

Although selecting a topic may be difficult or confusing, a careful decision is important for the ultimate success of a speech. While the topic is obviously a major factor in determining how the audience will respond to a presentation, it also has an immediate impact on the potential speaker. An interesting topic can make planning and developing a speech a pleasure. Preparing a topic that seems trivial or impossibly difficult, on the other hand, can be both tedious and unrewarding.

The topic guides the early stages of speech planning in several ways. Some subjects clearly require a particular presentation or organization. Others can be presented in many ways. The topic can be an essential guide to planning the strategy of a speech. If the needs of the topic are not met, even the most elaborate structure or elegant presentation may not save the speech. After all, the topic is the heart of the speech: It is what the speaker is talking *about*. For a speech to be effective, the speaker must want to communicate that subject to the audience. This requires putting the more formal aspects of speech making at the service of the topic. Thus, a thorough knowledge of the subject should be the foundation upon which all other plans are laid.

THE "GOOD" TOPIC: QUALITIES AND CONSIDERATIONS

Given that the selection of a topic is both difficult and important, how should the beginning speaker go about making a choice? What qualities should a good topic have? The answers to these questions involve both the audience and the speaker. Unless a topic can hold an audience's attention, they will not listen to a speech. Unless a speaker knows and cares about the subject, he or she will not be able to speak effectively.

The Topic and the Audience

Telling the Audience Something New. That a good topic should tell the audience something new may seem obvious; but it is often overlooked. Speakers who do not consider the audience's experience

An unimportant topic will not hold an audience.

and knowledge are apt to bore or even annoy their listeners. For example, the president of a large, urban university was asked to speak at graduation exercises for 7,000 seniors. The topic he chose was "bureaucracy." He informed the students that when they "went out into the world" they might be dismayed at first by the rigid structure in government offices and business. He talked about the loss of individual identity in a bureaucracy and lamented the lack of communication between bureaucrats and the people they supposedly serve. He spoke about the waste of time and energy that occurs when executives lose touch with their workers and the public. Despite all these problems, he said, bureaucracies must be accepted as a fact of life. He closed by encouraging the students to develop the humanism that could help them to live in a bureaucratic society.

The speech was not a success. As individuals in a mass graduation, the students hardly needed to be warned about depersonalization. They didn't need to go "out into the world" to encounter a large-scale bureaucracy. They had already dealt with one at school. They knew all about filling out forms, standing in lines, and waiting, waiting, waiting. Many of the students felt that the talk in itself proved one of the speaker's main points—that those administering a system are apt to lose touch with the people who have to live in it.

The president's speech might have been more successful if he had discussed the students' experience with the university bureaucracy. Then he could have offered them another point of view by talking about the problems, challenges, and rewards that come from managing such large organizations. As future business people, teachers, and administrators, the students might have been interested in his "view from the top." It would be a new perspective and one they might find themselves facing in the future.

Topic Relevancy.   A good topic bears some general relation to the listeners' past experiences, present lives, or potential futures. A speech about skateboarding could reveal much that was new to an audience of retired citizens. Yet, it is unlikely that the mere novelty of the subject would hold their attention for long. Skateboarding is a fairly recent amusement and would arouse few memories of the games the listeners had played in their youth. Nor would that audience include many present or future skateboarders. Some may have watched their grandchildren skateboard. Perhaps they admired their skill and speed. But, aside from such remote and passive experiences, the topic would bear no relation to them. Such irrelevance would probably produce a marked lack of interest among these listeners.

A better choice of topic in this situation might have been "bicycling"—an activity that the listeners might still be enjoying. This topic would relate to several aspects of retired citizens' lives—their age,

A topic should be relevant to an audience.

their health, and their need for safe, self-paced, and not-too-expensive recreation. A speech about bicycling would have a much greater chance of holding the listeners' attention.

Topic Importance.   Besides relevance, a good topic should be one that matters to the audience. Listener response is potentially much greater when the subject significantly affects them. When a topic is not important to an audience, their response is often merely "polite." A speaker may have their initial attention, but then it soon wanes. Speeches about topics that are unimportant to the audience may be marked by coughing, whispering, or the shuffling of feet. It is difficult to make eye contact with an uninterested audience and even harder to get any positive feedback from them—no expressions of interest, no questions, no comments. The reason is simple: The audience is not involved in the speech. They are only waiting for it to end.

The Topic and the Speaker: Knowledge and Interest

Speakers talk best about a subject they are interested in and already know something about (or can learn about very quickly). Choosing an already familiar subject offers both practical and personal advantages. As we mentioned above, interest in the topic can motivate a speaker to prepare a speech thoroughly and well. Knowledge about the topic can make the preparation easier and more effective.

Knowing Your Topic.

Consider the time and effort saved when speakers can consult their own experience instead of having to rely on research alone. If a speaker already knows the subject, he or she can do a minimal amount of research and spend most of the available time planning and polishing the presentation. Furthermore, if data are needed to support or expand the main points, the speaker with previous knowledge and interest will probably know where to find them.

At times, speakers have no choice—they have to discuss a certain subject. This happens in class, of course, or when someone is the only available source of information that is needed in a hurry. For example, consider Ms. Smith, the community theater member most skilled in backstage work. Two weeks before the scheduled opening of a play, the company's plans for hiring professional stagehands collapse. Whom do you think will be asked to talk to the amateur volunteers about how to do what needs to be done? Ms. Smith, of course, for she is the one with the knowledge on hand.

Whether a subject is chosen freely or under duress, the more knowledgeable speaker has a better chance of reaching an audience because audiences prefer to listen to experts.

Expertise or the lack of it can be perceived by an audience even when they are not particularly well informed about a topic. How can this be? Imagine yourself attending a talk about any subject remote from your own experience. The speaker gives many broad generalizations, but few facts to back them up. The explanations are shallow, unclear, or missing. Some of the information is contradictory; the speaker is unable to answer questions satisfactorily. How would you feel about the speaker and the speech? Would you accept that the speaker knows what he or she is talking about? Probably not. Would you value what you had learned? Probably not—after all, the speaker has not shown that he or she knows enough about the topic to justify your listening.

As we have seen, there are many advantages to choosing a topic that one already knows in depth. The speaker has more motivation and can use his or her preparation time more efficiently. When the speech is finally delivered, the speaker's expertise will establish credibility in the minds of the audience. Yet there is another dimension in the relation between speaker and topic, and that is the depth of his or her feeling.

Being Interested in Your Topic.

Strong belief or emotional involvement with the topic can give power to a speaker. Few speeches are more effective or persuasive than those delivered from deep conviction. By contrast, a halfhearted or overly cautious speech will ring hollow. A speaker who is indifferent to his or her subject will find it difficult to arouse or convince an audience.

Speakers, however, do not always speak from deep emotional or intellectual commitment, and it is unrealistic to expect it in every public speaking situation. But a speaker should always be interested in his or her topic. Without this interest, a speech—particularly one by a novice—will seldom be even minimally effective. Interest in the topic can be stimulated even when the speech is required, not given voluntarily. People in sales, advertising, or politics, for example, often have to speak about products or subjects that are not of their own choosing. To be effective in their jobs, however, they have to speak effectively. To do this, they have to develop an interest in what they say. In other words, because they are interested in the *effect* of their speech—selling or promoting a product; winning votes—they also need to be interested in their topic. After all, would you buy a new product that was feebly sold? Would you vote for a candidate who was openly indifferent to the issues?

The Best Source of a Topic: The Speaker

By now it should be clear that the speaker's relation to the topic is important for the success of the speech. In seeking a topic, therefore, a speaker should first look to him or herself. As we shall see, excellent topics can be drawn from each person's experiences.

Unusual hobbies can make for fascinating speeches.

Hobbies. Hobbies are often good topics for speeches. The longer you have been interested in the hobby, the more you are likely to know about it. Unusual hobbies can make fascinating and informative subjects for speeches.

Social, Ethnic, and Regional Background. A speaker's social, ethnic, or regional background can also provide an interesting speech topic. This has the most potential when the audience is not from the same ethnic or social group. Contrast with audience experience is important here. Thus, a woman from the deep South could offer her audience of New Englanders a view of a decidedly different life-style. Most people want to hear about different backgrounds and experiences. Here is an example taken from a speech given by someone with an unusual background.

> *Our problem is so different from what most people imagine, that it is hard for them even to comprehend its existence. It is not our blindness, nor is it that we have lacked sympathy or good will or widespread charity and kindness. . . . Rather, it is that we have not (in present day parlance) been perceived as a minority. Yet that is exactly what we are—a minority with all that the term implies.[1]*

[1] Kenneth Jernigan, ''Blindness,'' *Vital Speeches of the Day*, August 15, 1975, p. 661.

Jobs.   Jobs, past and present, are another good source of topics. The day-to-day happenings of one person's job or profession can interest a listener with no similar experience. Even a part-time job like delivering the morning papers can suggest a topic that an audience might enjoy: "Our Town in the A.M." Many people have been employed in a variety of situations and places and therefore have a number of possible topics to choose from.

> *When I first went into business, my goal was to simply write speeches for other people and let it go at that. However, I found out rather quickly that many of my clients were not taking advantage of all the opportunities that giving a speech can generate, such as press coverage and printed copies distributed to various people and publishers. And so, I began offering advice in these allied areas.*[2]

Extraordinary Experiences.   Extraordinary experiences are another source of topics for speaking. If the speaker remembers the event clearly, his or her personal account can be vivid and interesting. Examples of topics drawn from unique experiences might be "My Summer in Chile" or "Conversations While Trapped in an Elevator." If an experience seems unique, entertaining, and important to the speaker, the audience will probably enjoy hearing about it.

> *Just over a year ago, I went to Communist China with a group from Penn State. I had studied communism and China for years before that, but here at last was an opportunity to see the faces behind the rhetoric. . . . We were shown around a fair number of universities, colleges, and high schools, and had ample occasion to talk with faculty, students, and administrators. . . . I should like to share with you a few of the impressions I gained in China.*[3]

Learning Something New.   Most of our discussion of the topic's relation to the speaker has been in terms of his or her prior knowledge and experience. But if a person sifts through jobs, hobbies, and personal history and still finds no inspiring topic, he or she must not despair. Speech building can be a way of learning about a subject that one has always been interested in but doesn't know firsthand. If the speaker is enthusiastic and willing to do some extra research, and if the topic is one that can be learned about fairly quickly, the final presentation can be both interesting and credible. (See Chapter 12.)

[2] Charles A. Boyle, "A Few Words about Speeches: Rhetoric Is Action," *Vital Speeches of the Day,* September 1, 1975, p. 682.
[3] Jan S. Prybyla, "Man and Society in China," *Vital Speeches of the Day,* July 1, 1975, p. 55.

I've tried to learn from this experience. Thus, these are certainly not the only ideas and views or environmental considerations and concerns about nuclear power to which you may be exposed; they may not even be the best; but they happen to be mine.[4]

FORMAL TOPIC CATEGORIES

Most of the speeches you will give will be either informative or persuasive. Chapters 12, 13, and 14 discuss speeches of information and persuasion in detail. In this section we will consider them more briefly.

Informational Topics

General Information.   Students are always familiar with this category since most of the large group lectures given in colleges and universities can be defined as general informational speeches. In general informational speeches, a particular content area is covered with the aim of sharing knowledge with the audience. Any lecture you attend will probably have a general informational format. It could be a talk on "The Four Aspects of the American Presidency," or "Trends in Contemporary Country and Western Music," or "Fixed-Rail Mass Transit Systems." Whatever the topic, the basic speaker-audience relationship is the same—the speaker tells what he or she knows about a subject to the listeners.

How to Do It.   Topics in this category explain a particular technique or process to the listener—"How to Shoot Foul Shots in Basketball," "Canning Your Own Fruits and Vegetables," or "Learning to Watercolor." The success of these speeches usually depends on how well the speaker has organized the material. The best approach is step-by-step, taking each phase of the process at a time to ensure that the listeners understand it.

How-to-do-it speeches require the speaker to spend extra time making sure that whatever demonstrations he or she plans to include are appropriate and will be clear to the audience. Visual aids or other graphic illustrations can help the speaker to get the necessary points across. This is especially true if what is to be explained is intricate or hard to slow down for the purpose of demonstration. Enlarged diagrams or stop-action films would be useful in these cases. Obviously,

[4] Melvin W. Carter, "Concerns about Nuclear Power," *Vital Speeches of the Day*, October 1, 1975, p. 5.

demonstrations for large audiences will also require visual aids. (See Chapter 8.)

All About.   In an "all-about" speech the speaker usually tries to show the audience how something works or how it is constructed. All-about presentations most often involve objects which have some actual or potential place in the listeners' lives. The speaker's aim is to promote a general understanding of the structure or function of the object. To do this, he or she should explain the basic technical information in terms that the average listener can grasp. For example, a speaker might try to explain as simply as possible how a car's engine works to a group of people who are not mechanically inclined.

Persuasive Topics

The informational speaker's aim is to share knowledge. His or her success can be measured by the degree of audience understanding that the speech produces. Persuasive speeches, however, seek to do more. The persuasive speaker tries to convince the listeners to take action. He or she will emphasize what "should be" instead of merely explaining the facts. There are two basic types of persuasive speeches: those that call for policy action and those that call for individual or personal action. (See Chapter 14.)

Calls for Policy Action.   These are attempts to persuade listeners of the need for change in policy on some subject. Typical policy-action topics would be "The State of Utah Should Abolish the Death Penalty," "Marijuana Should Be Legalized," or "Business Should Recruit More Women as Executives." Almost all political speeches, except those that are direct calls to vote for a political candidate, would be classified as policy-action speeches.

Although policy-action topics are usually important and worth hearing, they often fail to produce tangible results. A speaker may indeed convince an audience about what "should be," but whether the listeners can bring about the desired change is something else. For example, an audience of college freshmen and sophomores can't really do much about corporations hiring more women even if they agree with the speaker's argument that present corporate policy is wrong. Policy-action topics such as this are often somewhat less than immediate or directly relevant to the listener. Yet, because we live in a democracy, these topics should be discussed.

Moreover, policy-action speeches often concern questions of right and wrong to which there may be no absolute answers. Speakers who advocate moral or ethical policies must first convince the audience of the "rightness" of their view before persuading them to take one

SELECTING A TOPIC: SAMPLE CATEGORIES

Speeches of Information

General Informational	*How to Do It*	*All About*
Careers	Operate Machines	Car Engines
Sports	Cook	Home Appliances
Current Events	Select a Career	Checking Accounts
Foreign Affairs	Garden	Solar Heating
Politics	Administer First Aid	Natural Child Birth
Personal History	Pick a College	Jogging
The Arts	Dance	Cameras
Literature	Make Repairs	Audio-Visual Equipment
Food	Prepare a Resume	Pedigree Pets
Travel	Have an Interview	Building a House
The Economy	Fill Out a Form	
Science	Make Friends	
Energy		
Health		

Speeches of Persuasion

Policy Action		*Personal Action*
Inflation	The Right to Die	Vote for a Candidate
Unemployment	Drug Control	Work for a Cause
Taxes	Abortion	Contribute to a Charity
Government Regulation	Censorship	Join an Organization
Business Ethics	Pornography	Buy Something
The Energy Crisis	Crime	Go on a Trip
Pollution	The Death Penalty	Eat Healthier
Minority Rights	Legalized Gambling	Change Jobs
The Equal Rights	The Drinking Age	Work Harder
Amendment	The Draft	Relocate
Gay Rights	Public Transportation	Save Fuel
National Health Care	School Policy	Personal Reform
The Aged		

action rather than another. An example of this type of policy-action topic would be "Racial Discrimination: Let Us Work to End It." Or consider the problems of the speaker who attempts to convince an audience that the constitutional rights of homosexuals should be protected or that abortion is murder and should be outlawed. Topics such as these are even more controversial and could provoke disagreement or even anger from many in the audience.

Calls for Personal or Individual Action. In these speeches the speaker usually wants a tangible and well-defined response from the audience. A good example is the used-car salesperson who tries to get a customer to sign on the dotted line. Speeches that attempt to persuade the audience to vote for a candidate or use a product also belong in this category. The desired response is usually immediate and singular. The success of the speech can be judged according to how many people are "sold."

Some persuasive speakers want a tangible audience response.

A Reminder to All Speakers

Whether a speaker works with an informational topic or a persuasive topic, the ultimate value of the presentation rests on what the audience gets from listening. Perhaps listeners may have been persuaded to act or change their mind, or merely to think something over. The point is that the audience should be affected in some way by the speaker's presentation. This is the most basic requirement of successful speaking. Speakers who remember this when choosing their topics have the best chance to succeed.

RESEARCHING THE TOPIC

Research is an organized process of investigation, a search for facts and ideas that bear on the speaker's topic. All speakers have the responsibility to support their main points with proper evidence. Research is the process of locating this evidence.

Using the Library

Research is easiest and most effective when one has both experience and skill—that is, technique. For example, knowing how to ask questions, as well as whom to ask, helps the news reporter get the "scoop" on a story. Knowing how to examine the scene of a crime for clues helps the detective solve a case. Knowing how to use the library *efficiently* helps the public speaker find the information that will support his or her ideas.

Unless a person is a fairly experienced researcher, his or her first encounter with a library may be confusing. A large municipal or university library will have several floors and perhaps a number of wings or annexes. Some very large libraries may overflow into separate buildings! The student, standing in the main hall, may have little or no idea where to find anything. Only one thing is certain: Aimless wandering will not help.

Many libraries conduct guided tours that introduce newcomers to the facilities painlessly and systematically. If such tours do not exist, the newcomer can probably obtain printed maps or guides at the main desk or ask one of the staff to direct him or her to the right place.

In any case, familiarity with the types and organization of materials generally found in all libraries can make it easier to get to know any library. It is therefore worthwhile to spend a little time learning the basic classifications of material, as well as the use of the card catalog—*the* invaluable aid to efficient research.

Printed Matter. In general, almost all libraries contain three categories of printed matter. These are: (1) books in the general collection, (2) reference books, and (3) periodicals, bulletins, and pamphlets.

The *general collection* is usually the largest body of books in the library. It includes all books available to be checked out and taken home, that is, those generally circulated. In some libraries, the general collection is on "open shelves." This means that the user can simply walk to the appropriate aisle, take the book off the shelf, and check it out at the desk. The open-shelf system allows the researcher to browse. Many libraries, however, lack the space to use this system, and instead, keep their general collection in "stacks" which are off limits to the public. To get a book from the stacks, a borrower must consult the card catalog (to be discussed below) and look up the call number, title, and author. He or she writes this information on a call slip and gives it to one of the staff, who then brings the book out from the stacks.

The types of *reference books* generally found in all libraries are dictionaries, indices, encyclopedias, directories, handbooks, yearbooks, atlases, and guides. Reference books are almost always kept on open shelves, but users are not allowed to remove them from the library. Some libraries may keep their entire reference collection in a single main reading room. Others divide the reference collection among several different reading rooms, each devoted to a specific subject.

Periodicals are magazines and journals which are published at regular intervals throughout the year. Most libraries will have a reading room where newspapers and recent copies of popular magazines (*Time, Newsweek, Life, National Geographic,* etc.) are available. Back issues will probably be bound and kept on open shelves or in the stacks. But popular magazines are only a small part of most libraries' periodical collection. As with reference books, many libraries have special reading rooms where periodicals on specific subjects are kept. These are journals, bulletins, and pamphlets published for and by workers in a particular profession. The articles in them are apt to have greater depth and more detailed, professional information than the popular magazines. If a researcher already knows something about his or her topic, the terminology and content of professional journals should not be too difficult. However, a person with little or no background may find them hard to understand, because the authors assume that their readers are not new to the field. As with popular magazines, back issues of professional journals are bound and kept on open shelves or in the stacks.

Whether a researcher chooses to investigate popular magazines or professional journals, he or she should be aware that merely "thumbing through" any number of periodicals is not an efficient method of research. Most periodicals print a yearbook or index of the articles in their particular magazine or journal. These are invaluable time-savers. They list all the articles that have appeared in the periodical during the last year or decade and also group them under subjects. There are also indices of a more general nature. One such research tool is the *Reader's Guide to Periodical Literature,* which lists all the articles published during a given year. The staff in any periodical reading room can direct a researcher to the guides and indices for periodicals.

The card catalog.   The card catalog is the prime source of information about the materials available to the library user. It is essential for researchers to understand how to use the card catalog, because it contains all the information needed to locate books and/or periodicals. Most libraries maintain separate catalogs for books and periodicals. Our discussion will center on the general catalog for books.

The card catalogs in American libraries are organized according to either the Dewey decimal or the Library of Congress systems. The more commonly used is the Dewey system, which divides books into ten numbered classes:

000–099 General Works   200–299 Religion
100–199 Philosophy   300–399 Social sciences

400–499 Philology 700–799 Fine arts
500–599 Pure science 800–899 Literature
600–699 Useful arts 900–999 History

Each of these classes is further divided into ten subdivisions, for example:

800 General literature 850 Italian literature
810 American literature 860 Spanish literature
820 English literature 870 Latin literature
830 German literature 880 Greek literature
840 French literature 890 Minor literature

Further divisions of these are also made:

821 English poetry 826 English letters
822 English drama 827 English satire
823 English fiction 828 English miscellany
824 English essays 829 Anglo-Saxon
825 English oratory

Notice that with each division, the category becomes more specific and narrow. Decimals following these Dewey categories indicate an even finer level of classification.

The Library of Congress system assigns books to lettered classes according to content or subject area:

A General works
B Philosophy–Religion
C History–Auxiliary sciences
D Foreign history and topography
E–F American history
G Geography–Anthropology
H Social sciences
J Political science
K Law
L Education
M Music
N Fine Arts
P Language and literature

Q	Science
R	Medicine
S	Agriculture
T	Technology
U	Military sciences
V	Naval science
Z	Bibliography–Library science

Further divisions of the Library of Congress classifications are indicated with letters and numbers which show the call number assigned to a book.

There are usually three cards in the card catalog for each book that the library possesses: an author card, a title card, and a subject card. Following is a sample author card from a library that uses the Dewey system. It would be found in the catalog's *N* drawer since the author's last name begins with *N*.

```
784.4 N

    Nettl, Bruno

       Folk and traditional music of the western
          continents.
       Englewood Cliffs, N.J., Prentice-Hall,
       1965.  213 p.  illus.  (incl music)
       (Prentice Hall History of Music Series)

       Includes bibliographies and discographies.

       1.  Folk Music           I.  Title
```

The number in the upper lefthand corner is the call number (Dewey system) of the book. Beneath that is the author's name and then the title of the book. Next is the publishing information (location and name of the publisher; and date of publication). The card then indicates that the book is 213 pages long, is illustrated, contains printed music, and is part of a series put out by this publisher. This book also contains bibliographies and discographies (listings of recordings). The "1. Folk music" entry indicates that the book is also listed on a subject card (under folk music). The Roman numeral item (I. Title) indicates that there is also a title card on file in the catalog.

The title card would be exactly like the author card, except that the book's title, *Folk and Traditional Music in the Western Continents*, would be listed first, instead of the author's name. It could be found by going through the catalog alphabetically, looking for the first word in the title. (When titles begin with words such as *A* or *The*, the second word will be the one to look for.)

The subject card would also have all the data found on our sample author card, except that the top entry on the card would be "Folk music." Usually, a catalog's subject cards will all be grouped together and arranged alphabetically by subject headings. If a researcher begins with the subject cards, he or she will save time and effort. For example, if the researcher looked under the subject area "Folk music," he or she would find not only the card for Nettl's book (our sample) but also cards for all the other books about folk music that the library owns.

In the Library of Congress system, the appearance or content of any of these cards would not be too different. The only change would be in the call number, which naturally would be from the appropriate Library of Congress classification.

As we have seen, a single card from a catalog contains a lot of information about the book it represents. By paying attention to this information, the researcher can decide whether the book will suit his or her needs.

Taking Notes

The ability to take useful notes when reading is another important research skill. As we know, reference books and periodicals usually cannot be taken from the library and used at leisure. Even for books that are taken home, it is not a good idea to be constantly thumbing through and trying to find that interesting passage you read yesterday. You need to record the key information the first time you find it, so that it will be clear and available when you organize the speech.

Two types of information should be recorded when the researcher is taking notes. First is *content information*—facts, quotes, and comments that bear on what the speaker wants to discuss. Second is information about the source. The speaker should be prepared to tell the audience where the supporting material came from—who said or wrote it, when and where it was published. Giving this type of information is honest and establishes the credibility of the material.

Most researchers find that it is best to record both content and source information on 3-by-5-inch note cards. Some people prefer to keep one set of cards for content and another for sources. It is also a good idea for the researcher to record the source first, then compile the content cards as he or she goes through the book. Later, when it is time to organize the speech, he or she will have all the information cards, both source and content, at hand.

Interviewing

The personal interview is a face-to-face encounter between a questioner and a respondent, the person interviewed. It can be one of the most effective research tools for a speech. An interview has a very flexible structure. This allows the interviewer to focus on specific questions. Handled skillfully, an interview can yield factual, lively information that is not available from any other source.

How to Ask Questions for Information.   The success of an interview depends on the ability of the interviewer to ask questions. If he or she does not know what to ask or how to phrase the question, nothing useful is likely to emerge from the interview. When conducting an interview, keep the following guidelines for questions in mind:

• Be relevant. Ask only those questions that are related to your topic. Interviews are usually relatively short. Moreover, the person being questioned is extending a courtesy to the questioner. Don't waste either of your time by wandering off the subject.
• Don't ask questions that can be answered with a yes or no. Remember, you want to learn as much as you can in a short time. What, when, how, why, and where type questions will produce more data.
• Be sure that your respondent fully understands the question. If your questions are vague or puzzling, chances are that the answers will not be what you need to know. It takes a clear question to produce a clear answer.
• Do not ask questions that your respondent doesn't know how to answer. If your aim is to gather information, it is pointless to ask questions that are over someone's head. You will not find out anything, and the person being questioned will be confused or annoyed.
• Pay attention to feedback. Watch how your respondent reacts to questions. His or her reactions will help you frame your questions more effectively.

Summary

Topic selection is the first step in preparing a speech. Beginning speakers often have problems selecting a topic because they are unsure of their own skills and the needs and desires of the audience. Nevertheless, even with these problems the speaker who makes a careful decision will find that he or she can prepare a successful presentation.

Criteria that distinguish between "good" and "poor" topics concern both the audience and the speaker. A good topic communicates new information to the listener. It is also relevant and important enough so that an audience will give the speaker undivided attention. Speakers should keep themselves in mind when they select a topic. They should draw on their own knowledge and experience in their search for a topic and choose subjects they are familiar with, interested in, or feel strongly about.

Topics can be categorized as informative or persuasive; and within each of these broad categories, finer distinctions can be drawn. General information topics cover a particular content area and are often presented in a "lecture" format. How-to-do-it topics demonstrate a particular technique or process for the listener and often require visual aids or other graphic supplements. All-about topics usually serve to acquaint the listener with the structure or function of a particular object, usually as simply as possible.

Two basic types of persuasive topics are those that call for policy action and those that call for individual or personal action. Policy-action topics are important, but often the most completely persuaded audience cannot really do much to carry out the speaker's message. Some policy-action topics relate to issues of right and wrong and are often controversial. Individual-action topics are those that attempt to persuade the listener to take a singular and well-defined action such as buying a product or signing a petition.

All topics—persuasive and informational—may be evaluated in terms of what the audience will get in return for listening. This is a perspective that each speaker should bear in mind when selecting or sorting through possible subjects for a speech.

Research is organized investigation. It is most effective when one has mastered certain skills. Among them are the abilities to use the library, to take notes, and to conduct an interview.

Exercises

1. Make a list of 15 things that you like to do. Include such activities as hobbies, sports, leisure-time activities, travel, etc. After the list has been drawn up, develop a hypothetical speech topic related to each item on your list. After this, place an asterisk (※) by the five topics you think are best for a speech to be given in class.

2. Interview your mother or father about your family. Be sure to include:
   a. history
   b. ethnic background
   c. interesting members
   d. religious tendencies
   e. important geographical moves
   f. political tendencies

   Use the information to develop a hypothetical speech entitled "My Family."

3. In addition to those from this chapter, develop a list of three topics for each of the informational categories below:
   a. general
   b. how-to-do-it
   c. all about

4. In addition to those from this chapter, develop a list of topics for each of the persuasive categories below:
   a. policy action
   b. personal action

OUTLINING AND ORGANIZING THE TOPIC

Tips for Speakers

1. Organize your speech so that you can decide what information is relevant and crucial and what is not.
2. Write out your topic and thesis statements before organizing the rest of the speech.
3. Translate your topic and thesis statements into an outline that will be a "roadmap" for your speech.
4. For reliability and comprehensiveness, use a complete-sentence outline.
5. In an outline, make sure that there are at least two subdivisions of a concept, or no subdivision at all.
6. Good outlines are simple and easy to follow.

ORGANIZING THE TOPIC

After the topic has been selected and refined, its presentation has to be organized so that it can be understood by the audience. By organization we mean here breaking the topic down into manageable parts. This makes it easier for the speaker to communicate the relevant information and for the audience to receive it. It is important to remember that speech organization is a methodical process. Carefully followed, it will yield a solid *speech outline* that can be used to make a successful speech. In fact, organizing consumes most of the speaker's time as he or she prepares the presentation.

In this chapter, we consider first why it is important to organize a speech. Next, we discuss the topic and thesis statements of a speech and how to use them. We also study the process of outlining and examine some examples of good and poor outlines. Finally, we explore the approaches that are available to a speaker as he or she organizes a speech.

Why Organize a Speech?

More than one student has asked, "Why do I have to organize my speech anyway? Isn't it enough that people can understand my ideas?" In fact, students sometimes do simply stand before a class and ramble through their ideas without any attempt at organization. Even "professional" speakers occasionally make a formal presentation that lacks recognizable organization. Because some people neglect organizing their speeches is no reason for not learning how to do it (or, then for not doing it in an actual speech). Organization is one of the important steps in speech making. After you have read some of the reasons for organizing your ideas, you will understand its significance.

WHY ORGANIZE A SPEECH

1. To help the speaker develop a complete idea.
2. To help the speaker discuss a topic in a limited time.
3. To help the audience manage the information that the speaker gives them.
4. To help the audience recognize what the speaker thinks is important.
5. To help the audience remember key concepts.

---

1. Organization helps the speaker develop a complete idea. When asked what topic they plan to discuss in their informative speech assignment, students often respond with a global answer such as "solar energy." But a topic such as solar energy is much too broad to be covered in a five- to seven-minute informative talk. What, in fact, about solar energy do you want to say? Deciding what to talk about is done in the organizational process. A speaker defines and limits his or her ideas by organizing them. Organizing the speech is a built-in technique for making a general topic into a more specific one.

2. Organization helps the speaker discuss a topic in a limited time. Almost all public speaking situations are ruled by the clock. With the possible exception of Premier Fidel Castro of Cuba who will talk for hour after hour, most speakers possess their audiences only for a limited amount of time. Literally and figuratively people will not sit still for long. The president of the United States may, under extraordinary circumstances, speak for an hour. In your public speaking class, you will probably get only seven minutes. So you have to decide what to talk about and what not to talk about. In the end, almost every speaker has to drop material from the final speech plan. (This, believe it or not, is a more common problem than not having enough to say. You will find this out yourself as you develop more experience in public speaking.) Organizing provides a "rule" that lets you decide whether questionable material should be included in the speech. If the material is relevant and crucial to your organizational plan, you will want to keep it. If it is not, you may want to drop it.

3. Organization helps the audience manage the information that the speaker gives them. A speaker should never forget that he or she is speaking for only one reason—to convey a message to the listener. All speakers should have as their primary goal one thing only—communication with the audience. Let us return to our example about solar energy. If a speaker rambles on and on about solar energy with little rhyme or reason, is it realistic to expect the audience to focus on his or her ideas?

4. Organization helps the audience learn what the speaker thinks is important. Of course, within any speech some ideas will be more important than others. Not every point in the speech should be given equal value. Organization helps the speaker tell the listener what is important and what is less so. This helps both the speaker and the listener. The speaker conveys this by how he or she emphasizes certain points—through repetition, for example, or by making a startling statement. But regardless of the particular technique used, it is the organizational plan that provides the methodology.

5. Organization helps the audience remember key concepts. Speakers want members of their audience to remember the significant

Organization lets a speaker relax and speak more effectively.

ideas in a speech. A good speaker will organize his or her speech to emphasize the two or three most important ideas. What you want your listener to take from the speech should be identified and highlighted in the organizational pattern.

Developing Topic and Thesis Statements

The Topic Statement.   The first stage in organizing is developing a topic statement. A topic statement is a short summary that identifies what a particular speech is about. Let us return to our old example and consider two topic statements about "solar energy."

Topic Statement No. 1: In this speech, I am going to talk about how everyone can convert their homes by installing solar heating panels to save electrical energy.

Topic Statement No. 2: This speech will examine the history of solar heating; how solar heating can be used in the home; and the cost of converting a typical 1400-square-foot home from conventional heating to solar heating. The purpose of the speech is to make the audience aware of what solar heating can accomplish, given our existing technology.

The first topic statement outlined a general informative purpose with no specifics. It does not tell the audience what the speaker really intends to say. The speaker has overgeneralized. The audience has only a vague idea of why the speaker chose to discuss this topic.

The second topic statement is much better, although it may be too detailed for the limited time available in a classroom. The audience knows what the speaker intends to discuss and what the speaker is not going to do. (He or she is not going to try to persuade us to put solar heating immediately into our homes.) The topic statement provides the audience with a good summary of what the speech is about. Now let us examine three other topic statements that effectively present what the speech is going to be about.

Topic Statement No. 3: Lately, the prices of food have begun to "skyrocket." In response to high food prices, some people within our community have started food cooperatives. This speech will explain what a food coop is, how it works, and how you can join. It will also compare prices at a food coop with prices in a conventional supermarket. The speech will conclude by comparing the quality of food from coops with that bought in supermarkets.

Topic Statement No. 4: Since football season is again upon us, the television sets of America will soon be tuned in to the games of the National Football League. To help you understand more fully and better enjoy your football watching this fall, this speech is going to examine three different types of running backs—football players who run with the ball—represented in the NFL. First, the speech will examine big, hard-charging backs. Second, we will look at versatile backs who can run, pass, and catch. And, third, you will learn about speedy "scatback" running backs.

Topic Statement No. 5: Should we invest our tax money in steel-wheeled (trains) or rubber-wheeled (buses) mass transit in our community? This speech will examine the advantages and disadvantages of each system. It will conclude by offering an opinion of each and a recommendation as to which system should be adopted in our community.

In each of the three topic statements, the listener is aware of what is to come. There is never any doubt about the flow or direction of the speech. To learn to develop topic statements is essential to good public speaking.

The Thesis Statement.   The thesis statement spells out the main point of your speech as clearly and completely as possible. It represents the core idea around which the speech should develop and should include your value judgment about your topic. Moreover, a good thesis should also briefly state the important points that support this judgment.

Poor thesis statement: "In this speech, I would like to discuss some of the ways in which inflation adversely affects your daily life."

Effective thesis statement: "Today I would like to discuss how inflation, by eroding the value of the dollar and causing prices to rise faster than most incomes, makes it more difficult to feed, clothe, and house your family."

The thesis is usually presented in the introduction, but speakers frequently give it additional emphasis by restating it in their conclusion. (See Chapter 7.)

It should be clear that the thesis is different from the topic statement. It is not a summary. Nor does it contain the purpose of the speech. The purpose is why you are giving the speech and how you want the audience to react. The topic of the speech is simply what it is about. Both of these should be included in the topic statement. The thesis is your central idea and value judgment about the topic of your speech. Any of the following, for example, could be the *thesis* of a speech on the *topic* of inflation:

· Inflation makes it easier to pay off debts.
· Inflation is impossible under communism.
· Inflation is part of the natural economic rhythm.

Saving the thesis for the end of a speech can make a dramatic impact.

Should you state your thesis within the speech? There are two sides to this issue. It can be argued that you should spell out your thesis statement early in the speech, so that the audience knows exactly how you stand. The other approach suggests that you should keep the thesis from the audience to build suspense. To some extent both approaches are "right." Under some conditions you should state the thesis almost immediately. At other times, for dramatic impact, you may want to leave the thesis implicit. It depends on the situation and circumstances. The inexperienced public speaker who is giving an informational speech would be wise to state his or her thesis directly.

Thesis Development: Some Tips. There are five points that you should keep in mind when developing a thesis statement.

It is exact. The thesis is the main point of your speech. It contains the exact purpose of your presentation. Be prepared to stress it.
It is written. Write the thesis out early in the planning process. Do this after the topic has been picked but before the outline is completed.
It is useful. To be effective, a thesis must be related to the overall speech plan. Otherwise, problems will develop.
It is complete. It lays out the entire speech. The main point that the speaker wants to cover should be in the thesis.

It is emphatic. Since the thesis contains the core idea of the speech, it should be highlighted by the speaker. It can be used in the introduction as a "signpost" for the body of the speech that follows.

PRINCIPLES OF OUTLINING

The next step in the organizing process is to develop a speech outline. The outline is really a *roadmap* for the speech. It takes the thesis and the topic statements and translates them into a guide to be used to communicate with the audience.

An Outline: What Is It?

The outline has three characteristics—structure, logic, and utility—that we should look at briefly.

Structure. An outline has the following structure:

```
I.
     A.
     B.
          1.
          2.
               a.
               b.
                    1)
                    2)
                         a)
                         b)
                              i.
                              ii.
     C.
     D.
II.
     A.
     B.
```

This structure is consistent regardless of the type of outline you develop.

Logic. There is logic to an outline. For example, if there is a I level,

The outline is the skeleton of the speech.

there is also a II level; if an A, then a B; if a 1, then a 2. The principle here is: *If there are not at least two subdivisions of a concept, then there cannot be any subdivision at all.* Furthermore, an outline lets you determine the relative importance of a point. You know that a I level is of equal importance with a II level; an A is equal to a B, etc. This helps the audience focus on the relative value of points within a speech.

Utility.   As suggested above, an outline is a skeleton of a speech, not the speech itself. Good speakers learn how to develop a complete outline before a speech because it helps them plan. Later, they reduce the complete outline to a compact model which they can use while actually speaking to an audience.

Types of Outlines

Some speakers develop their own shortcuts in outlining. For experienced speakers this may be reliable. But as a beginner, you should rely on one of the methods below.

Complete-Sentence Outline.   The complete-sentence outline is comprehensive. It provides all relevant information.

RUNNING SHOES
I. When you begin a program of running, you should have a quality pair of running shoes.
   A. Your feet need the protection from the terrible pounding running inflicts.

      1. Orthopedic surgeons recommend quality running shoes.

      2. Podiatrists also recommend quality running shoes.

  B. The more you run in terms of time and/or distance, the greater the need for good shoes.

      1. As you run over six miles, the stress you give your feet increases markedly.

      2. Running greater distances increases the likelihood of stress fractures, but good shoes reduce the chances for this injury.

  C. Hard pavement is not good for the foot.

      1. Most people run on blacktop.

      2. Others run on cement.

      3. Even on grass your feet take a beating.

II. There are some important things to look for when selecting running shoes.

  A. The shoe should be flexible.

      1. It should bend easily.

      2. It should move with the foot.

  B. The shoe should have a strong durable "upper."

      1. Most good running shoes have either a nylon fabric or nylon mesh upper.

      2. Older running shoes may have a leather upper, but while durable they may not be comfortable.

  C. The shoe should have a thick sole that can cushion the foot.

      1. This means that the upper part of the sole should be soft.

      2. The lower part of the sole should be of harder rubber than the upper part.

  D. The shoe should feel stable to the foot.

      1. You do not want your foot floating around inside the shoe.

      2. Both the front part and the back part of the shoe should be secure.

  E. The shoe must be light.

      1. After a few miles of running, the shoe will become heavier and heavier.

      2. The light shoe is generally a better shoe than the heavy one.

  F. The shoe should fit well.

      1. You should concentrate on fit and ignore such factors as color or style.

      2. The shoe should allow your foot to breathe, so you might want to select a shoe a half to a full size bigger than your street shoe.

  G. The shoe should not be bought before you have run in them.

      1. Good shoe stores will even insist that you at least run around the block in the shoe.

      2. If you have the slightest doubt after running in the shoe, do not buy it.

  H. The shoe will cost between $30 and $50.

III. There are two basic types of running shoes.
   A. Training shoes are intended for the casual and serious runner.
      1. They will render much mileage before they become worn.
      2. They come in two varieties.
         a. A waffle sole has ridges to give extra cushioning.
         b. A flat sole will give longer wear but less cushion than a waffle sole.
      3. Most runners you see out on the highway are in training shoes.
   B. Racing shoes are intended for the serious runner entered in a race.
      1. They provide very little cushioning.
      2. They are very light.
      3. The serious runner may change from training to racing shoes for a race.

Short-Phrase Outline. The short-phrase outline is much quicker to do than the complete-sentence outline, but it is a less reliable planning tool. The full-sentence outline forces you to develop your thoughts fully. Completing it advances you further into the planning task.

LIVING IN LOS ANGELES

   I. Los Angeles' special life-style
      A. Freeways for transportation
      B. Smog a problem
      C. Hot summers
      D. Little change of seasons
   II. Outdoor life.
      A. Barbecuing in the backyard
      B. Year-round golf
      C. Boating and water sports
      D. Trips to the mountains
      E. Sun shining 250 days a year
   III. Los Angeles' social problems
      A. Transient existence
         1. Lack of roots
         2. People move often
      B. Suburban existence
         1. Limited sense of community
         2. Emphasis on "me" and "mine"
      C. Hollywood image
         1. Everything make-believe
         2. Hard to distinguish between the image and the essence
         3. Television image of Los Angeles

IV. Geographical problems
    A. Spread-out city
        1. No mass transit
        2. Dependence on automobile
    B. Los Angeles really an irrigated desert
        1. Little foliage
        2. Very sandy and dirty when the wind blows
    C. Nearby mountains
        1. Wind cannot blow smog away
        2. The basin effect

Single-Word Outline.   The third type of outline is the easiest to complete, but it is the least preferred because it does not make you go far enough into the planning process.

CAMPING OUT

I. Tents
    A. Types
        1. 2-man
        2. 3-man
        3. Larger
    B. Uses
        1. Backpacking
        2. Family camping
II. Sleeping Bags
    A. Types
        1. Rectangular
        2. Mummy
        3. Semi-mummy
    B. Buying
        1. Materials
        2. Costs
III. Ice chest
    A. Plastic
        1. Light
        2. Easy-to-handle
    B. Metal
        1. Heavy
        2. Durable
IV. Stoves
    A. Types
        1. 2-burner
        2. 4-burner
    B. Fuel
V. Lanterns/Lamps
    A. Battery-powered
    B. Kerosene

The single-word outline is often used by students. But it does not provide as much information as the two previous ones. It may also lull the speaker into a false sense of security. The outline makes it seem that a speaker has enough information for the speech. But when the time actually comes to talk, the speaker may well be underprepared.

To repeat: Of the three types of outlines considered here, the full-sentence model is by far the best for the inexperienced public speaker. Many speech teachers require students to use only the complete-sentence outline in preparing their speaking assignments.

Guidelines for Outlining

In his book *Message Preparation*, Glen Mills presents some effective guidelines for good outlines. They will be considered briefly here.[1]

Simplicity.   Good outlines are simple and easy to follow. Nothing is gained by doing an extremely complex outline that neither you nor anyone else can follow. A good rule to follow is to keep an outline as straightforward as possible. To do this, make sure that you have only one idea in each item on the outline.

Coordination.   In an outline, a list of things should have a generic or common factor. For example:

Wrong	*Right*
I. Great eastern universities	I. Great eastern universities
A. Harvard	A. Harvard
B. Yale	B. Yale
C. Stanford	C. Brown
D. Brown	II. Great western universities
E. Berkeley	A. Stanford
F. USC	B. Berkeley
	C. USC

Subordination.   Outlines, of course, have main points and subpoints. Subpoints are subordinate to main points. But there should be a relationship between the main points and the subpoints.

Wrong	*Right*
I. Problems encountered in college	I. Problems encountered in college
A. Finding time to study	A. Finding time to study
B. Expenses	B. Getting part-time jobs
	C. Meeting tuition costs

[1] Glen Mills, *Message Preparation: Analysis and Structure* (Indianapolis: Bobbs-Merrill, 1966), pp. 53–55.

C. Having fun at football   II. Fun aspects in college
   games   A. Dating
D. Finding part-time jobs   B. Football games

Discreteness.   As you develop an outline, each topic or point should be separate and distinct. There should be no overlapping or merging of ideas. If there is overlap, both the listener and the speaker may be confused.

Sequence.   There is an implied sense of chronology about each outline point. The topic in I is to be considered (and/or to have taken place) before the topic in II. This is true for all of the items in the outline.

If you follow Mills's five guidelines, you should be able to design outlines that are logical and consistent.

Approaches to Speech Outlines

There are five patterns that can be used to develop a speech outline: topical, spatial, chronological, step, and advantage/disadvantage.

Topical Pattern of Outlining.   This pattern works by dividing a speech into topics and subtopics. It is probably the easiest to use and the most popular among student speakers.

THE DEPARTMENTS OF A NEWSPAPER IN A LARGE CITY

I. The news department is responsible for gathering the news.
   A. City room covers local news.
   B. Metro bureau covers regional developments.
   C. Sports division reports on sporting events.
   D. Society column covers social news.
   E. Business desk analyzes financial affairs.

II. The advertising department is responsible for selling advertising and collecting revenues.
   A. There are two kinds of newspaper advertisements: classified and display.
   B. The collection bureau generates the paper's advertising revenues.

III. The administration department is responsible for the ongoing administrative functions at the newspaper.
   A. Hiring is handled by the personnel division
   B. Accounting division handles all of the paper's finances.
   C. Labor relations represents management in negotiations with the unions.

IV. The composition department is responsible for the makeup and printing of the newspaper.
   A. The composing room sets type.
   B. Letter press and page proofs divisions handle art work and design the paper.
   C. Press operations division prints the paper.
 V. The circulation department is responsible for making sure that the newspaper gets distributed throughout the community.
   A. Commercial deliveries are made to newspaper stands across the city.
   B. Home deliveries are handled by "paper boys."

Spatial Pattern of Outlining.   The speaker should use this pattern when his or her speech topic has a spatial or geographical focus. For example, a speech on a particular city or place—"A Walking Tour of New York City," "A Guide to My Favorite Hotel," "What You See in a Classroom"—naturally lends itself to the spatial pattern. But other topics can also be organized using this technique, for example, "A Look at the Parts of the Human Body," or "The Functional and Working Parts of an Automobile Engine." The example below deals with a tour of a college.

A TOUR OF MIDDLETOWN COLLEGE
  I. Entering the campus from the main road, you encounter Founders' Hall.
   A. Notice the door that was original in 1719 when the building was built.
   B. Looking toward the roof you can see the ivy that has been growing since the nineteenth century.
   C. Up the stairs on the second floor of the building is the president's office.
     1. There is a great, large oak desk that was given the college for the president in 1910.
     2. The president's office is laid out in an oval like the one used by the president of the United States.
 II. Coming out of Founders' Hall, you will discover the great quad where students lounge in the spring and fall.
   A. Around the quad you will see a number of large evergreen trees that have been growing at the college as long as anyone can remember.
   B. The quad is surrounded by a long hedge that must be maintained by the freshmen at the school.
     1. This is an old tradition.
     2. If the freshmen do not keep the hedge maintained properly, it is the responsibility of the sophomores to punish them accordingly.

III. Leaving the quad and turning south, you immediately see Alexander Hall, the main classroom building.
   A. Alexander Hall was a gift to the college from the Alexander family in 1860.
   B. After it was built, it was used to quarter Union troops in the Civil War.
   C. The building is the oldest entirely brick structure in this part of the state.
IV. Moving farther east from Alexander Hall, you observe the college dorms.
   A. The older buildings were originally for men students and were built in 1910.
   B. The newer buildings were constructed under a government grant in 1963 for women students.
   C. Now both men and women share the dorms equally.

The spatial pattern is not widely used, but it can be very effective with the right topic.

Chronological Pattern of Outlining.   When a topic can be subdivided chronologically, the speaker probably should use this pattern. It is especially useful for speeches on "the history of . . . ," as we can see in the following example:

IMPORTANT DEVELOPMENTS IN THE HISTORY OF COUNTRY MUSIC
I. Early RCA recordings were made in Bristol, Virginia, 1920–1930.
   A. Jimmy Rodgers recorded the "Blue Yodeler."
   B. The original Carter family recorded several songs.
II. The Grand Ole Opry developed in Nashville, Tennessee, 1925–1935.
   A. Radio station WSM had the original idea.
   B. The first Opry broadcasts were from several locations.
   C. Eventually the Opry settled at Ryman Auditorium in downtown Nashville.
III. Roy Acuff was the first singing star of the Grand Ole Opry, in the late 1930s.
   A. Before that, Acuff's music had been primarily instrumental.
   B. He became a national figure with his recording of "The Wabash Cannonball."
IV. Country music spread to Southern California in the 1940s.
   A. The major labels became interested in country music.
   B. California talent began to develop:
      1. Roy Rogers and the Sons of the Pioneers
      2. Tex Ritter
      3. Gene Autry
      4. Lefty Frazell

C. The "singing cowboy" was a popular phenomenon.
V. Hank Williams became country music's greatest superstar in the early 1950s.
   A. His early work was in the South.
   B. He caused the great popularity of the Grand Ole Opry.
   C. He had many runaway hit records:
      1. "Your Cheatin' Heart"
      2. "I Can't Help It If I'm Still in Love with You"
      3. "Hey Goodlookin'"
   D. He died in 1953 at the age of only 29.
IV. The "Nashville Sound" emerged in the 1960s.
   A. Major artists came to Nashville to record with background musicians.
   B. Many radio stations throughout the country began to play records by country artists.
   C. Major stars were created:
      1. Johnny Cash
      2. Glen Campbell
      3. Waylon Jennings
      4. Loretta Lynn
VII. Country music has had a tremendous growth and acceptance since 1970.
   A. Nashville stars now play in Las Vegas.
   B. Television programs are devoted to country music.
   C. Several country stars have national audiences:
      1. Willie Nelson
      2. Linda Ronstadt
      3. Crystal Gayle
      4. Kenny Rodgers

The chronological pattern lets the speaker begin his or her outline either with the most recent date or the most ancient one and work backward or forward. It makes no difference. To repeat: If your topic can be broken down into chronological phases, you should probably use this pattern of speech outlining.

Step Pattern of Outlining. The step pattern, like the chronological, implies a progression. But the step pattern does not depend on the progression of time. For example, almost any topic that tells someone how to do something—"How to Shoot Free-Throws in Basketball," "How to Tune the Automobile Engine," "How to Select a Physician"—can be organized in the step pattern.

SELECTING THE RIGHT COLLEGE FOR YOU

I. The first step is to do a complete self-assessment.
   A. Decide what your talents are.
   B. Take stock of your educational background.
   C. Critically analyze yourself to see what things you want to do vs. what abilities you have.
II. The second step is to collect as much information about colleges as you can.
   A. Write for catalogs and admission materials.
   B. Visit nearby colleges.
   C. Talk with alumni of various colleges.
   D. Visit with your guidance counselor.
III. The third step is to narrow your list of possible colleges to not more than five.
   A. Consider the important variables for you.
      1. What does each cost?
      2. How good are their faculties?
      3. What living facilities do they offer?
      4. How attractive are their academic programs?
   B. Make contact with each college on the list to get specific information.
      1. Do you qualify for financial aid?
      2. Can you live in a dormitory?
      3. What are the admission requirements?
IV. The fourth step is to apply for admission to all of the colleges on the list.
      1. Complete application forms.
      2. Mail in applications.

Advantage/Disadvantage Pattern of Outlining. When the speaker wants to present both sides of a question, he or she can use the advantage vs. disadvantage outlining pattern. This is also sometimes called the pro-and-con pattern or the two-sided presentation pattern. Most often it is used to persuade, with the speaker making stronger arguments for the side he or she advocates.

There are three ways to outline using the advantage/disadvantage format:

1. *Interwoven:* alternating between advantages and disadvantages.

2. *Anticlimax:* all of the arguments on the side advocated followed by all of the arguments on the side not advocated.

3. *Climax:* all of the arguments for the side not advocated followed by all of the arguments on the side advocated.

Any of these approaches could be effective given the right circumstances. In the example below, the climax order is used to consider the question of whether a city should have a rubber-wheeled or a fixed-rail mass transit system.

RUBBER-WHEELED TRANSIT SYSTEMS

I. Rubber-wheeled mass transit systems have some inherent disadvantages when compared with steel-wheeled systems.
   A. Rubber-wheeled systems have a higher per-passenger cost than rail systems.
      1. It takes more people to run the system.
      2. The economy of scale is smaller.
   B. Rubber-wheeled systems use the wrong kind of fuel.
      1. Almost all use gasoline.
      2. All use other oil products.
   C. Rubber-wheeled systems carry fewer passengers per unit than fixed-rail systems.
II. Rubber-wheeled systems have some inherent advantages over fixed-rail systems.
   A. The initial start-up cost of a rubber-wheeled system is less than a quarter of the fixed-rail system.
      1. The initial bus system can be used.
      2. Start-up for a fixed-rail system involves a huge capital expenditure for equipment.
      3. If no tracks are available, the start-up cost of acquiring right-of-way for land acquisition is prohibitive.
   B. The flexibility of the rubber-wheeled system is much greater than the fixed-rail system.
      1. Rubber-wheeled vehicles can use the existing roadway.
      2. Anywhere a car goes a bus can go.
   C. The per-unit replacement cost for a bus is much less than a train.
   D. Generally, throughout the country people are used to riding the bus, so there would not have to be a great change in people's attitudes.
Conclusion: Therefore, for these reasons, I would submit that the rubber-wheeled system is preferable to the fixed-rail system for our city.

As you can see, the speaker using the advantage/disadvantage technique appears to be analytical and reasonable. It is apparent to the audience that he or she has presented both sides of the argument. The speaker gives the impression not of being an advocate, but rather of having thoroughly researched the issues. In fact, however, before the audience's eyes, the speaker turns from analyst to advocate.

Summary

Organizing a speech is an important process because it requires breaking a topic down into manageable parts. Organization helps the speaker define and limit his or her ideas by deciding what information is relevant and what is not.

The first step in organizing is to develop topic and thesis statements. A topic statement is a short summary that identifies what the speech is about. The thesis statement is the central idea and value judgment about the topic of the speech.

Developing a speech outline is the next step in the organizing process. The outline has structure, logic, and utility. It can be used both in the planning stage of the speech and as a guideline when the speaker is actually talking to the audience.

The best type of outline for the beginning speaker is the complete-sentence outline, because it is comprehensive and provides all the relevant information. Making one up forces the speaker to develop thoughts more fully and advances him or her further into the planning process. The other two types of outline are the short-phrase and the single-word.

There are five patterns of speech outline: topical, spatial, chronological, step, and advantage / disadvantage. The outline pattern the speaker uses is determined by the nature of the speech.

Exercises

1. Develop a complete-sentence outline for one of the five speech topics below or for a topic of your choice.
   a. parking on campus
   b. my favorite sports
   c. my favorite hobby
   d. cars
   e. clothes

2. Develop a chronological outline for one of the five speech topics below. The outline should be in complete-sentence form.
   a. the best day of my life
   b. my town's history
   c. my family's history
   d. my years in high school
   e. a typical day at my job

3. Develop a spatial outline for one of the five speech topics below. Make sure the outline uses complete sentences.
   a. around my town
   b. visiting New York
   c. visiting Los Angeles
   d. visiting Chicago
   e. around my home

A SPEECH TO INFORM

The following speech was given to fulfill an assignment in which students were asked to speak for three minutes from their personal experience on an informative topic. The object was to organize and present their ideas as logically and clearly as possible. Ms. Taylor begins by establishing rapport with her audience and by giving her credentials. She then provides very clear topic and thesis statements from which the body of the speech is developed.

Hidden Opportunities of Campus*
Gloria Taylor

Throughout the speech the speaker goes to great lengths to identify herself with the audience's need for campus social life.

If you are as I was, you may look on campus life at CSULA as a "vast wasteland." Since we attend a commuter school with no on-campus living facilities and little fraternity or sorority life, even the most objective analyst would have to conclude that the typical student here has rather limited opportunity for widespread participation in campus activities. At our neighboring campuses, such as USC or UCLA, as you walk across campus on a Friday or Saturday night, you are impressed by the liveliness. There are parties, classes, and celebrations of all kinds. But the same Friday or Saturday, an evening stroll across CSULA finds almost nothing going on, with the possible exception of a lonely student leaving the library after putting the final touches on a term paper due the first thing Monday morning.

Speaker credibility is established in this passage. The speaker is saying "learn from my mistakes." Her strength is that she has personally investigated these opportunities for participation on campus.

This situation is a fact of life at CSULA. We are probably going to have to accept it. After my first two years on campus, the lack of social life really depressed me. But last year I made up my mind that I was going to thoroughly investigate the opportunities for social life that did exist on campus. So I spent about two months making daily pilgrimages to the Dean of Students' office and the student union to see what was available to students. I would like to share with you the results of my investigation so that you can learn from my faulty impression that there was nothing available at CSULA for the student.

Here the speaker "signposts" the speech by telling the listener what is going to come next. The three opportunities referred to are the thesis of the speech.

In this speech I would like to discuss three important activities on campus: the Outing Center, the EPIC program, and the office of Commuter Students. Since I discovered each of them, I have become active in each. I hope, after my speech, that you too decide to be active in one of them or in one of the other programs.

The Outing Center on our campus is designed for nothing more than the fun and relaxation of the students. The center is located on the third floor of the student union building and is supported by student fees. The primary activity of the center is to arrange low-cost trips for students. Most of the trips take place during quarter break but some

* Speech given in an oral communications class, California State University, Los Angeles, May 21, 1979. Reproduced by permission of Gloria Taylor.

are arranged during the quarter as well. For example, I just returned from a three-day weekend trip at Lake Tahoe to ski. For the three days at a good hotel with food and airfare, I paid only $150.00. Airfare, alone, from Los Angeles to Lake Tahoe is more than that. But because we had a group of 30, we got plenty of cost breaks. During the trip I got to know a number of students. We skied together during the day and attended some of the Nevada attractions during the evening. I had a great time and enjoyed the trip thoroughly. And, this time last year, I didn't know the Outing Center existed.

Again the speaker emphasizes her personal experience with what she is talking about.

Over the coming months the center will be organizing trips to Yosemite, Vancouver and Victoria, British Columbia, Salt Lake City, a weekend trip to San Francisco, and during the spring break, a great one-week trip to Cancun in the Yucatan State of Mexico. If you like to travel and like to do it cheaply, let me recommend the Outing Center.

Since Cal State is located right in the middle of one of the world's great urban centers, there are a number of opportunities to become involved in the community. An organization on campus called EPIC (Educational Participation in the Community) coordinates these opportunities for students. You can presently be involved in such projects as tutoring disadvantaged children, volunteering for nursing and convalescent hospitals, working in senior citizens' centers, registering voters, office work in community development centers and many others. Normally students are not paid for their EPIC work, but they can receive academic credit through such departments as Chicano Studies, Pan-African Studies and Urban Studies.

Since I joined EPIC I have tutored fourth graders in reading at an elementary school in southeast Los Angeles and have volunteered to teach watercolor at the Boyle Heights Senior Citizens' Center. Both of these activities were highly rewarding and interesting. If you are looking to gain more experience working in the community, why don't you contact the EPIC office in the Student Activities Center?

Although the speech is intended to be informational there is an obvious persuasive quality running through it. The speaker is saying "become involved."

Since almost all students at CSULA are commuters, it would seem appropriate to have an office on campus that caters only to the needs of the commuter. There is such an office in Bungalow D, but I bet most of you didn't even know it existed. The Commuter Student Services Center has all kinds of activities for us, the commuting student. Among the most popular are the ride-sharing clearinghouse, the part-time job board, and the discount corner, where information about stores that give special discounts to CSULA students is provided. In addition, the center has begun to sponsor noontime programs, weekend dances, and special after-school activities. If you are a commuting student, why don't you walk down to Bungalow D and see what's happening?

In this passage the speaker reviews the three opportunities for campus participation.

Even though you may have thought that the campus offers little in extra-curricular activities for students, let me review by again calling your attention to the programs of the Outing Center, EPIC, and the commuter student center. Each has something unique to offer students.

thinking critically and logically

Tips for Speakers

1. When preparing your arguments, avoid confusing inference or assumption with concrete fact.
2. Be aware of the tendency to label and to use oversimplified, single-cause arguments.
3. If you remember that "change is constant," you will prepare up-to-date, flexible arguments.
4. Use deductive reasoning, syllogisms, and hypothetical discussions to help you present your arguments.
5. Be alert to errors in logic, such as using inaccurate information and making false generalizations.
6. Be aware of the differences between propaganda and logical argument.

In previous chapters we discussed several steps necessary for preparing a public speech—analyzing the audience, selecting, researching, and outlining the topic. The next step is to develop the topic by using appropriate supporting materials. Much of this chapter, therefore, is devoted to critical thinking and logic, which are necessary for selecting, evaluating, and applying the materials that will most effectively support a presentation.

SUPPORTING MATERIALS

To be taken seriously, every speaker must "build a case" to support his or her topic. Supporting materials do just that: They are the evidence and documentation that underscore and expand the major points in the speech. These materials enrich the speaker's arguments and encourage the audience to understand and to believe what they are hearing. The best supporting materials make the point of the speech clearer. They are thus useful and practical.

But whenever possible they should also add color and interest, the way a sauce can perk up the flavor of food. Suppose, for example, a historian states that the excesses and frivolity of the nobility helped cause the French Revolution. As a simple statement, this may or may not mean much to the audience. They are probably unfamiliar with

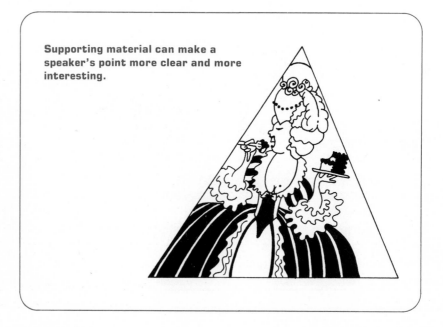

Supporting material can make a speaker's point more clear and more interesting.

both aristocratic excess and revolutionary violence. But suppose also that the lecturer supports her statement by reading an account of a feast given by a nobleman, detailing the variety and luxury of the food, the richness of the setting, the number of chefs and waiters needed to serve such a meal, the expense and waste involved. She contrasts this with another account of the near-famine conditions that prevailed at the same time for much of the peasantry. Her audience can thus more easily understand how hostility could have been aroused by such waste in time of need. The use of supporting material has made the speaker's point both clearer and more interesting.

The Speaker's Responsibility

It would be an error, however, to consider supporting materials solely in terms of their usefulness to the speaker. To support your position is more than convenience—it is, in fact, a responsibility. A speaker must be willing and able to document and stand behind a speech. In other words, an audience has the right to hold each speaker responsible for what he or she says in a public speaking situation.

A speaker might fulfill this responsibility to support his or her position by using visual aids or figures of speech. (See Chapters 8 and 10.) But the primary support is the argument, or the speaker's statement of why the audience should believe a particular proposition that he or she sets forth. The preparation and development of good, solid arguments is an intellectual process and involves *critical thinking*. It is critical thinking and logic that make the difference between a sound argument and a poor one.

IMPORTANT ELEMENTS IN CRITICAL THINKING

The skilled critical thinker is, above all, a careful thinker. He or she realizes the inadequacy of hasty judgments and impressions based on the surfaces of things. When developing arguments, the critical thinker is disciplined and keeps the following elements in mind.

Fact vs. Inference

The essential difference between fact and inference is the distinction between what *is* and what *appears to be*. Objective truth, or fact, is not always the same as perceived truth, or inference, and we should avoid confusing the two.

The Nature of Fact.   A fact is concrete, definite, and invariable: The sun sets in the west; mammals require oxygen to sustain life; a dropped ball falls downward. We can observe and test these facts directly on any given day and in any given place—they will never vary. Aside from such laws and characteristics of physical reality, there are very few general facts in our daily lives.

Suppose we want to present as fact something we have observed which is not as invariable as the facts given above. In other words, it might not be true on any given day and in any given place. To resolve this, we qualify our statement and present a limited fact. For example, on a clear night in the late summer, it is often possible to see a shooting star. When exposed to temperatures lower than those of their normal environment, reptiles are inactive. A majority of American males between the ages of 10 and 20 engage in some form of sports activity. These are specific, limited facts. They are confined in scope and do not masquerade as universal truths. They are valuable in that they are true for the *particulars* that they describe.

The Nature of Inference.

An inference is the conclusion that one thing is true because other things related to it are true. The truth or validity of the inference itself is not proven but inferred from the truth or validity of something that can be proven true or valid. For example, one inference of historical note was the belief that the sun traveled around the Earth. Our ancestors' perception of the daily path of the sun across the sky led them to accept as fact that the sun was a satellite of the planet Earth. Centuries went by before the real organization of the solar system was recognized and the inferred belief was shown to be false.

Almost all our opinions about human behavior are inferences drawn from our perceptions of and experiences with people. We build up expectations about the events and interactions in our daily lives and infer that what was true yesterday will be true today and tomorrow. We may assume, based on past association, that Mary is patient, that Henry is a romantic, and that Anne tells the truth. Our perceptions cause us to believe that these are the facts. But what happens when Mary suddenly loses her temper, Henry laughs during the love scene in our favorite movie, or Anne tells a lie? Our cognitive expectations collapse. The point is that with inferences it is best to recognize the possibility of inaccuracy. While inferences based on perceptions impose a pattern on and lend predictability to our lives, they should not be relied upon as if they were concrete facts.

The Map-Territory Relationship

The relationship between words and the objects they symbolize is like a map and the territory it represents. The word is the map, the thing is the territory, and the two are distinct—both in reality and in one's mind. An awareness of this relationship should stop us from confusing labels with realities. Apply this concept, for example, to the phrase "war against crime." It becomes clear immediately that the map is designed to inspire people with visions of soldiers marching off to meet the foe. The territory this phrase represents is another matter. It consists of changing, or putting into effect, specific social, civic, judicial, and penal policies. It is a complex situation which may be approached in several ways. Above all, it requires more than the efforts of "good soldiers." Uncritical acceptance of the map implies that a simple solution to crime was readily available. The person who considered the territory, on the other hand, would recognize that this was false.

As we shall see when discussing language in Chapter 10, the map-territory concept is especially important in terms of the labels applied to people. When we react to words such as "redneck," "dame," or "honky," we are reacting to the map, not the territory. You should recognize this distinction and remember that such words tell us very little about the people they are applied to. That is, they tell us very little about the territory.

The Tendency to Abstract

Listeners tend to abstract reality.

One trait that we all share is the tendency to abstract. It is impossible to perceive and intellectually process all the different stimuli in our environment at the same time. Instead, we focus on the relevant details—those that directly affect us—and filter the rest out. The result is an abstraction from reality, an abstraction as unique as the person who made it.

In social situations, a person's abstractions are influenced by his or her values, interests, beliefs, likes, and dislikes. A critical thinker should understand this and respect another person's view, even if it differs from his or her own. Such respect may lead to useful understanding. Consider Gail, a dancer and choreographer, who worked for many months on a program of improvised music and movement. Gail had always believed that the arts, especially dance, should reach as wide an audience as possible. When her project was finished, she asked permission to put it on in a local park.

When she presented her plan to the community board, Gail was surprised by the resistance she encountered. One older member of the board, Mrs. Harris, was especially opposed. The meeting broke up before a final decision was reached and Gail was instructed to come the next week and be prepared to present her plan in more detail.

Gail went home disappointed and angry, but she realized that to dismiss Mrs. Harris as an "old stick-in-the-mud" would be a mistake. Instead, she asked herself what element or elements of the plan would cause this woman to react so negatively. (Essentially, Gail was trying to learn what Mrs. Harris had abstracted and why.)

After making a few calls, Gail had the information she needed. It turned out that Mrs. Harris lived near the park and had helped raise money for planting flowers and shrubs there. Gail also discovered that many of the elderly people living around the park had been annoyed by frequent nighttime "jam sessions" of jazz and rock musicians.

When she went back to the meeting the next week, Gail was prepared. She had included in her plan a strategy for keeping the spectators from walking over flower beds and newly seeded areas. She explained that her music would not be amplified and would be played on flutes and light percussion instruments—finger cymbals, thumb pianos, gourd rattles, and the like. Mrs. Harris kept her peace and the board approved Gail's plan.

Gail's critical thinking and awareness of the human tendency to abstract allowed her to construct solid arguments to support her project. By changing or clarifying those facets of the plan which would annoy a woman like Mrs. Harris, Gail was able to save the whole. Had she shown less respect for Mrs. Harris' position, this would not have been possible.

Multiple Causality

A speaker can support his or her view of a complex event or situation by giving the audience some background information (that is, how and why things occurred). This promotes audience understanding and also shows the logic of the speaker's conclusions. In preparing this background information, the speaker should remember that most things have multiple causes. He or she should consider the broad range of factors—political, historical, economic, biological, environmental, and so on—that affect major events. While simple, single-cause explanations may be attractive, the critical thinker should realize that they are also usually inadequate. Offering listeners more than a single-track argument can make the difference between success and failure in public speaking.

Change

Change is the final element that the critical thinker needs to consider when developing supporting arguments. Nothing in life is more constant than change. We experience it every day: in our cultural and social institutions, in the people around us, and in ourselves. It is illogical to assume that time leaves events, places, or persons unaltered.

A speaker's awareness and acceptance of the potential for change can help to prepare arguments that are up to date and flexible. He or she should use sources of information that tell the audience what is true today and what seems likely or possible in the future. If a statement is based on "yesterday's news," he or she lets the audience know about it. For example, a speaker might say, "I base my conclusions on the data gathered in the federal census of 1970. This was the last large-scale compilation of data about the conditions that I am discussing." Such "dating" of information lends authenticity to the speaker's views. Besides being honest, it shows the audience that the speaker has not made the logical error of ignoring the possibility that changes may have occurred since 1970.

The Elements Together: A Work of Quality

In the light of these five elements, it should be clear that making decisions about the content of our arguments is hard work. Awareness of fact vs. inference should make us strive for truth and precision. The map-territory concept demands that we check our initial reactions to labels and try to remain objective. Awareness of the tendency to abstract forces us to question our own perspective (or at least acknowledge its limitations) and respect how others see things. Multiple causality should force us to look at the "big picture," no matter how complex it may be. Finally, awareness of change should make us admit that what we knew yesterday may do us little good today. All these elements together make critical thinking sound like a painstaking process. But it pays off in arguments that are logical and complete, arguments that make a better and more effective speech.

THE STRUCTURE OF ARGUMENTS

The elements of critical thinking that we have discussed thus far should ensure that our arguments in content are "the truth, the whole truth, and nothing but the truth." But we must also consider the structure of arguments and try to arrange the materials in a logical and communicative manner. Fortunately, there are some time-honored methods and conventions of logical reasoning which can help us do this.

Deductive Reasoning

Deductive reasoning moves from the general to the specific. Consider how this process might be used in a speech presentation. Ken, a salesman, is opposed to a new policy adopted by his company. Because the new policy has only been in effect for a short time, there is little that Ken can say about its impact personally on himself and his clients. But he has assembled a lot of general data about the ill effects of the same policy on similar companies. His argument is that the policy will cause the same problems for his company. Essentially, Ken's argument is a form of deductive reasoning:

Generalization: This policy has caused nothing but trouble in companies all over the country.

Specification: If we continue this policy, we'll wind up with the same troubles.

Inductive Reasoning

Inductive reasoning is just the opposite. It moves from the specific to the general. Let us give Ken a new job: He is now on the board of directors. For a year, he has been disturbed by reports from several branches of the company. It seems that none of them has had any luck with a certain new procedure. Ken thinks that the board should issue a directive to *all* branches of the company advising them not to adopt this procedure.

To convince the other board members, Ken argues inductively. He demonstrates that the procedure has failed in the sales department. He shows that it costs twice as much to implement as planned. Finally, he reads a report which states that the procedure will break down if the company continues to expand. Ken hopes that his listeners will induce that the procedure is an overall failure. The scheme of his inductive argument is:

Specific Cases: It hurt sales; it costs too much; it inhibits growth.

Generalization: It is a *complete* failure.

Syllogistic Reasoning

In a syllogism, two pieces of information provide a basis for drawing conclusions about a third piece of information. For example:

A. The production workers at the shoe factory are unionized.

B. Jean is a production worker at the shoe factory.

C. Therefore, Jean is a union member.

In a persuasive presentation, the separate elements of a speaker's syllogism might not be as clearly or directly verifiable as in this example. Instead of presenting the audience with facts, the persuasive speaker often uses value statements. For the speaker's aim is similar—to provide a reason for getting the audience to accept his or her argument. For example:

1. America has a duty to protect world peace.
2. The nuclear arms race is a *direct* threat to peace.
3. Therefore, America has a duty to slow down or limit the production of nuclear arms.

The first statement of this example is typical of many persuasive syllogistic openings because it is something that the audience already knows and is likely to believe in. The speaker probably won't need to defend the idea of "our duty to protect peace" to any great extent. Almost everyone values peace. By using such a commonplace to open the argument, the speaker has paved the way for the second statement which is more debatable: "The nuclear arms race is a *direct* threat to peace." This is an opinion, but the speaker wants the audience to accept it as a *fact*. The speaker could present statistics and probabilities to try to convince the audience that the stockpiling of nuclear arms must end in war. He or she could also seek to demonstrate that "arms deals" disrupt the balance of power and contribute to global instability.

If the listeners accept the first and second statements, then the speaker has a good chance of persuading them to accept the third statement, which is the main point of the speech. If we have a duty to protect peace, and the arms race threatens peace, then we logically have a duty to do something about the arms race.

Hypothesis

An hypothesis is a conjecture or assertion, an intellectual speculation that we think or predict to be true. To test the validity of an hypothesis, we work out its logical implications and see if it agrees with facts that we know to be true.

An hypothetical argument can be very powerful, but the speaker who decides to use one should realize that he or she is dealing with an assumption, not a given fact. This should always be made clear to the audience. The speaker should be ready to justify the assumption. The second element in the syllogism given above—"The nuclear arms race is a direct threat to peace"—is an hypothesis, an assertion on the speaker's part. Because its validity is open to question, the speaker has to support it with as much data as possible. This is not only fair to the audience, but it can go a long way toward convincing them to share the speaker's point of view. It is often impossible to prove an hypothesis objectively; by giving his or her evidence, however, a speaker can persuade others to share it.

The Toulmin Model

The philosopher Stephen Toulmin has made an important contribution to the understanding of argumentation. His model can be used to evaluate the strength of an argument before it is actually presented to an audience. Or, it can be used to locate weaknesses in an argument that we plan to refute.

Basic Elements and a Basic Scheme.   According to Toulmin's analysis, all arguments share three basic elements: data, a claim, and a warrant. On the basis of the data, the speaker makes a claim. But there has to be a reason, or warrant, for the listeners to accept the claim.[1] The basic relation among the data, claim, and warrant is illustrated in the accompanying figure.

Consider how the data and the warrant in this example work together to support the claim. Neither the warrant nor the data alone would be enough. Just saying that a company is a monopoly (that is, just offering the data) does not justify government action. We must also know something about how monopolies operate. That "something"—supplied by the warrant—is that they destroy free enterprise. When the data and the warrant are taken together, the full implications of the claim become apparent—by dissolving the Epsilon Company, the government will be protecting free enterprise.

Supporting Materials and the Toulmin Model.   Having arranged the three basic elements of the argument about the Epsilon Company, we should now consider the potential weaknesses or points of vulnerability in the argument. Begin with the warrant (monopolies destroy free enterprise). Could it be questioned? By definition, a mo-

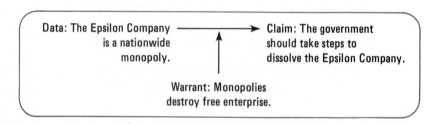

Data: The Epsilon Company
is a nationwide
monopoly.
Claim: The government
should take steps to
dissolve the Epsilon Company.

Warrant: Monopolies
destroy free enterprise.

[1] Stephen Toulmin, *An Introduction to Reasoning* (New York: Macmillan, 1979), pp. 23–28.

nopoly eliminates all competition, so factual support is probably not called for. But we might feel obligated to say something about the value of free enterprise in American history and its importance for our future. This can be documented. It would add strength to the warrant because it would imply that monopolies are destructive to the fabric of American life when they interfere with free enterprise.

The statement of the data (the Epsilon Company is a monopoly) obviously needs to be proved. It is not proof merely to accuse a company of monopolistic practices. We would have to be prepared to prove—with facts and figures—that the Epsilon Company really controlled an entire industry. To accomplish this, we could offer the audience the results of our research. We would name the smaller companies they had forced out of business, show that they were manipulating prices, demonstrate the full extent of their stranglehold on the market, and so on. The point is, that unless we can convince the audience, our argument will fail.

What are the potential weaknesses of the claim (the government should take steps to dissolve the company)? How could it be questioned or qualified? The audience would probably want to know what "steps" we think the government should take. A Congressional investigation? An antitrust suit? Charges against particular people in the company? We should be prepared to present a specific program.

ERRORS IN LOGIC

Arguing in a Circle

Circular arguments are a common type of logical error. When people argue in a circle, they claim that *A* is true because of *B* and that *B* is true because of *A*. Such arguments may appear logical, but they are merely "closed."

Don't argue in a circle.

Consider the statement "Women are unfit for careers because they naturally belong at home." The circularity of such an assertion is obvious: (*A*) Women are unfit for careers because (*B*) they naturally belong at home, and (*B*) they naturally belong at home because (*A*) they are unfit for careers. The same sort of merry-go-round can be seen in other statements: "We must obey him because he is our leader." Why must we obey him? Because he is our leader. But what makes him our leader? The fact that we must obey him.

As these examples demonstrate, circular arguments leave little room for dispute. But this is not a source of strength; in fact, it makes them weak. Because they are closer to "blind belief" than to logical thought, they fall apart under critical analysis.

Truth vs. Logic

Merely using a formal scheme of argument—inductive, deductive, or syllogistic—does not, of course, ensure that an argument will be logical. Any of these types of argument can be faulty if the speaker has (1) used "facts" that are false; (2) overgeneralized; or (3) drawn an irrelevant conclusion.

For example, during the 1940s, the English psychologist Sir Cyril Burt maintained that intelligence was largely an inherited trait. To support his position, he used in part the results of studies of identical twins who had been separated from birth. These children had been reared in different environments but measured the same on intelligence tests. Burt therefore argued that genetics and not environment were the major determinant of intelligence. His argument sounded logical. Unfortunately, it was recently discovered that Burt *manufactured* the data about the twins. His proof that intelligence is inherited was not based on scientific study. The data on similar intelligence in twins never really existed. As a result, psychologists no longer accept many of Burt's arguments.[2]

Overgeneralization is a logical error that is most often found in faulty inductive arguments. Consider the following:

- Rattlesnakes are dangerous.
- Cobras are dangerous.
- Coral snakes are dangerous.
- Copperheads are dangerous.
- All snakes are dangerous.

The speaker who argued this way could have gone on listing poisonous snakes for as long as he or she could name them. No matter how many species were cited, the conclusion that all snakes are dangerous would be both illogical and untrue. The conclusion is based on a sample of specific cases which is not true for all the snakes in the world. Because four types of snakes, or ten, or a hundred, are poisonous does not justify the inductive conclusion that therefore all snakes are poisonous. The speaker has overgeneralized on the basis of limited information.

The third potential fault in logical reasoning is that of irrelevant conclusions. This type of error often occurs in syllogisms

[2] Boyce Rensberger, "Data on Race Role in IQ Called False," *The New York Times*, November 9, 1978.

where the facts presented are not really related to the issue at hand. For example:

- Congressman P. advocates socialized medicine.
- The American Communist Party advocates socialized medicine.
- Congressman P. belongs to the American Communist Party.

The error occurs because the syllogism offers no proof that Congressman P.'s views on socialized medicine have been influenced by those of the American Communist Party. That he happens to share an opinion espoused by them is irrelevant, as is the conclusion that he belongs to that party.

When speakers use formal arguments they must be sure (1) that their information is true; (2) that their generalizations are based on enough specific cases; and (3) that their facts and conclusions really do relate to each other.

Argument to the Person

Argument to the person (from the Latin phrase *ad hominem* meaning "to the man") is an error of focus. Instead of concentrating on the issues, speakers sometimes attack the person or group concerned or involved with the issues. When speakers attempt to discredit a person instead of his or her ideas or actions, they are not arguing either logically or honestly.

A common example of argument to the person is political "mudslinging." This often involves insinuations about an opponent's private or past life: "Senator R.'s 17-year-old son has been arrested twice in the last year. His eldest daughter's marriage recently ended in a bitterly contested divorce. Do you really want a man whose family is troubled to represent you and your family in the United States Senate?"

The answer to this should be: "Why not?" This is no argument. It is audience manipulation. Intelligent listeners will probably recognize this and feel insulted. Their hostility ought to be directed toward the speaker rather than toward the senator whose ability to do the job has not been questioned.

Some speakers, of course, may not consciously set out to manipulate their audience by using to-the-person arguments. Even so, they fall short of the standards of good public speaking. Arguments to the person are not logical. Moreover, speakers who use them deprive themselves of the opportunity to be truly informative and persuasive.

Argument to the person is an error of focus.

Compare the strength of the following statements:

1. "The director of the realty company is a cold, unfeeling, and opportunistic woman who only cares about profit."

2. "The policies carried out by the current director of this company have had disastrous effects on both properties and people. Sites purchased and buildings supposedly scheduled for renovation have been neglected and allowed to deteriorate. The low-income families and elderly people who live in them have been threatened with eviction each time they voiced their complaints."

The second example is much more powerful because it tells the audience exactly what the speaker is concerned about in the most direct and informative way. The personality of the director is not very important; the results of her actions are.

Argument to Tradition

When a speaker claims that we should follow a particular course of action because "we have always done it that way," he or she is arguing to tradition. Such an argument may have sentimental appeal, but it should not be considered logical.

The most obvious potential flaw in an argument to tradition is that what has been done in the past may have been wrong. For example, social policies that discriminated against minority groups were continued for many decades in the United States on the basis of "tradition." This particular tradition, however, was one of ignorance and ill-will.

Secondly, arguments to tradition ignore change. This is particularly illogical given the rapidly changing nature of our society. Consider our present retirement age of 65 years. This tradition is being challenged by many people and for many good reasons. Today's 65-and-over population are much healthier than their counterparts of yesteryear. The Grey Panthers, a senior citizens group, point out that retirement and pension policies that once protected and sustained the aged are now restrictive and unrealistic. No argument to tradition will convince them that able people should be pushed out of their jobs and forced to live on fixed incomes in an age of rapid inflation.

Argument to Authority

By arguing to authority, the speaker tries to support his or her position entirely on the grounds that it "has been accepted by the experts." Certainly, expert studies and opinions can be cited as evidence during a speech. But the speaker should remember that agreement with the experts does not, in and of itself, prove that he or she is right. The responsibility to provide logical arguments still stands.

One problem with argument to authority is that with controversial issues, authorities tend to conflict with each other. For example, if a speaker is giving a speech about the energy crisis, he or she will doubtless find that all the experts do not agree. Scientists and economists representing the oil companies, for instance, may argue that the best solution is to develop new oil sources. This opinion implies that the oil companies be given a profit incentive and not be asked to pay higher taxes. On the other hand, experts representing conservation groups hold that the best solution is to put taxpayer dollars, including taxes paid by the oil companies, into developing clean energy sources such as solar power. Both positions are authoritative, and who can be sure in a particular case that one is right and the other wrong? Which authorities we choose to believe will depend largely on our own values.

Looking Out for Persuasive Devices

As consumers of public speaking, we should be aware of how other speakers may try to manipulate us into accepting their views. Instead of offering logical arguments, manipulative speakers try to reach their listeners by appealing entirely to their emotions, needs, or fears. These are really the techniques of propaganda. If we recognize propaganda when we hear it, it can lose most of its power to sway us.

Name Calling.   Name calling is often used when a speaker wishes to distract attention away from the important issues. For example, a speaker might continually refer to an opponent as "a crazy fool" as an excuse for dismissing his or her views offhand. After all, if the person is crazy, why should we waste time considering his or her views?

Name calling can sometimes arouse the audience and make them forget the issues. This is known as "mob appeal." It seeks to propel the audience into hasty and ill-considered action. One good example of this occurs in the film "Gone with the Wind." The news that the Civil War has begun is delivered to a group of people at a picnic. Someone gets up and delivers a fiery speech about the need to "teach those Yankee cowards a lesson." A few reasonable men try to remind the group that fiery words won't win a war, but they are shouted down. Within minutes, everyone rushes off to join the army.

Name calling, whether it is used to avoid issues or to fuel the emotions of an audience, has no relation to logical argument. If anything, it undermines the listener's desire for the truth.

Transfer. Transfer occurs when a speaker tries to "borrow" the high status or credibility of another person by claiming some connection with him or her. For example, a minor political figure might open a campaign speech by telling the audience that the president has endorsed his or her candidacy. Of course, the speaker will not also say that the endorsement was practically automatic because he or she is the only Democrat in the race. The speaker is only making this statement because it sounds good, not because he or she really has the personal support of the president.

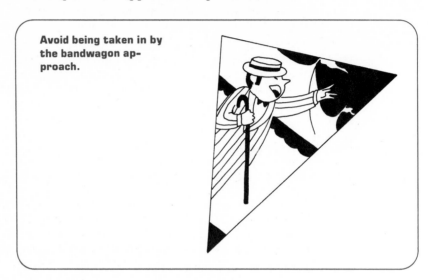

Avoid being taken in by the bandwagon approach.

Bandwagon. We are all familiar with the bandwagon approach. This is the basic "do it because everyone else is doing it" argument. The bandwagon device manipulates the human need to belong—a very strong need felt by most people.

Again, the bandwagon device ignores the real issues. Instead of discussing the accuracy and worth of his or her view, the speaker merely focuses on how many people support it.

Probably the most common use of the bandwagon approach is in advertising. We have all been exposed to messages that tell us to "buy while the supply still lasts." "Don't be the last on your block to own this delightful article." "Everyone is going to be there; don't miss out on the fun." The idea is always the same—if you don't do what everyone else does, there must be something wrong with you.

Plain Folks. The plain-folks device is an attempt by the speaker to identify him or herself as being "just like you folks out there." This is permissible, but it can be a substitute for logical argument. It takes advantage of the human tendency to mistrust outsiders and to support those most similar to oneself. The plain-folks argument can backfire if an audience feels that the speaker is being patronizing or phony. If a high-salaried professional addresses a group of laborers and claims to be "a working man" just like they are, he or she probably won't convince them.

Cardstacking.   Cardstacking occurs when a speaker is overly concerned with defending the exclusive credibility of his or her views. He or she may try to do this by "warning" the audience away from other approaches to the issues or advising them to ignore information that might contradict his or her position.

Summary

Supporting materials are the evidence and documentation that a speaker uses to build a case for his or her position. They can clarify the speaker's ideas and thereby promote audience understanding. They can also make the speaker's message more memorable by adding color and interest. Above all, supporting materials fulfill the speaker's responsibility to back up the ideas stated in the speech.

The development of sound supporting arguments depends largely on critical thinking. When deciding whether to use materials in a speech, the critical thinker should discriminate between facts and inferences and avoid being manipulated by language alone.

He or she should keep an open mind and consider all potential causes. Finally, critical thinkers should be aware of the constancy of change. They know that to be powerful, their arguments must be up to date.

Critical thinking also applies to how arguments are structured. Certain formal, time-honored schemes of reasoning can help a speaker present materials in the most effective way. These include deductive and inductive reasoning, syllogisms, and developing hypothetical arguments.

It is always possible to clothe a false argument in a logical form. The most typical errors in logic are arguing in a circle; using inaccurate information; making false generalizations; and building irrelevant syllogisms. Certain other types of argument are illogical by nature. These include arguing to the person; arguing to tradition; and arguing to authority.

As consumers of public speaking as well as potential speakers, we need to be aware of the difference between propaganda and erroneous argument. Propaganda devices include name calling; transfer; attempts by the speaker to ingratiate him or herself with the audience (the "plain-folks" argument); and the "bandwagon" type of argument in which speakers try to convince by citing the number of their supporters. All of these devices avoid discussing the real issues.

Exercises

1. Using the Toulmin model in the chapter, build an argument for each of the topics below.
    a. limiting nuclear power
    b. affirmative action programs
    c. quitting smoking
    d. limiting water pollution
    e. the need for more national parks

2. Give an example of each of the following:
    a. arguing in a circle
    b. cardstacking
    c. abstraction
    d. fact-inference confusion

3. Take a particular topic and develop six arguments for it. There should be three logical arguments and three emotional arguments. Which type of arguments do you think are stronger. Why?

7

building introductions and conclusions

Tips for Speakers

1. Remember that the introduction, the body, and the conclusion form a complete ''speech package.''
2. The introduction sets the stage for the speech.
3. The introduction should also secure the audience's attention.
4. The conclusion should emphasize the main idea of the speech.
5. In addition, the conclusion ties up loose ends.

In this chapter we shall be discussing the relationship between good introductions and conclusions and effective public speaking. Together with the body of the speech, they form a speech "package." Each element of that package is both important in itself and important to successful public speaking. The introduction, for example, should set the mood a speaker wants an audience to reach. It also can highlight what the speaker will be saying, so that the audience is prepared to listen to the main points of the speech contained in the body. While the body of a speech is obviously very important, the audience will appreciate it better if the speaker engages their interest first in the introduction. The audience needs to have a reason to listen. They need to know that what they are about to hear is important to *them*.

But an introduction and a body still need an effective conclusion to make a good speech. As we shall see, there are several types of effective conclusions. Any one of them must make a lasting impression on the audience. Especially, however, when the speaker wants the audience to do something—to make a contribution, to sign a petition, to vote for a candidate—the conclusion should translate words into deeds by motivating the audience to act.

BUILDING GOOD INTRODUCTIONS

What an Introduction Does

The introduction, very importantly, "sets the stage" for a speech. It should include what you intend to talk about and why you have chosen this topic. If there are specific points you intend to cover, these should be indicated exactly as they will occur in the body of the speech. This has psychological value. Not only does the audience know the major points of your talk in advance but they are made more receptive by being told briefly what is to follow. When you discuss these points in detail later in the body of the speech, you will be talking about something with which they are already somewhat familiar. Psychologically, the listener is prepared for what you are going to say in the body, and what you say reinforces (and expands) what you have begun in the introduction.

Builds Rapport with the Audience.   Besides introducing the topic of your speech, a good introduction should also help to build rapport between you and the audience. This is particularly important because you want the audience to like you and respond positively to the speech. Remember that the object of public speaking is communication. It is very difficult for a speaker to communicate with an audience unless he or she has built this sense of rapport with them. There are three easy ways in which you can develop rapport with your audience: through humor, especially humor directed at yourself; by identifying areas of common interest between you and the audience; and by stressing concern for the audience's welfare. The most effective displays of humor are often those in which the speaker pokes fun at him or herself. Presidents Franklin Roosevelt and John F. Kennedy were masters at building audience rapport through this technique. Kennedy, for example, once delighted an audience by beginning a speech with the remark that his father, a former ambassador to Britain, had stopped contributing to his campaign after JFK had announced that in his administration ambassadorships would not be given as rewards to generous campaign contributors as they had been under previous presidents.

Establishes Speaker Credibility.   While the words you choose and the way you organize your speech reflect your knowledge about a particular topic, an audience will still want to know *why* they should believe what you are about to tell them. They need to know what credentials you have that will make your opinion or knowledge about a subject more valuable than that of someone else. (See Chapter 9.) Often, all a speaker needs is a single statement: "I've been a racing car driver for fifteen years, and today I'd like to tell you about how it feels to be behind the wheel at the Indianapolis 500." Simple and direct—the audience will have no problem accepting that speaker's creden-

WHAT AN INTRODUCTION DOES
1. **Builds rapport with the audience**
2. **Establishes speaker credibility**
3. **Presents the topic**
4. **Personalizes the speech**
5. **Makes the first impression**
6. **Makes a smooth transition into the body of the speech**

tials. He or she may also have aroused their curiosity and perhaps, excitement. Or again:

> *For twenty days in July, along with a group of educators, retirees, social workers, and businessmen, I visited the People's Republic of China.*[1]

Presents the Topic.   As stated earlier, an introduction should highlight the points that follow in the body of the speech. These should be mentioned in the order in which they will be covered. The listeners then know how the speech is to develop and have some idea of what they are going to hear. This allows them to make mental notes about possible associations between the points outlined and what they already know about the topic. When the speaker gets to the heart of the speech, the audience's attention will then focus more easily on what the speech is chiefly about.

Personalizes the Speech.   Not all audiences are going to be closely involved with every speech. If they do not know the speaker personally, or if he or she is not a recognized expert or a celebrity, their interest and attention initially may be low. As a student of public speaking, how are you going to make your audience sympathetic and interested in your speech?

One of the best ways to do this is to personalize your topic, so that the audience's interest is aroused. Personalizing a topic makes the audience feel that the topic is important to them. This can be done by asking questions: "Did you know that it takes only five years to pollute a river the size of the Ohio by chemical dumping?" This kind of question immediately puts an audience on the spot and makes each listener feel as though the question is asked personally of him or her.

Then, once the audience is engaged, you can further involve them as individuals with the topic: "Each of us contributes to this kind of chemical dumping by the products we buy." If the audience is able to feel that they are a part of what you are discussing, their interest is going to be that much greater:

> *I've always felt a certain kinship with journalists because I began my own career by selling life insurance; and when you get right down to it, I think insurance and journalism are both based on the same grand and noble principle—persistence.*[2]

[1] Billy O. Wireman, "The People's Republic of China," *Vital Speeches of the Day,* January 1, 1979, p. 178.
[2] Robert A. Beck, "Business, the Press, and the Zero-Risk Society," *Vital Speeches of the Day,* October 1, 1978, p. 758.

Makes First Impressions That Are Lasting. Few statements are as true as this one. While impressions can change as you get to know someone better, in public speaking there simply is not time. As a speaker you encounter an audience for a relatively short time, and everything you say and do is going to be judged by them. The first impression you make, therefore, is the most vital one. With it, the audience judges much of what is to follow. If you make an unfavorable impression in the introduction, your audience may "tune out" much of what you want them to hear, and respond to.

Is a Transition. Last of all, the introduction allows a speaker to make a smooth transition into the first point in the body of the speech. It is a vehicle for leading into the main ideas of your topic and prepares the audience to receive them. Basically, this lead-in should be as smooth as possible. It should not be particularly obvious, but it should alert the audience to what is to follow and make the progression from one part of the speech package to the next easy to follow.

Harvard's motto is "Veritas." Many of you have already found out and others will find out in the course of their lives that truth eludes us as soon as our concentration begins to flag, all the while leaving the illusion that we are continuing to pursue it. This is the source of much discord. Also, truth seldom is sweet; it is almost invariably bitter. A measure of bitter truth is included in my speech today, but I offer it as a friend, not as an adversary. [3]

[3] Alexander Solzhenitsyn, "A World Split Apart," *Vital Speeches of the Day*, September 1, 1978, p. 678.

A speaker's first impression is the one that sticks in the audience's mind.

Adolescence is the limbo of family life: a time for moving away from total dependence on parents toward full independence—never as fast as the teenager would like; always faster than parents think wise.[4]

How a Good Introduction Works

By now, you think that introductions are easy, that it is the body of the speech that you have to worry about. Although the body is certainly very important—in effect, the substance of the speech—good introductions and conclusions do much to enhance its effectiveness. All three, remember, constitute the speech package. The introduction prepares your audience for what you are going to tell them. If the listener is not "tuned in," is not motivated to look forward with interest and enthusiasm to what you are going to say, your speech may fall on figuratively deaf ears. However brilliant the body of your speech may be, its impact may not be recognized if you have lost your listener back in the introduction.

There are both constructive and less than constructive ways to involve an audience in your topic. For example, you might ask a question. What sort of question you ask, of course, will depend on the topic of your speech, as well as on the interests and perceptions of your audience. "How many of you feel that the building of nuclear reactors should be halted?" If you are addressing an audience of pronuclear people, this question could be disastrous in an introduction. If you believe that the audience may be fairly evenly split on the issue, however, and you want to involve them in a discussion after the speech, the question could be appropriate. Remember, always think in terms of your audience and how you want them to react.

An ineffective approach would be to assault the audience with a negatively phrased comment. For example: "I suppose most of you think nuclear power is a pretty bad idea." Again, in some circumstances this statement could be effective, but it is more likely to antagonize, to set speaker and audience at opposite poles. The speech to follow, it might be presumed, will be seen as a hostile declaration from you to the audience. This kind of statement places you in opposition to how the audience may view a certain situation. Confrontations may get an audience actively involved, as in a debate, for example, but they will rarely help to convince them to share your views.

Getting the Audience's Attention.   The chief function of the introduction is to make the audience pay attention to the speech itself. There are as many ways of gaining listener attention as there are

---

[4] Joseph A. Califano, Jr., "Adolescents: Their Needs and Problems," *Vital Speeches of the Day*, August 15, 1978, p. 647.

It is seldom
effective to
assault your
audience.

public speaking situations and public speakers. The Duke of Devonshire, a nineteenth-century English statesman, once told Winston Churchill that he liked to begin his speeches by staring at his audiences and remarking that he had never seen such a bunch of idiots in his life. Apparently, this made the duke feel more confident and rarely left his listeners indifferent to what he had to say.

In general, however, it would be unwise for you, as a student of public speaking, to attempt to get the audience's attention in your introduction by using highly unusual or dramatic techniques, such as slamming a book on the podium. These often come across to an audience as theatrical and can easily backfire and defeat your purpose.

There are, however, some techniques that the speaker can use to make sure that the audience has "tuned into" the speech. Among these are the following:

- Making a surprising statement at the beginning of the speech.
- Showing a visual or graphic that highlights an important aspect of the speech.
- Doing something interesting physically (for example, a hand gesture or making special eye contact) that is consistent with the purposes of the speech.
- Quoting a famous person about the topic of your speech.
- Referring to something unusual about your audience ("I see I have here an island of lovely and talented Republicans in a Democratic sea").
- Paying a special compliment to the audience ("You are the best looking group of listeners that I have seen during my tour").

Signposting the Speech.   Any audience appreciates being told what is going to be covered in a speech and how long it will last. This

NYPL

OLIVER CROMWELL was born in Huntington, England, on April 25, 1599. A stern speaker, he entered Parliament in 1640, joining the Puritans against King Charles I. In 1642 civil war broke out between the King and Parliament. Cromwell emerged as the most dynamic general in England, leading troops to smash the Royalists in 1645. In 1653 King Charles was executed, and Cromwell dissolved Parliament in a famous speech that began: "It is not fit that you sit here any longer." He became king in all but name until his death in 1658.

An introduction should signpost the speech.

is what is meant by signposting in the introduction. As a speaker you should use specific phrases, such as: "Today, we'll be spending the next twenty minutes examining how you can become a more knowledgeable consumer. First of all, how do you go about shopping? Second, do you make comparisons between one item and another or between one shop and another? Third, when you have made a purchase, do you feel you've been cheated because you haven't looked around long enough? These points represent comments I have frequently heard consumers make. I've researched them extensively, and I want to share the results with you now."

You do *not* want to be vague: "Today, we're going to look at some things which have greatly interested me, and I think they will you, too." What things are you referring to? And just because these things (whatever they may be) happen to interest you, can you presume they will also interest someone else?

Nor do you want to be overly direct and say: "These are the points to be covered in my speech today. First . . . ," merely listing them in the order in which they will be given. Signposting should be direct and informative. It should not be mechanical.

My purpose today is to focus your attention:
—on the dimensions of the energy challenge confronting our nation;
—on the major reasons why the energy outlook remains so uncertain, and finally,
—to offer what I feel is a realistic perspective on what America must do to assure a more stable and expanding supply of energy in the years ahead.[5]

Connecting the Speech to the Speaker.   In some public speaking situations the relationship between the topic and the speaker is immediately clear. A talk by a NASA engineer on the mechanical problems involved in the space flight to the moon would not make the audience wonder why the speaker chose that particular topic. The relationship is self-evident.

In most cases, however, the connection is not so obvious. The listener will want to know why you have chosen your topic and how much you know about it. Usually, a very simple and direct statement is best. Consider the following example. The speaker, in this case, is talking to a community organization about how to handle simple repairs around the home: "I am certain that you all would agree with

[5] H. J. Haynes, "A Rational and Effective Energy Program for America," *Vital Speeches of the Day,* July 15, 1978, p. 600.

me that it is in your best interest to know how to make certain repairs around the house. I learned, and you can, too."

While the statement may contain some truth, it presumes that what is in one person's best interest necessarily follows for others. It might have been better to say: "I was standing alone in my basement one day watching water gush from a leaking pipe. It was the sixth time that month I had had to call a repair service, and I hated the thought of having to do it again. I decided then and there to learn how to make such repairs myself." This version allows the relationship between speaker and topic to become self-evident from the facts, rather than from the self-assessment of the speaker.

Establishing Parameters.   Certain types of speeches need to be explained during the introduction. For example, a speech about only one aspect of a controversial or complex topic might require some preliminary statements about why the subject was to be approached in that fashion: "Although I realize that the feminist movement has many ramifications, I have decided to focus only on the need for day-care centers, so that you can get a better idea of what is involved in women's liberation and will perhaps wish to consider other areas of the movement yourself." This lets the audience know just what is being discussed by delimiting the topic of the speech within the much wider limits of feminism.

Leading into the Body of the Speech.   The final major purpose of the introduction is, of course, to lead into the main points contained in the body of the speech. In other words, something you said in the introduction should relate directly to the first main point of the speech. Compare the following two examples: "Many people feel that both marijuana and tobacco smoking may be harmful. We shall talk about both, but the main point of our discussion is how to go about cutting down on smoking tobacco." AND "Many people who think it terrible to smoke marijuana see nothing wrong with smoking two packs of cigarettes a day. They can see why they should not smoke 'pot,' yet cannot conceive of curbing their use of tobacco."

The problem with the first statement is that, while a correlation may exist between cigarette smoking and the smoking of marijuana, the relationship to the topic of the speech is not immediately evident. Moreover, the approach is disjointed and may make the listener feel that the speaker has composed his or her speech haphazardly. The second example, on the other hand, not only makes an effective psychological point, but lets the speaker move comfortably into his or her first point: how to cut down on cigarette smoking.

CONCLUSIONS AND THEIR PURPOSES

Having introduced your topic and discussed the main points contained in the body of the speech, you still have to finish it. Literally, the conclusion ends the speech; it is the last element of the speech package. It rounds out the speech by tying up any loose ends that may be left from the points discussed in the body. It completes the purpose of your talk, and it lets the listeners know that the speech is about to end. Remember what we have said about communication being the key to successful public speaking. You have an idea that you want to get across to your audience. The conclusion should emphasize this idea so that it will be firmly etched in the listener's memory. Hence, the conclusion is often the most dramatic part of the speech. Here, you can sum up your argument and try to make it as clear and forceful, indeed, as dramatic, as possible. Particularly in speeches of persuasion or information, you will want the audience to remember vividly all that you have said. We shall now discuss in detail a number of specific points to follow when planning the conclusion of a speech.

What a Conclusion Does

Reviews the Speech's Main Points. This review stresses only the essential ideas without going into detail. In the body of the speech, you have already explained why you feel the listener should agree with you. Now, in the conclusion, you only want to remind the listener of the most important points in your argument. The review serves as a kind of "mind conditioning" by leaving your listeners with what you most want them to remember. By process of association they will recall the rest of your argument.

Stresses the Strongest Argument. While reviewing the main points of the speech, you should also stress the key argument. If that argument is that conservation begins with each individual, then this is what you should underline most strongly in your conclusion. You may, in fact, want to stress it by restating it in several different ways or perhaps by introducing arguments which all lead to the same conclusion. For example, you might say: "Many of us think of the air we breathe and the mineral deposits in the ground as infinite. But reflect on how life around you has changed in the last ten, even five years. There is less 'empty' land available; increasing populations require more housing, more services. These increases have to be met and paid for somehow. Or, think about how much paper you use or

WHAT A CONCLUSION DOES
1. **Reviews the speech's main points**
2. **Stresses the strongest argument**
3. **Can be a call to action**
4. **Resolves loose ends**
5. **Creates a positive climate**
6. **Disengages the speaker from the audience**

come in contact with everyday, multiply that by the 200 million people in the United States, and you have some idea of our dependence on paper products and the natural resources (trees) that they come from. Our natural resources are not something which government alone has to worry about. They are something which affect, and are controlled by, each one of us."

Should Be a Call to Action, When Appropriate. Many speeches, particularly those which seek to persuade, ask for some kind of action from the listeners. It might be to go out and vote for a candidate, to sign a petition, or simply to reconsider a problem. Whatever action the speech advocates, the conclusion is the place to jolt the audience into acting. It is also why conclusions are appropriate for dramatic appeal. You will want to build an emotional "pitch"—to make your audience think of very little else than the message you have given them.

A good conclusion is often a call to action.

Inscribed on the Statue of Liberty is still the invitation, "Give me your tired, your poor, your huddled masses yearning to breath free. . . ." We have work to do. And the time is short. Let's be about our business![6]

Resolves Loose Ends. If there are any points which the body of the speech has left unclear, the conclusion is also the place to resolve them. For example, in a discussion of voter apathy in the inner cities, you might also discuss those problems—changing population, foreign immigration, and the like—which contribute to it. While your objective had been in part to explain why such apathy exists, you also wanted to call attention to the fact that voter apathy is a serious

[6] Billy O. Wireman, "The People's Republic of China," p. 178.

problem. The body of the speech may not have made this distinction perfectly clear. Therefore, you will need to make it in the conclusion, so that your audience will understand that voting is important. The conclusion is also the place to pass out relevant literature, to inform your audience of sources for further information or help, to let them know about forthcoming meetings on the same or similar topics, and the like.

Should Be Positive.   Leaving a positive impression with each listener can contribute to how well your audience retains, or acts on, the main points of your speech. People tend to react favorably toward an idea if they like, admire, or respect the person who expressed it. In part, the ability to inspire this feeling is a function of personality and natural charisma. But any effective speaker can leave his or her audience with supportive rather than controversial or uncertain feelings.

If the world has not approached its end, it has reached a major watershed in history, equal in importance to the turn from the Middle Ages to the Renaissance.... This ascension will be similar to climbing onto the next anthropological stage. No one on earth has any other way left but—upward.[7]

Together, we must try to move from today's environment, replete with anxiety, struggle, and existential victimization, to a new vision of America more closely attuned to the idealism of our forefathers.[8]

Then will our educational institutions have earned the right to call themselves truly creative enterprises. Then will our students find that life is not irrational wandering but a journey with a homecoming, a voyage with a port of call. So may it come to pass.[9]

Disengages the Speaker from the Audience.   An obvious function of a conclusion is to signal that the speech will soon be over. Your conclusion, therefore, should make this immediately clear. You may be specific and say: "And now before I close, I want to remind you...." Or, you may imply it by your tone of voice or by the content, which may recap what has already been said but should

---

[7] Alexander Solzhenitsyn, "A World Split Apart," p. 678.
[8] William J. McGill, "Simple Justice and Existential Victims," *Vital Speeches of the Day*, December 1, 1978, p. 107
[9] Harver H. Bernstein, "Learning as Worship," *Vital Speeches of the Day*, December 1, 1978, p. 122.

not contain anything new. The speaker should also make the conclusion as graceful as possible by not being either excessively wordy or redundant.

Summary

Good introductions and conclusions are important to effective public speaking. They "round out" the speech package by letting your audience know what to expect, how long it will last, and when it will be over. They each, in their distinct ways, contribute to the effectiveness of the speech by building up interest (in the introduction) and by reemphasizing (in the conclusion) the main points presented in the body.

Exercises

1. Develop an introduction for a hypothetical speech on two of the following topics, or those of your choice.
    a. skiing in Colorado
    b. the need to take mass transport
    c. playing backgammon
    d. why one should go to college
    e. politics in our state
    f. energy needs in the year 2000
    g. tuning up your automobile
    h. getting a job after graduation
2. Develop a conclusion for a hypothetical speech on two of the following topics. If you prefer, you may select your own topics.
    a. tuition-free higher education
    b. cruelty to animals
    c. reading a book a week
    d. ending violence on television
    e. the rising costs of raising children
    f. getting along with parents
    g. jazz, America's music
    h. whether the U.S. should compete in the Olympics

usinq visuAl aids

Tips for Speakers

1. Use visual aids:
   a) to save time and speed up communication
   b) to make a subject easier to understand
   c) for dramatic effect and to gain listener attention.
2. Prepare your aids and check equipment in advance.
3. Use aids to supplement your speech—not to substitute for it, or to ''decorate'' it.
4. Make sure that your aids are immediately clear—that they simplify rather than complicate your subject.

Some may think that a visual aid is the answer to any speaking problem. Get a few good visual aids and your speech is certain to be a success. Unfortunately, it is not quite that easy. Aids to public speaking should be enjoyable to use. Handled well, they can enhance a speaker's potential impact. They increase the listener's understanding of the subject and make the speaker more credible. They facilitate the message of a speech and make it easier to understand. One picture *can* be worth a thousand words. Choosing the kind of aid to improve your speech—or even whether to use one at all—can be as important to a speech as content and style.

Generally, aids are useful in speeches which give detailed information. They can also be helpful in speeches of persuasion. Most aids are visual, but occasionally an audio aid (such as a record or tape recording), or one which combines both (such as a videotape), can help make a speech a success. In special circumstances, even an aid that involves a form of tactile stimulation (for example, a model the listener can hold) can also be effective.

Just when should you use an aid? Is it absolutely necessary for effective public speaking? And if you decide to use one, how and when should it be used? These are some of the questions we will explore in this chapter.

PUBLIC SPEAKING AND VISUAL AIDS

Basically, a visual aid is anything the audience can see that helps the speaker get his or her message across. Remember, communication is the object of public speaking. Like the content and delivery of your speech, the visual aid should make it easier for you to get your message across to the listener—and easier for the listener to receive and understand it. It should bring speaker and audience closer together. It should help to develop rapport.

Aid and Audience

When deciding whether to use a visual aid, you should keep your audience in mind. Again, we are reminded of the importance of audience analysis. What are their interests? Are they old, young, or a mix of both? Some aids may distract, while others perfectly illustrate the point you want your audience to understand. Graphs, for example, would probably be inappropriate for a group of amateur gardeners

Graphs can be useful aids but will not work for every audience or every topic.

listening to a talk on how to care for houseplants. For different reasons, graphs might also be a poor choice in a speech before a neighborhood group considering whether to vote for municipal improvements. For the amateur gardeners, graphs would not illustrate anything specific about how to care for plants. A graph might tell an audience about the differences in plant growth from one year to the next but such information is irrelevant to caring for them. It might even distract the audience. With our group of voters, graphs could be useful, but they might also think them too complicated.

On the other hand, a meeting of business executives would probably be comfortable with graphs used as visual aids. Most executives are already familiar with graphs because businesses often compare percentages. The point is that each speaking situation is unique. Public speakers have to decide whether and how to use aids, based on the subject of their talk and the kind of audience they will have.

Other points to look for in an audience include their level of education, whether they are from an urban, suburban, or rural area, or whether their politics happen to be liberal or conservative. A printed handout that quotes from a liberal political observer such as Gore Vidal might annoy an audience whose members would feel more comfortable with the thoughts of William Buckley. The quote might relate well to the point of the speech, but its source—liberal rather than conservative—could make some people less receptive to the speech's message.

Aid and Topic

The aid you use in a speech should also be appropriate to the topic. Ideally, it should help to clarify an idea, to sharpen an audience's focus, so they have a better concept of what the speaker is saying. It should also help to enliven the topic, to give it a kind of psychological adrenalin shot. But to do this effectively, it must extend the point of the speech, so that the connection between the speech and the aid will be obvious. This requires choosing a visual aid carefully. For example, a speech explaining how a mechanical device works might be helped by a diagram of the device, showing its various parts. Each one could be labeled and separated from the whole, so that the audience could see exactly how they work together. A drawing of the device as a complete object would not be nearly as effective. Both could be used, but the drawing by itself would not strengthen or extend the meaning for the listeners unless they were already familiar with the device itself.

Another example of an appropriate aid involves the use of a recording. The speaker is talking about the invasion of Normandy during World War II. While describing the invasion, the speaker plays a recording of waves beating against a shore, of men sludging through water, of gunfire. The recording would not be loud enough to drown out the speech, but it would intensify its dramatic element, making it much more vivid.

There are times when a particular aid may be inappropriate. One which shows the opposite of what the speaker is saying becomes distracting and confusing. Consider the case of a speaker talking about the pleasures of Caribbean travel. He or she shows slides which depict inviting beaches and lush tropical plants but include the poverty and underdevelopment found on some of the islands. By showing such pictures, the speaker may have made the prospect of a Caribbean holiday much less appealing to the audience. *Remember, an aid must closely follow the topic.*

Types of Aids

Projecting an enlarged picture is one of the most effective ways to use visual aids.

There are any number of aids, each of which can be used differently. The trick is to pick the type of aid that will best deliver the message of the speech. For a speech about comparative facts and figures, a graph chart might be appropriate. To explain how a machine works, however, as we saw, a diagram would probably be more suitable. The speaker must *think* about his or her subject and use the aid that best suits both the topic and the audience.

Some of the aids which can be used in speaking situations include the following:

Pictures.　These may be photographs or drawings. The important factor here is size: The picture must be large enough for everyone in the room to see. A photograph 11 by 14 inches (or better still 14 by 18 inches) would be visible in an average-sized room, say 20 by 30 feet. (A speaker may even want to pass a photo around. As we have pointed out, however, passing anything around the audience can be distracting and should be done either before or, preferably, after the speech is finished.) For a speech in a large auditorium, of course, the picture would have to be considerably bigger. An opaque projector is a useful mechanical aid that enlarges a picture, so that it can be seen in a large room. Better still, if the photos can be put onto slides and then shown on a screen, their effectiveness will be increased.

Blackboards and Flip Charts.　Perhaps the most basic visual aid is the blackboard. Since almost every classroom has one, availability and access is no problem. It is best to come into the room ahead of time to prepare your visual on the blackboard. In this way, you can be sure that your diagram accurately represents what you are discussing in your speech.

Flip charts are widely used in industry. A flip chart is a large pad of blank paper attached to an easel that can be used to display a series of visuals. As each visual is needed the speaker can flip to the appropriate illustration. Flip charts allow the speaker to complete his or her visuals ahead of time without breaking up the continuity of the speech by drawing during the talk.

Regardless of whether the blackboard or the flip chart is used, the speaker needs large and clear diagrams that are appropriate to the speech. Speakers often like to use a pointer to call attention to a feature in the visual.

Films. Many large businesses, the government, libraries, and foundations produce films that can be used in public speaking. They are most effective when they parallel a speech. In a talk on China, to cite an obvious example, a film could convey pictorially and immediately what could only be partially described in words. Few Americans have firsthand knowledge of the country. A film could make it easier to understand those differences based on culture, terrain, climate, and the like, with which we are unfamiliar.

Yet films, whether in black and white or in color, can have disadvantages. They take up time and can delay the speech itself. In speeches of information or explanation, the time lapse might not make much of a difference; but for speeches of persuasion, it could hamper the speaker's effectiveness.

Filmstrips. Unlike movies, filmstrips let the speaker stop or go backward or forward according to need. Moreover, filmstrips can be held at any frame (or shot), which can be extremely useful if the speaker needs to emphasize a particular point illustrated by that image. The speaker may spend as much time as needed on that one frame.

Audio Aids. These include tape recordings and records. Unlike visual aids, they are usually only a background to actual speaking. But they can also be used to illustrate a point, as in a discussion on various types of regional accents. The speaker could discuss Southern or New England accents, for example, and then illustrate his or her point with a tape recording of the actual accents he or she has just been describing.

Written Handouts. These are useful as something for the audience to take with them after a speech. The handouts should make the same point as the speech, so that its impact will be strengthened each time the material is read. Remember, it is less distracting and more effective to wait until the very end of a speech before distributing handouts.

Videotapes.   Videotapes can be effective learning tools for the beginning speaker who wants to practice giving a speech, tape it, and then play it back to see how it looks and sounds. They can also be used as a two-dimensional aid when giving a speech. A speaker advocating a political position, for example, could show videotapes of interviews with voters to buttress his or her argument. Videotapes can also be used to demonstrate something that cannot be duplicated at the time or place of the speech.

Graphs.   Graphs are best used to draw attention to differences in comparative figures (percentages, growth rates, and so on). They are most effective for audiences of professionals—business people, technicians, academics—who are used to them and thus more likely to appreciate their value. They should, however, always be used sparingly since too many graphs can become uninteresting to any audience.

Full-scale Models.   These, including reproductions, have a certain immediate value. They enable the audience to see what is being discussed and to associate the model with it. There are also "schematic" models, two-dimensional drawings of something, for example, of a building facade or interior. They are line-drawings of what the finished product will look like.

Charts and Diagrams.   These will often accompany statistical data, or scientific/mechanical items that are not easily understood. Listeners are first told what the object is supposed to look like or how it is supposed to operate. They then see a diagram that shows the thing and how it works. The speaker thus gives his or her listeners two images of the object—a verbal and a visual one—each of which supports the other and helps to make a lasting impression.

A working model can make the topic of a speech much easier to understand.

People.   Surprisingly enough, people make effective aids—perhaps the most effective aids. People can be used in countless situations. For example, a person might be called on to model what the speaker has been saying. A presentation of lifesaving techniques could be clarified by using two members of the audience to demonstrate how to rescue a drowning swimmer or the proper way to administer artificial respiration.

Tactile Aids.   These can be effective in special circumstances. For example, a talk about a new form of synthetic rubber that is exceptionally soft but durable would make a more lasting impression if the speaker passed around a sample to the audience and asked them to guess what they thought it was. It could thus make the audience much more eager to hear the talk.

Why Use Aids

Not all speeches need aids. Topics with which an audience is already familiar, for example, do not require them. The important factor is how well an aid improves the level of understanding between speaker and listener. As we have emphasized throughout this book, giving a speech should be a two-way communication. Sometimes aids can accomplish what words cannot. When this happens, they are invaluable. When they do not increase the level of understanding, however, omit them.

How does a speaker determine when aids help? The reaction of the audience is an obvious sign. Is the audience distracted? Are they paying more attention to the aid than to the speaker? When this happens, the speaker has lost his or her rapport with the listener. The aid should have accomplished just the opposite—it should have brought speaker and listener closer together. Should this occur to you as a speaker, go back and look at the aid. Remember where in the speech you introduced it. Perhaps there is nothing wrong with the aid. It may have fit your topic well. Perhaps it was used at the wrong time. Many speakers make the mistake of handing out written material while trying to speak. The audience, of course, tries at once both to read the handout and to listen—an almost impossible task. Throughout the speech there is a low rustle as paper shifts from hand to hand down the rows. Some handouts fall and make more noise. The audience is distracted and the speaker can become demoralized.

To Save Time.   One of the chief values of aids in public speaking is that they speed up communication, the primary purpose of a speech. One picture can capture with a single image what it may take five minutes to explain in words. It can thus save time. A talk about pollution of rivers, for example, would be more effective—and clearer—if the speaker showed a picture of a contaminated river. This is what pollution looks like. See for yourself. In this instance, a picture not only saves the time that the speaker might have to spend describing pollution, but it is also a statement more dramatic than any made in words. The picture would also give tangible meaning to the remainder of the speech, to statistics about pollution, perhaps. Thus, here the speaker could use a visual aid to double advantage. And as a result, it is more likely that the listeners will be persuaded to accept the speaker's argument.

The results of river pollution. Carefully chosen and presented, a visual aid can give a powerful impact to a speaker's message.
© Gilles Peress / Magnum

To Clarify Complex Subjects.   Some subjects are so complex that aids have to be used for them to be understood. A speech describing photosynthesis, for example, might be more effective if the speaker used a diagram showing how it worked. It might also be useful simply to display a houseplant. The plant would be a tangible object to which the audience could relate the abstract concept of photosynthesis.

Speeches about machines and other mechanical concepts are also relatively difficult for many listeners to absorb without some visual or other aid to give them meaning. The speaker could provide a diagram, a drawing, or a full-scale model of the machine. Having a workable model is especially helpful to show how the parts of the machine work.

To Help Maintain Listener Interest.   Aids are often useful for holding an audience's interest. They act as a sort of "pick-me-up" from the routine of just listening to a speaker's voice and give the audience something else on which to concentrate. When a topic is difficult to follow, an aid can help keep the audience's minds from wandering. The audience may have "tuned the speaker out," simply because the topic is too complex to concentrate on for long. An aid wisely used could help to refocus their attention on the speech. Finally, in an age of television, many audiences have also come to expect aids when they hear a speech. They look forward to them, particularly to a film or other visual image that may be interesting or entertaining in its own right.

USING AIDS EFFECTIVELY

Using aids effectively is much like giving a good performance. You as the speaker are also an actor. You must introduce your material carefully and wisely. All aids should work to enhance audience interest in the main point of your speech. They should be part of the gradual buildup to the speech's climax. For this reason their timing is of obvious importance. An aid, particularly a visual aid, should not be carelessly displayed or presented without reason. In most instances, it is best to conceal a visual aid until the exact moment when it is needed. Obviously, this will vary from situation to situation, and *you* must decide the best timing for your aid. Practicing on a friend or relative is a good way to help decide. Select two places in a speech that seem appropriate. Try each in turn on your "audience" and test his or her reaction. You may have to use different individuals in order to get a fair reaction. If there is no difference, use the aid in the spot that works best for the points that are to follow in your speech.

Of course there are times when you as a speaker will simply want to clarify your point by using an aid. The momentum of the speech should make using an aid the logical next step. It will "just seem right" to your audience that the aid be introduced there. In fact, it should seem so logical that listeners will not be surprised to see it. There should almost be a feeling of inevitability.

When an aid is used in this way, the audience will not linger over it. They will see it, or feel it, or hear it. It will tell them something more than they already know. But it will only complete an idea that had been begun by you, the speaker. They will be satisfied by what the aid has helped them to understand; it will have made its point. The audience will then be ready to pay full attention to the next idea in the speech.

Preparing Aids

One of the worst things you can do when speaking in public is to present your aids ineffectively. This includes not knowing how to run equipment like projectors, film reels, and tape recorders. An aid of this sort—the movie, film, record, tape—should be ready to be used

Talk to the audience. Point to the aid.

when the speech calls for it. The speaker or the person operating the machine should have practiced how to run the equipment and should be sure that it is in good working order. A test run can save a speaker from an embarrassing disaster.

When using photographs, drawings, or other stationary aids, be sure that they can be clearly seen by the audience. Before the speech, set up the visual and then walk to the back of the room to see how it will look to the audience. Sit in different seats and notice how the view changes from each. When speaking, be sure not to block the aid from the audience. When referring to your visual aid, talk to your audience, not to it. Stand to one side and point. When you have finished with the aid, remove it from view. Leaving it in place can be distracting.

Graphs, charts, or diagrams should be drawn as simply and clearly as possible. Bright, distinct colors help to distinguish different objects. Overlapping transparencies are useful for explaining relationships between the different objects of the graph, diagram, or chart, especially with complex material.

Choosing the right aid also depends on the kind of room where it will be presented. A large room will require visual aids that can be enlarged, or are already large to begin with. In a small room, on the other hand, a movie could easily overwhelm the audience. Here, a filmstrip or slides would be a better choice if a visual of this type has to be shown. You might also use drawings or photographs to accomplish the same purpose.

Check out the acoustics of the room before deciding to use sound-related aids. This can be done when you are testing your equipment. An otherwise useful aid can be rendered completely ineffective because the sound was drowned out by too high ceilings or multiplied by echoes off a wall.

Points to Remember

There are certain questions a speaker must answer in deciding when, how, and whether to use an aid:

• Does it really further communication between speaker and listener?
• Can the aid be used with competence *and* confidence? To show a movie, for example, a speaker must know how to operate the projector and have the film already threaded and ready to go. Most of us have been in classes when the teacher was unable to work a projector. While the teacher labored with the machine, the class often went into a mild uproar.
• Can the aid be seen (or heard, or touched) by everyone in the room? This is crucial because listeners who are unable to "experience" the

SHOULD A SPEAKER USE A VISUAL AID?
1. Does the aid further communication with the audience?
2. Does the speaker know how to use it?
3. Does the aid provide additional information?
4. Is the aid appropriate for the room?
5. Will the aid overshadow the speech?
6. Is the aid interesting?
7. Does the aid further the speaker's credibility?
8. Does the aid support the main point of the speech?

aid will feel "left out." Their interest in the speech may suffer. Visuals which are difficult to see force the audience to crane their necks, stand up, or change position to see better. Sounds which cannot be heard accurately are simply annoying. Except in a small group, it is hard for everyone in an audience to touch or taste an object simultaneously—people are distracted waiting for their turn. The consequent commotion usually upsets the mood of the talk and overshadows interest in the speech itself.

• Does the aid provide additional information? Some speakers simply use an aid here and there as though they were adding ornaments to a Christmas tree—they were in the box, why not use them? Unfortunately, these speakers ignore the relevance of the aid to their topic. Someone told them they should have a visual or two in a speech, so they included some.

• Do the aids tend to replace the speech itself? An aid, remember, is supposed to supplement a speech. It is not intended as a substitute for it. Some speakers simply rely on aids to do their work for them by bombarding their audience with slides or recordings, for example. The result frequently confuses the listeners, who may easily forget what the speech is supposed to be about.

• Does the aid support the point of the speech? Some speakers use aids to provide additional information that has little to do with the topic of the speech. In itself the information may be interesting, but it may also puzzle the audience. How does this item fit in with what has already been said? Their attention is diverted from the point of the speech to the meaning of the material presented in the aid. In effect, the speaker has lost his or her audience.

• How interesting are the aids? Complicated diagrams, charts, graphs,

A visual aid should be big enough to be seen without strain.

or maps can bewilder the audience instead of helping them understand the subject. Visuals, for example, should be immediately clear. Again, this requires choosing aids with the audience in mind. A highly educated adult audience could be expected to understand technical charts, maps, or graphs, but they might go over the heads of some junior high school students.

• Does the aid further the speaker's credibility? Effective public speakers should have a command of their topic. The audience regards them as an authority. If the aids contradict what the speaker is saying, however, or show poor judgment either in terms of the type of aid or what it depicts, the audience's belief in the speaker will decline. A speaker talking about gourmet cooking who passed out samples of bad food would not convince an audience that he or she was a skilled cook, able to judge good food from bad.

Summary

A visual aid is anything the audience can see that helps get the speaker's message across. There are also audio and tactile aids. Good aids supplement the speech by making it more interesting and easier to understand. No aid should distract an audience or interfere with the message of the speech.

When deciding whether to use an aid, a speaker should remember both the nature of his or her audience and that of the speech. Every aid should be appropriate to both. Aids work only when they further communication between speaker and audience. Aids should be used competently. They must be able to be seen or heard by everyone in the room. They should clarify or provide additional information. No aid should be merely decorative. Aids should support the point of the speech and enhance the speaker's credibility.

There are many types of aids including pictures, blackboards, flip charts, films, filmstrips, records and tapes, handouts, videotapes, graphs, full-scale models, charts, diagrams, and even people.

Exercises

1. Visit the audiovisual center at your campus. Make a list of the available resources for your classmates to use in giving their speeches. Make the list available to all the members of the class.

2. Compile a list of films and recordings dealing with speech communication that are available in your library. Make the list available to all of the members of the class.

3. What are some "natural" visual aids for the following speech topics:
   a. a tour of historical castles in Europe
   b. photographing birds in Central Park
   c. playing badminton
   d. sports injuries
4. Obtain a catalog of filmstrips available for purchase. From the catalog, determine what filmstrips would be best utilized in public speaking. Make the list available to your classmates.

PART II: SUGGESTIONS FOR FURTHER READING

Brown, J. W., and R. B. Lewis. *Audio-Visual Instruction: Technology, Media, and Method*, 5th ed. New York: McGraw-Hill, 1976.

Cathcart, R. *Post Communication Criticism and Evaluation*. Indianapolis: Bobbs-Merrill, 1966.

Clevenger, T. *Audience Analysis*. Indianapolis: Bobbs-Merrill, 1966.

Cronkhite, G. *Persuasion: Speech and Behavioral Change*. Indianapolis: Bobbs-Merrill, 1969.

Ehninger, D. *Influence, Belief, and Argument*. Glenview, Ill.: Scott, Foresman and Company, 1973.

Henle, M. "On the Relation Between Logic and Thinking," *Psychological Review*, 69 (July 1962), 366–378.

Mills, G. *Message Preparation Analysis and Structure*. Indianapolis: Bobbs-Merrill, 1966.

Rokeach, M. *Beliefs, Attitudes, and Values*. San Francisco: Jossey-Bass, 1968.

Ross, R. *Speech Communication: Fundamentals and Practice*, 5th ed. Englewood Cliffs, N.J.. Prentice-Hall, 1980.

Vatz, R. "The Myth of the Rhetorical Situation," *Philosophy and Rhetoric*, 11 (1973), 154–161.

Woolbert, C. "The Audience," *Psychological Monographs* (June 1916), 37–54.

Speaker Variables

PART III

building speaker credibility

Tips for Speakers

1. In order to establish credibility, you must convince your audience that you are trustworthy, reliable, and concerned about them.
2. The greater the skepticism of an audience, the more important it is to establish credibility.
3. Cite your qualifications regarding your topic at the beginning of the speech.
4. Tell your audience why you have chosen your topic.
5. Deliver your speech in a relaxed yet serious and involved manner.
6. A logical, well-supported speech goes a long way to establish credibility.

CREDIBILITY IN PUBLIC SPEAKING

In public speaking situations, the credibility of the speaker is crucial to the effectiveness of the speech. A speaker whom the audience considers credible will be accepted much more readily than one whose credibility the audience questions. Acceptance, of course, does not mean that the audience will necessarily or easily be converted to the speaker's point of view. How likely a speaker is to win over an audience depends on many factors besides his or her credibility, including how far apart the audience and the speaker are in belief before the speech. In extreme cases, the edge that credibility gives to a speaker may mean only that the audience will consider his or her point of view. But even this is significant because unless the audience is willing to listen, the speaker cannot hope to reach them.

There is no denying it. The overall effectiveness of a speech depends largely on the speaker's credibility. This, in turn, depends on two variables: the impression the audience forms of the speaker as a person and their opinion of the speech as a presentation. The speaker must strive to impress the audience favorably so that he or she will be accepted as a credible person. The speaker must also make sure that the speech itself is logical and well supported. In this chapter we shall focus our discussion primarily on the first variable—the interaction between speaker and audience.

What Is Credibility?

The words "credible" and "credibility," "charisma" and "image" are all familiar to us. Journalists have written about "credibility gaps," disparities between what public figures say and what those who hear and read their statements believe. Lawyers speak of the importance of putting a "credible" witness on the stand in jury trials. Voters yearn for a candidate with "charisma," and public relations firms campaign to improve the "corporate image" of industrial clients. In each case, these terms refer to the degree to which one person or group succeeds in securing the belief or trust of another.

The importance of these concepts of public speaking cannot be overstressed. Every student of public speaking should therefore learn as much as possible about what credibility is and how to achieve it. But the examples just given should not mislead us into believing that the need to establish credibility arises only in times of media "hype" and mistrust. The greater the skepticism of an audience, of course, the more important it becomes to establish credibility. But speakers have always had to convince their listeners that they are trustworthy, reliable, and concerned about their audience.

It is, in fact, these three elements that every speaker needs to es-

There can be a gap between what you believe and what you see and hear.

tablish credibility. A trustworthy speaker is one who listeners judge deserves their confidence. A reliable speaker can be depended on by an audience to act consistently and responsibly. A speaker concerned for the listeners' well-being identifies with their interests or even places their interests before his or her own.

Credible People and Credible Roles

Americans cherish credibility. As citizens in a democracy, we want to admire and trust our leaders. As consumers, we often buy products that have been endorsed by well-known people in whom we have faith. We are likely to adopt beliefs, support causes and spend money in ways that have been identified with the beliefs, actions, and habits of prominent, admired contemporaries. Each year lists of the "most admired," "most beautiful," "most believable," and other superlatives are published in this country. The people whose names appear on these lists achieve high credibility as a result, even though the reasons for their inclusion often have nothing to do with being trustworthy or reliable, as in a list of "most beautiful" women.

One name that appears on nearly every list of credible Americans is the newscaster Walter Cronkite. Even though Cronkite works for a large broadcasting corporation that is as concerned about its rating as it is about world events, many people put more trust in his account of the news than they do in that of any other broadcaster. He may be the most credible man in America today. In fact, he has come to be almost an elder statesman, above commerce, above politics—and above suspicion.

Some people have credibility. Others don't.

Among the women rated highly trustworthy and respected are first ladies—for example, Jacqueline Kennedy Onassis and Rosalynn Carter—and professional women—Dr. Joyce Brothers and Katherine Hepburn. The most credible woman in America today may be Betty Ford, another former first lady. Because Mrs. Ford has for several years discussed personal medical and family problems openly and honestly, she has won the trust and sympathy of much of the public.

Certain individuals enjoy tremendous credibility by virtue of their title or job. The American presidency provides an excellent example of this. While in office—and in some cases even when out of it—an American president is believed or at least given the benefit of the doubt by most of his constituents on nearly every issue of domestic and foreign policy. Because of the prestige of the office, there is even a considerable carryover to areas where presidents may not be experts. When a president loses the confidence of the public, however, as Richard Nixon did after the Watergate Affair, his loss of credibility can be abrupt and absolute. Nixon, of course, was forced to resign.

Members of certain prestigious professions—doctors, ministers, and judges, for example—also have considerable credibility because many people have to place their trust in them. By contrast, members of some other professions or occupations enjoy very low prestige and credibility—used car salespersons, for example. Overall, a person's professional role can largely determine his or her credibility.

CREDIBILITY IN PUBLIC SPEAKING: THE SPEAKER AND THE AUDIENCE

How Audiences Assess Speaker Credibility

Within a single group or profession not everyone, of course, is equally credible in the eyes of others. Despite the influential role that professional membership plays, individual credibility is affected by several factors. When you address an audience, your own credibility will depend to a large extent on how your listeners perceive you, how they judge you as compared to themselves, the cause or point of view you represent, or the group or organization you represent. Before we describe how you can improve your credibility with an audience, therefore, we need to analyze how audiences assess speakers.

How Others See You.   You may be eminently qualified to speak on a specific subject, but your listeners will admit your qualifications only if they perceive them. Credibility is, therefore, a perceptual variable. Various audiences will notice various things about the same speaker. Moreover, even when two audiences notice the same thing, they may interpret it in different ways. For example, let us suppose that you are addressing a group of people to promote a new weight-reducing program. You yourself are fifteen or twenty pounds over-weight, but your audience is made up of people who are much heavier than that. Therefore, when you tell them how much weight you have already lost since starting the program, and how close you are to reaching your goal, you will probably become a highly credible speaker. But if your audience is a group of thin people seeking to lose their last ounce of fat, you will appear comparatively obese and not credible at all on the subject of weight loss.

Your listeners, then, will often judge you by their standards. They may judge your behavior in the same way. If you speak in favor of a candidate for city council, for example, some of your listeners may misjudge or suspect your motives. With them you will lack credibility. You may support Mrs. Young because she favors improved schools and new programs for the elderly that you consider important, but your listeners may suspect that you hope to advance your own career or that you hold a personal grudge against the incumbent, Mr. Smith. These listeners judge your motives as unsound or selfish and therefore rate you low in credibility. If your listeners believe that you are right to support Young because of the issues or to oppose Smith because he has been corrupt or ineffective, you will win high marks for credibility. People who do not know you well, however, will tend to be skeptical of you and your motives, especially when you speak about something controversial.

The Causes You Represent. A speaker's credibility will often vary with the cause he or she represents. Sometimes a "label" identifying your point of view will establish your credibility with an audience—or alienate you from them. A Republican addressing a predominantly Democratic audience would have low credibility, as would a liberal before an audience of conservatives or a speaker known to represent the interests of young people before an audience of the aged. Once a speaker is associated with a specific viewpoint, most audiences will connect him or her with it. For example, Protestantism is the most widely followed religion in the United States; and the Reverend Billy Graham is one of the most visible and popular Protestant spokesmen. Doctor Graham's name appears regularly on lists of credible and influential people in this country. When he speaks out on an issue, therefore, many of his listeners will believe him because they are already sympathetic to his viewpoint. They assume that he will always represent the views of Protestant Christianity. Equally, people who disagree with Doctor Graham's convictions will tend not to believe him regardless of the specific content of his message.

The Groups You Represent.   As a speaker, you will often represent, formally or informally, an organization or group. Some groups have consistently high credibility, some consistently low. Others vary according to circumstances and audience. Examples of groups enjoying high credibility in this country include: the Supreme Court, the Red Cross, and the Public Broadcasting Service. Groups whose credibility is low would include the Communist Party and the Ku Klux Klan. A speaker for one of the first three groups could expect his or her listeners to believe what they heard. A speaker for one of the latter groups would begin with a negative credibility rating and perhaps even with the hostility of the audience.

The credibility of many organizations depends on the audience and other factors. A speaker from the United States Marine Corps might be either highly credible or highly suspect, depending on an audience's view of the marines and the military in general. A speaker advocating better treatment for illegal aliens in this country would also be neither credible nor unbelieved in every case. A liberal, middle-class audience sympathetic to the hardships these people suffer would tend to believe the speaker. An audience of working people afraid of losing their jobs to foreigners willing to work for low wages might not find the speaker credible. A speaker's credibility, then, is influenced by the ideas and groups he or she represents and the audience's opinion of them.

Audience Expectation of Credibility

The audience will almost always expect speakers to demonstrate their credibility on a specific topic. If the speaker neglects to detail his or her qualifications, including experience and expertise, the audience may decide that he or she has no genuine expertise. The audience cannot be expected to confer expertise or credibility on a speaker without concrete reasons for doing so. Therefore, it will usually be necessary for the speaker to cite his or her qualifications and to show during the speech that he or she is indeed an expert.

Suppose, for example, that in class you choose to speak about recreational programs for senior citizens. Both you and the audience are college students. They will therefore assume that you are not an expert on the aged. But you may have worked for a center for senior citizens, have studied the subject, and have even written a research paper on it in another course. To establish your qualifications, you should refer to this background and reveal the breadth of your experience in your speech. If you do so, you should earn the credibility you deserve.

Credibility-Content Interaction

As a speaker, the opinion of you held by the audience will depend to a great extent upon what they thought about you before you began to talk. If that opinion is already high, you can improve it still further. If it is low, you must use your speech and demeanor to try to improve it. Suppose, for example, you decide to run for student body president at your college when you are a sophomore. This office, however, is normally held by a senior. Many of your fellow students may consider your candidacy as arrogant or pushy. Your campaign will have to overcome that image and replace it with one of a dedicated person, motivated by the desire to contribute to the college and its students, with both the intelligence and the zeal to be an effective president. When you speak to students, you should try to establish these credentials. Let others know how your background qualifies you for the position and what programs you propose for the student body. In this way you can improve credibility both in yourself as speaker and in the content of your speech.

"Sounding Credible"

Demonstrating Credibility. A speaker must sound authoritative, that is, as if he or she knows what he or she is talking about. We call this demonstrating credibility within the speech. Some true experts are such poor speakers that they cannot address an audience of any kind without losing credibility. These people simply do not sound like experts, despite vast knowledge. Other speakers may know nothing about a subject but can deliver a memorized text and give the impression of knowing all about a complex subject. Actors who portray lawyers or scientists often do this with great success. The audience is convinced that they really are experts, although they may know nothing but the script they memorized. Of course, the best situation for a speaker is to be both well versed in a subject and to sound convincing. Nevertheless, a speaker who can show credibility within the speech will appear credible to an audience, even if he or she is not truly an expert.

Being Confident and Relaxed. One of the ways that a speaker can appear credible is to seem relaxed and confident. Unfortunately, this is not easy, especially for inexperienced speakers. Generally, you will be less uneasy as you become more experienced. But even proven speakers succumb at one time or another to an attack of nerves or stage fright. Typical stage fright symptoms are wet, clammy palms, perspiration, butterflies in the stomach, some nervousness, rapid breathing, and a dry mouth. You may have some of these symptoms whenever you speak in public. Even though most speakers learn to control them, some nervousness usually remains. In fact, according to the *Book of Lists*,[1] more Americans are frightened of speaking in public than of any other thing. The ten most common fears are:

Biggest Fear	% Naming
1. Speaking before a group	41
2. Heights	32
3. Insects and bugs	22
3. Financial problems	22
3. Deep water	22
6. Sickness	19
6. Death	19
8. Flying	18
9. Loneliness	4
10. Dogs	1

Controlling Stage Fright.   As you can see, speaking in public scares people even more than death. So you are not alone: Relax. Let us look at five ways to help you overcome your fears of speaking in public:

1. *Learn not to brood about a speaking assignment.* If you are already scared or nervous, the more you worry about it, the more the fear will grow. So, try to put it as much out of your mind as you can.

2. *Be prepared.* Most teachers agree that prepared speakers show less stage fright than speakers who are not well prepared.

3. *Try to relax physically before the speech.* If you run around before you speak instead of sitting down and collecting your thoughts, you are inviting stage fright. Some student speakers actually lie down, prop up their feet, and daydream for a half-hour before they are scheduled to talk.

4. *Don't worry about entertaining the audience.* Speakers sometimes feel that they have to perform in front of an audience. The speaker is not an entertainer. You talk to an audience because you have something to say, not to be amusing. Concentrate on speaking. Don't worry about putting on a successful show.

[1] David Wallechinsky et al, *The Book of Lists* (New York: Bantam, 1978), pp. 469–470.

5. *Develop delivery habits that lead you to move around during the speech.* You will be more at ease when you are not rigidly planted in one position. Your delivery should let you use the whole speaking area to unlimber.

Audience Needs to Know

A speaker's credibility with any audience will be the sum of what they already know about the speaker, the impression the speaker makes during the speech, and how the speaker is introduced or introduces him or herself. If the audience is told nothing by the speaker or by anyone else to encourage belief in the speaker's credibility, it will be hard for the speaker to earn a very high credibility rating. Speakers often prefer to "let the facts speak for themselves." They avoid trying to impress audiences with their qualifications and achievements. This is not realistic. An audience may know next to nothing about the speaker and his or her subject. In any case, they have little time in which to form opinions about either the speech or the speaker. If the speech is given to persuade, and the speaker genuinely wants to be persuasive, he or she should give the audience whatever will encourage them to grant the speaker high credibility. Some of this information may be presented by the person who introduces the speaker. But if there is no introduction, the speaker should present the relevant personal information—even if this means "blowing his or her own horn."

CREDIBILITY IN PUBLIC SPEAKING: HOW SPEAKERS ACHIEVE IT

Ten Components of Credibility in Public Speaking

Several factors consistently determine the credibility of individual speakers. The ten most important are reliability, expertise, dynamism, consistency, sociability, honesty, sincerity, concern for the message, concern for listeners, and personal attractiveness. Each of these should be kept in mind whenever you speak in public. Some may seem to promote image over substance, but all of them can help you to put your message across.

Reliability.   This is the ability to inspire confidence. A reliable person can be counted on to stand by what he or she believes in. A speaker who is reliable will take the same position whether the audience is sympathetic or not. A person who favors abortion on demand,

Reliability inspires confidence.

for instance, will support that belief even when addressing a "right-to-life" group that strongly opposes it. By the same token, a reliable candidate for political office would take the same position on an issue without regard for how many votes might be won or lost as a result. Let us say, for example, that the candidate favors raising property taxes to build new schools. He or she should defend that position whether the audience is a group of property owners concerned about high taxes or a group of parents who want better schools. The candidate might well discuss issues with property owners other than taxes. But he or she should not duck the issue if it arises. In this sense, then, a reliable speaker is a trustworthy one.

Expertise.   A credible speaker must know what he or she is talking about. Usually this means that the speaker should be both knowledgeable and experienced in the area. This, of course, is an ideal. Few people can become experts through firsthand experience in every area about which they speak. How much expertise is required will also depend upon the audience. For example, a person who addresses a group of workers about health and safety hazards in their own factory would be expected to know a great deal about the specific conditions and risks that exist at that plant. This is crucial, since the workers are experts themselves through day-to-day experiences, even if they lack technical information and formal education in the subject. A speaker who addresses a group of white collar workers about factory-work conditions, however, might not be expected to know as much at firsthand. The speaker might, however, need to know more statistics: the proportion of workers who suffer serious injuries, the loss of time due to injuries, and so on. In either case, the speaker needs expertise appropriate to the specific audience.

So far we have been discussing an expert who speaks in his or her own field. When an economist discusses whether inflation will increase, decrease, or hold steady in the next year, he or she is on home

TEN COMPONENTS OF CREDIBILITY

1. Reliability	6. Honesty
2. Expertise	7. Sincerity
3. Dynamism	8. Concern for the message
4. Consistency	9. Concern for listeners
5. Sociability	10. Personal attractiveness

turf. But sometimes a speaker who is an expert in one field will decide to move into another field, as when the same economist tries to predict whether there will be a major war in Asia in the near future. Generally, an expert's credibility will be limited to his or her own field. There are exceptions, of course. Winston Churchill and Bertrand Russell, for example, wrote and worked in a number of different fields, in each of which they were regarded as authorities. And Albert Einstein, who made no claim to expertise outside of physics and mathematics, was constantly invited to make statements about many subjects.

Dynamism. Speakers who are active, energetic, and enthusiastic earn more credibility from their audiences than passive, lethargic, indifferent speakers. The failure of a speaker to embrace both subject and audience in an energetic, affirmative way often leaves the audience feeling that the speaker cares neither about the subject nor the speech. Apply this standard to your professors. Can you easily stay interested in a course taught by a bored lecturer? A professor of history lecturing on the causes of the Civil War, for example, needs to present his or her material in a lively manner. Otherwise, the students may treat the events as so many "dead" facts. They become indifferent partly because the professor's apathy is contagious.

Consistency. Consistency is the quality of holding the same position over time and of holding positions that agree with one another. In this sense it is closely related to reliability. A consistent speaker does not propose on Monday that the local football team replace its coach and then announce on Tuesday that the coach is doing an excellent job simply because the team won its Monday night game. Nor should a speaker place the entire blame for the team's poor record on the coach in one speech and then blame the defensive line in another speech. Mulish inflexibility is not appealing either, of course. Speakers should change their minds when new facts or arguments arise to convince them that their earlier positions were wrong or premature. But they will not be credible if they switch sides whenever they are challenged or each time the winds of fashion on an issue change. Consistency means holding to positions as long as they are reasonable.

Sociability. Sociability is the quality of being friendly and pleasant. Audiences warm to speakers they perceive as sociable and tend to grant them more credibility than they give to speakers who are distant and unfriendly. A speaker should stress the similarities between him or herself and the audience. In addition, likability, pleasantness, and lack of snobbishness are all traits that improve one's credibility with an audience. Although most speakers and audiences have little chance to socialize or even to meet informally, audiences are more apt to believe a speaker who addresses them as equals than one who talks down to them as inferiors.

Honesty.   Speakers must satisfy their audiences that they are telling the truth and that they are generally honest. An honest speaker—that is, one who is perceived by an audience as honest—has great credibility. A speaker suspected of dishonesty will find it hard to shake the suspicion that he or she is not telling the truth. Even when the matter a speaker lied about (or is thought to have lied about) is unrelated to the subject of the speech, the audience will tend not to believe him or her. For example, suppose a speaker describing the desperate conditions of Vietnamese refugees is suspected of having lied about his or her business interests. The two subjects are in no way connected, but the speaker's credibility will suffer. By the same token, a speaker who is perceived as generally honest will carry his or her credibility over to most occasions and subjects.

Sincerity.   Sincerity is meaning what we say and believing it to be true. It is the opposite of hypocrisy. Sincerity is especially important to a speaker, since its presence encourages listeners to find the speaker credible even if they do not agree with what the speaker says. Suppose the president of a college speaks to the student body to explain why tuition costs must be raised for the following year. The students may think that tuition is already high enough. If the president is to convince them, the president must show that he or she sincerely has the best interests of the college at heart and considers the proposed solution reasonable and necessary.

Concern for the Message.   A credible speaker must believe not only that a statement is true but also that it is important. The audience should perceive this concern in the speaker's presentation. They may find a concerned speaker credible even if they do not share the speaker's sense of urgency. Consider the many commercials that feature endorsements of products by celebrities who are paid for their recommendations. The people who see, hear, and read these advertisements know that these famous people are paid for their endorsements. They may, nevertheless, find the endorsements credible if they believe that the endorsers really do believe in the excellence of these products and want others to enjoy them. If a speaker takes his or her statement seriously, the audience will be encouraged to do so too.

Concern for Listeners.   The speaker should project concern for the best interests and welfare of the audience. An author who appears

Attractive people tend to be perceived as credible.

on a talk show to promote a new book is, after all, trying to stimulate sales and increase his or her own income and fame. But to do this, the author will have to convince viewers or listeners that they have some reason for buying and reading the book. What the author will stress, then, is what is useful, interesting, valuable, or amusing about the book to potential readers. The audience will therefore have some reason to consider reading the book and also to believe that the author has at least their pleasure in mind.

Personal Attractiveness.   A speaker who is physically attractive is more likely to be a credible speaker than one who is unattractive. Look at the anchorpersons on television. The more specialized reporters (sports, crime, etc.) may or may not be good looking, but the anchorpersons are almost always attractive, well groomed, and able to project affability and charm. Not every speaker can be glamorous, but everyone can take pains to be as attractive as possible.

The Speaker and Credibility: Tactics

The speaker should work during a speech to maintain and even to improve his or her credibility. A number of procedures and safeguards can be used to further this aim. In this section we will discuss the most important credibility-making tactics.

1. *Introduce yourself or have someone introduce you.* Your impact upon an audience is enhanced by an introduction. Even if it seems pompous or unnecessary, make sure that you receive an introduction, if possible by someone whom the audience respects. The introduction should always include your qualifications to speak about your topic. If no one is available to introduce you, introduce yourself. We repeat, do not be afraid to blow your own horn. Try to weave your introduction of yourself into the opening passages of your speech, so that it will strike the audience as both modest and relevant.

2. *Tell the audience why you are talking about the topic.* Speakers too often neglect this basic point. Your audience is curious and entitled to know why you have chosen—or have been chosen—to discuss this subject with them. You should answer this unspoken question early in your speech. For example, suppose you grow orchids as a hobby and decide to make this the subject of a speech. Your audience (your classmates) probably do not share your interest in orchids and will be curious to know why you thought it important enough to talk to them about it. A straightforward explanation will encourage them to share your interest, at least temporarily.

3. *Tell the audience about any special expertise you have that relates to the topic.* Since you chose the topic, you probably have some experience, skill, or knowledge in the area. You should tell your audience about this, even if it seems insignificant and not worth mentioning. Remember you are trying to establish yourself as a qualified expert in the eyes of your audience. Even if you see yourself as a rank beginner in your subject, you may yet be an expert compared to them. Suppose you are still talking about your orchid-growing. While you are no true expert, you have displayed your orchids at an exhibit, were an assistant to the Parks Department horticulturist last summer, and have pursued your hobby for several years. These achievements will probably be more than enough to establish your credibility on the topic with your audience. If you neglect to mention them out of misguided modesty, you will reduce the effect of your speech.

4. *Do not admit to limited knowledge easily.* No one knows *everything* about *anything.* You may feel that you know much too little about the topic of your speech. Nevertheless, you should emphasize what you do know. Be positive, even if you admit that your knowledge is limited. It is better to answer a question by saying, "In my reading on this topic, I've never come across that idea," than to say flatly, "Well, I've only been reading about orchids since April."

5. *Suggest that you have the best interests of the listener at heart.* You chose a subject because you have something to say to an audience about it. This is true even when the subject and audience are classmates in a course where topics are assigned and students required to listen to each other's speeches. You want to give the listeners the impression that you have chosen your subject—or the approach to it—with them in mind. And you should do so. Don't ask only what you know about orchids. Ask also what your audience will gain from learning what you have to tell them. Make your listeners aware that you have shaped your speech with their needs in mind, and they will respond more favorably. For example, perhaps no one in your audience will be as interested in growing orchids as you are. But they may enjoy looking at them, learning to distinguish between some different varieties, and understanding the unusual conditions under which these flowers grow. As you present the speech that addresses these interests, inform your audience that you had them especially in mind.

6. *Maintain a competent and relaxed style.* A simple concept, this may appear a tall order. But remember that even experienced performers often have stage fright. However, they learn to keep their actions under control, so that the audience perceives them as self-assured. You must learn to do the same. One sure way to lose credibility is visibly to lose control or confidence. The audience should perceive you as someone accustomed to talking about your subject before large groups.

Audiences prefer a relaxed speaker.

7. *Take the speaking situation seriously.* You need not be somber, but your manner should assure your listeners that you have thought about your subject and believe it to be worth their consideration and yours. Consider how you will deliver your speech. If you are too serious, neither you nor they may enjoy it. But if you are too spontaneous or lighthearted, you risk giving the impression that the subject or the speech itself is not worth taking seriously.

8. *Appear involved.* This is the tone you should aim for, neither overserious nor flighty. You want your listeners to feel that you are involved both with the topic and with them, and you want this feeling to be contagious. The more your listeners get caught up in your speech, the easier you will find it to maintain interest and credibility. Speakers who appear listless and uncommitted alienate their audiences. The ideal speaker is lively, involved, and dynamic.

These tactics should be studied and practiced. When you master them, you will be able to establish yourself as a credible speaker. The person who can establish credibility with a variety of audiences under a variety of conditions will succeed as a public speaker.

Summary

Every public speaker should understand credibility and how to achieve it with audiences. To achieve credibility, speakers must be seen as trustworthy, reliable, and concerned about their listeners. Certain people and professions carry high credibility. Your credibility as a speaker will depend on how the audience sees you, how you compare to the audience, the causes and groups you represent.

Ten important components of credibility are: reliability, expertise, dynamism, consistency, sociability, honesty, sincerity, concern for message, concern for listeners, and personal attractiveness. Audience acceptance depends upon your credibility, which you must establish before and during the speech.

To maintain and enhance credibility, you should be introduced, let the audience know why you have chosen and are qualified to speak about your topic, show the audience that you are interested in them, and deliver the speech in a relaxed, yet serious and involved manner.

Exercises

1. What do you consider to be the most important factors in speaker credibility? List five factors and tell why you have placed each on your list.

2. Identify five men you consider to be the most credible in America. Tell why you have placed each on your list.
3. Identify five women you consider to be the most credible in America. Tell why you have placed each on your list.
4. Develop a brief position paper entitled "My Personal Credibility." In the paper, discuss what the audience might think of you as a speaker. On what topics are you likely to have good credibility? On what topics are you likely to have poor credibility? Why?

AN INFORMATIVE SPEECH

When this speech was given to an audience of General Motors executives in 1972, Mr. Cole was president of GM. His speech is a good example of an acknowledged expert talking about his area of expertise—in this case, business. With this audience and on this topic, the speaker's credibility is taken for granted. Notice how the assumption of competence and authority colors the entire speech.

Two Myths and a Paradox✻
Edward N. Cole

Since Cole already has high credibility among GM employees, he spends very little time establishing his expertise. They know he *has it.*

For much of the day you will be hearing about technology. To help orient you for the talks you will hear and the things you will see, I would like to talk for a few minutes about two myths and a paradox.

In recent years it has been popular to talk about the rapidity of change—particularly scientific change. It has been said that scientific knowledge doubles every ten years. No doubt it does. One writer has predicted that the rapid change of products and processes will make obsolete the work of 60 million Americans in the next generation. Again, this probably is true.

Still others have pointed out that we are shortening the time from scientific breakthrough to market application. Photography took 112 years from invention to application. The telephone took some 56 years, radio 35, radar 15, television 12, and transistors 5; but laser rays made it from the laboratory to application in only 10 months.

The speaker uses rhetorical questions to set the stage for the speech and then he "signposts" his organizational pattern (two myths and a paradox).

If all this is true—and it is—doesn't this mean that new technology in the automobile industry can move in months from the laboratory to the assembly plant and the production of 8.5 million cars a year in the United States?

Absolutely no—and that is the first myth. Automotive breakthroughs cannot be translated quickly into production cars. Production lead time, intensive testing, customer acceptance, and cost-benefit analysis determine what and when innovations can be safely and effectively added.

* Delivered at the GM Technical Center, Warren, Michigan, February 10, 1972. Printed in the 1972 *Report on Progress in Areas of Public Concern* (General Motors Corporation). Copy supplied by Paul R. Miller. The printed version was slightly revised from reading copy.

Automotive developments are coming fast. But unlike other products, they apply to very complex products involving safety, health, and the commerce and life of communities. They apply to millions of vehicles requiring a high degree of uniformity, reliability, and long life. Both because of the products, the volume and nature of their materials, the manufacturers are faced with expensive tooling and space and manufacturing problems. These characteristics make every automotive decision a major investment and every investment a commitment for several years.

The automobile industry is highly competitive. A wrong engineering decision may affect not only one model, but by creating or destroying customer loyalty, it may affect product success for several years. Every change must go through careful cost-benefit analysis, establishing the priorities for the customers' dollars.

Currently, the industry is in the process of developing an energy-absorbing bumper. In the customers' interest, very detailed studies have been made—such as, the nature and frequency of various types of accidents, the cost of accident repair, and, of course, the cost of the bumper systems themselves. These have been related to the savings that motorists might reasonably expect from reduced insurance premiums. The cost-benefit results are interesting.

The owner of a car with a bumper system that provides protection to all safety-related components at front and rear barrier impact speeds of 5 m.p.h. (as required by Federal regulations for 1974 models) would have to wait over 8 years to recover his bumper investment—*if* the premium is reduced 10 percent, or over 5 years *if* the premium is cut 20 percent.

There is another reason why it is a myth to expect automotive developments to be instant additions to automobiles.

The automobile industry depends not only on *research* and *development* but also on long and careful *demonstration* before cars are put in the hands of customers. This is a necessity because of the nature of the products, their use, and the requirements of Federal standards. Customers do not want to be guinea pigs for research—and they shouldn't be.

New developments must work not only under the controlled conditions of the laboratory, but also in the subzero of northern Montana winters and in the high temperatures and high humidity of Florida. They must be engineered and tested for a variety of drivers and for frequently casual or no maintenance.

The timing of Federal standards does not always take into consideration all the essential time factors involved in the development, testing, production, and use of innovations demanded of the automobile industry by those standards.

First, there is the time it takes to develop the new equipment from engineering specifications to laboratory performance under carefully controlled conditions.

Within his first point the speaker develops some important subpoints.

Then, after the new device has been tested and retested and refined sufficiently for production, the machinery has to be ready to mass produce it. Some federally required innovations are highly sophisticated items—emission control systems, for example, and some day, perhaps, air cushions. They require sophisticated production equipment, which takes time to develop, build, and teach people to operate.

Crash programs can shorten the lead time preceding mass production of some items, but they can also increase the risk of error, especially with complex equipment. In our development work on air cushions, for example, we are very conscious of our liability as a manufacturer. When you are dealing with explosive devices—which air cushions are—you want to know the answers to a lot of touchy questions, such as:

By using a list, the speaker makes it easy for the audience to remember his information.

(1) What is the life expectancy of these systems?

(2) What will happen when the vehicle equipped with an air cushion is scrapped?

(3) What is the manufacturer's liability if the cushion deploys and causes an accident? Or if it doesn't deploy quickly enough?

Our first concern, of course, is for the safety of our customers; but, if we are required by law to provide certain equipment to the public at a certain time, we would be remiss if we did not very seriously consider our risks and liabilities as the manufacturer of that equipment.

To protect ourselves against excessive risk, it will be necessary for us to recommend that cars be maintained as if they were being operated by owners who give them the hardest use—the 2 or 3 percent who drive at the highest speeds, over the worst roads, in the most severe weather.

This will not please the average owner. We have no alternative because we have not found a way to simulate all the various kinds of use and misuse that a car will get over a 5 year period. We can run a car 50,000 miles in about three and one half months, operating around the clock. But we just do not know how to give a car 5 years of all kinds of driving, weather, road conditions, and maintenance in a relatively short test period.

With an easy transition, the speaker moves to his second point.

There is a second myth I would like to mention. Several years ago an idea was widely promoted that there are two worlds—a world of science and technology on one hand and a world of humanism on the other. The two worlds have two languages and very different objectives and goals.

There is a grain of truth in that theory, but only a grain. In industry, the two-world concept is a myth. The worlds of science and nonscience come together in the common objectives of a company. Industry takes the theory of the laboratory and translates it into the practical hardware of the marketplace. It provides motivation for individuals with a variety of talents. They do talk the same language—when they have the common goals of improved service and products for customers.

We do recognize that there has been a problem of language, but it is not so much within a company, as it is between the progress of technology and the understanding of the public. Frequently, technology has moved faster than the public has been able to keep up with it.

Here the speaker examines some of the current thinking critical of GM. He gives the "company position" on the criticism.

For example, judging by our mail and the press, many still feel that the car is the major contributor to air pollution. They believe that the nation's air pollution problem would disappear overnight if we turned off the ignition of every car, truck, and bus in America. Careful studies by several competent researchers show that this is not true. If all cars, trucks, and buses were parked, we would still have 60 percent of our air pollution problem measured by weight, and about 90 percent of the problem as it relates to health. The public has not realized that the automobile's percent of the air pollution problem has been reduced—even though the car population has increased.

These points have been emphasized in literature and on public platforms, but we continue to have a language problem or, perhaps more accurately, a credibility problem. More than ever in the history of our country, we need the factual, objective findings of technology as a basis of discussion and decision. To this extent there is a language problem.

In addition to the two myths of instant progress and two worlds, there is also an important paradox that we must recognize. Technology is both a cause and a cure—a saint and a sinner, depending on how it is directed. Critics have pointed out that technology has polluted our environment. It has wastefully used our natural resources and created an impersonal, mechanistic society.

No one would deny that in many cases this has been true.

As a result, some critics have even insisted that we return to a simpler life—that we turn back the clock to the agrarian society of one hundred years ago, reduce our consumption and Gross National Product, and set a goal of zero growth.

Note the use of rhetorical questions and the comparison and contrast technique in this passage.

Do they want to go back to the days before the Salk vaccine for the prevention of polio? Do they want to do without modern bathrooms, telephones, electricity, or other modern conveniences? Would they be willing to go back to the hand-cranked car with two-wheel brakes and boiling radiator, or even further back to the horse and wagon? The answer is not to stop technology but to redirect it with new environmental assignments. Technology can do the job. It can protect and restore our environment, and it can do it to whatever degree the public and the customer want it done. Or, putting it more accurately, to the degree they are willing to pay the cost.

Technology, in itself, is neither good nor bad. It does what people direct it to do.

USING LANGUAGE AND STYLE

Tips for Speakers

1. In wording your speech, make sure you say what you mean simply, directly, and clearly.
2. Make your speech interesting by varying the sentence patterns and by being imaginative in your choice of words.
3. Tailor your language to fit the audience you are addressing.
4. Make your language relate to the occasion—serious and formal, or light and informal.
5. Make the most of your own personal style.
6. To enhance your style, use figurative language.

> **Perhaps of all the creations of man, language is the most astonishing.**
>
> **—Lytton Strachey**

LANGUAGE AS CONCEPT

People communicate in many ways. When a woman is given an engagement ring, she communicates her pleasure by holding her fiance's hand and kissing him. When a police officer conducts traffic at a busy intersection, he or she gets cars to stop and go by gesturing or blowing a whistle. At the theater, raising and dimming the lights in the lobby indicates that the play is about to begin.

All of these nonverbal communicators are effective for particular situations. But many things—such as ideas, concepts, and theories—cannot be so easily communicated. It takes more than a waving of the hand or a dimming of the lights to communicate Einstein's theory of relativity or even how you spent your summer vacation. Admittedly, you could show silent movies that chronicle your experiences over the summer, but how would you communicate the way you *felt* about watching a particular sunset or what you *thought* when you were sunbathing at the beach?

To communicate thoughts and ideas, mankind devised language. And, as Lytton Strachey said, language *is* a most astonishing creation. Unlike animals, which have communication but not language, we use symbols, or words, to represent the thought, emotion, or concept we wish to discuss but cannot point to. Language enables us immediately and efficiently to communicate experiences that occurred tens, thousands, or even millions of years ago, as well as to speculate about what might happen in the future. A kiss on the cheek communicates one thing—although even its meaning may be ambiguous—but what nonverbal communication technique can one use to describe the agony of the Holocaust or the sufferings of the dying.

What Is Language?

People study language from many different perspectives. To the linguist, the basic element of language is sound, a continuum of sounds in fact. These sounds do not exist externally, but in our heads. Called phonemes, these internal sounds are the smallest pieces of language. As we hear "language," we are really hearing a series of phonemes being strung together. We make the conversion from a stream of external sounds into a sequence of internal phonemes in order to understand what has been said to us. By themselves, sounds mean nothing. It is the structure we give them, the meanings we attach to them, that make sounds intelligible to us. It is language that gives structure, or understandability, to sounds.

What then, exactly, is language? Basically, it is a system of recognized sounds that expresses or symbolizes thoughts and feelings. When these sounds, or words, are strung together in sentences to convey meaning or ideas, they become language. Used appropriately, by people who know what the words represent, language becomes a method of communication.

We are bombarded with language—written, spoken, heard.

Each day, in almost everything we do, we rely on words to understand and to be understood. Newspapers, magazines, books, television, radio, discussion groups, telephone conversations, meetings, seminars, classroom lectures, personal encounters, journals, and reports all utilize a language of words. We use them to give and get information; to explain attitudes and feelings; to report experiences from the past and present; to discuss what will happen in the future. We use words to entertain people; to teach them; to impress them; to deceive them; to influence their thinking and their actions. Our ability to use language and to understand the messages it conveys depends only on our familiarity with the words that are being used.

Experience Structures Language

The meanings we attach to words come from our own personal experience. Our ability to use language is developed through our experience in a range of situations. As we read, travel, interact with people from varied backgrounds, attend classes, listen to experts, we develop language skills which we use to communicate with others. Let us consider some specific examples.

Before visiting Europe during the summer, Joe had never considered the European contributions to American culture. When he returned from his trip, during which he visited museums, cathedrals, and art galleries, Joe had the direct experience which helped him to understand words such as impressionism and romanticism.

Sally grew up in an affluent midwestern suburb. She had never seen anything that even approximated urban poverty. Her lack of familiarity with the problem prevented her from discussing the situation knowledgeably. After college, Sally spent a year as a VISTA volunteer. Her firsthand experience with the poor, the sick, and the disadvantaged of a big city gave new meaning to the words "hunger," "poverty," and "unemployment."

Language Is a Tool

As we use language, we must realize that it is only a tool; it is symbolic. Symbols, or words, do not have meaning in and of themselves. They represent—they stand in place of—whatever thought, idea, or thing the speaker wants them to represent. The word "justice," for example, has no inherent meaning. Depending on the point of view, "justice" can mean the administration of law, the quality of being fair, or the principle of right action. Let's examine two situations in which one person's concept of justice might not match someone else's meaning for the same word:

1. A woman is killed by an intruder. The police arrest a man who fits a witness's description of the intruder. The police and the victim's husband are convinced that the suspect is guilty. They want him convicted and punished. The prisoner maintains his innocence and demands that the police find the real criminal. Each party wants "justice."

2. A student hands in her assignment late. Her professor refuses to accept the paper and fails her for the course. The professor considers this is a just penalty. The other students in the class had to do the work within the time allotted. Each of them met the deadline although they might have preferred to take longer. The student who had been failed considers this grade to be unjust. She was delayed because of the pressure of an outside job that she needed to stay in school. Both professor and student are convinced of the "justice" of their position.

Justice can be a subjective term.

In each of these examples, justice meant different things to different people. All of them, however, used the same word—"justice"—to express their own ideas.

Language cannot give a precise representation of things or ideas because there are simply not enough different words to express the subtlety of every shade of thought. If we had words for everything, their numbers would be astronomically large and beyond our powers of memory and skill to use them.[1]

Given the limited number of words available, our primary function is to express what we have in our heads to the person or people we are addressing. We must do this in a way that is both understandable and

[1] M. Andersen, W. Lewis, and J. Murray, *The Speaker and His Audience* (New York: Harper and Row, 1964), p. 91.

interesting, whether we are talking on the phone to a friend, speaking behind closed doors to a colleague at work, or addressing a political rally.

Public speakers, whose primary tasks are to inform and influence an audience, are constantly challenged to use language creatively. Indeed, whether they are politicians, schoolteachers, lawyers, or business executives, their livelihood often depends upon their ability to affect an audience through the use of language.

USING LANGUAGE IN PUBLIC SPEAKING

Aristotle said that a speech has two parts. You state your case, and you prove it. That is simple and true enough. But, as any student of public speaking knows, how a speaker goes about stating and proving his or her case is the difference between a great orator and a bumbler.

Goals for Language Use

The public speaker has four main objectives in wording his or her speech. A speaker wants to use language that is (1) clear, (2) interesting, (3) relevant to the audience, and (4) related to the topic and the occasion. Of these, the most important is clarity.

Making It Clear. Language must be clear if we expect to be understood. We must say what we mean—as simply, directly, and unambiguously as we can. Compare the following two ways of saying the same thing:

> *I see one-third of a nation ill-housed, ill-clad, ill-nourished.*
> *—Franklin D. Roosevelt*

> *It is evident that a substantial number of persons within the continental boundaries of the United States have inadequate financial resources with which to purchase the products of agricultural communities and industrial establishments. It would appear that for a considerable segment of the population, perhaps as much as 33.333 percent of the total, there are inadequate housing facilities, and an equally significant proportion is deprived of the proper types of clothing and nourishment.[2]*

The first statement goes directly to the point. It uses as few words as possible to say exactly what it means. The second statement *means*

[2] Stuart and Marian Chase, *The Power of Words* (New York: Harcourt, Brace, Jovanovich, 1954), p. 249.

roughly the same as the first, but the language used is so inflated and imprecise that the reader is inevitably confused about what the writer is trying to say.

When we make a highly informative presentation or give any instructions, we must be careful to use language that highlights the information as opposed to language that obscures the points we are trying to make. The speaker who complains that an audience fails to "get" what he or she is trying to say would be wise to review the speech, keeping the following aids to language clarity in mind.

1. *Be specific and concrete.* The best way to achieve this is to explain ideas in easily understandable language and to provide real incidents as illustrations. Generalized statements are often misleading and can confuse an audience about what the speaker really means. For example, instead of saying something abstract, such as, "I am a feminist," be precise. Say: "Not only am I a strong supporter of liberation for women, but I advocate the adoption of the Equal Rights Amendment." By using a specific example to illustrate an abstract idea, you can clear up any confusion your audience might have as to what your idea of a "feminist" really is.

2. *Avoid language that is too technical or overly specialized.* If you want to be understood, you should use words that mean something to your listeners, not just to yourself. The problem with overly technical or arcane language, or even with words that have too many syllables, is that you risk losing your audience. Although you may find big words impressive, they often alienate listeners. The audience is very likely either to consider the speech affected and artificial or to have no idea what the speaker is talking about.

Three different coats: One word can have many meanings.

3. *Be aware of the multiple meanings of the words you use.* We discussed the map-territory relationship between words and the objects they symbolize in Chapter 6. As we saw then, language is perceived by listeners in two distinct ways. Words are used as symbols that stand for, or *denote*, certain ideas or objects, such as "lamp," "table," "radio." But words also express personal feelings or attitudes that give them a range of meanings beyond their objective definition. This type of language is known as *connotative*. Because of their connotations, some words are blatantly designed to trigger a strong emotional response. Words like "commie," "pervert," or "hood," have such unsavory connotations that they inevitably provoke a strong reaction from anyone who hears them. Other words are less sharply emotional, but, nevertheless, connote very different meanings to different people. The word "communist," for example, has entirely different connotations for Angela Davis and Barry Goldwater. Everyone would agree that motherhood *means* the state of being a mother, but it *connotes*, or suggests, different meanings to radical feminists and old-fashioned housewives.

Because each person's initial understanding of a word—both its denotative and connotative meanings—is unique, no two persons' reactions to a word will be exactly the same. The word "bar," or "barre," for example, means something very different to a ballet dancer, a cocktail waitress, and a Supreme Court Justice. Similarly, "coat" has different meanings to a horse breeder, a painter, and a tailor.

It is important to select the one word which best expresses your idea, that expresses it exactly as you want it expressed. Many speakers settle for a word that is *almost* right. But effective public speakers, such as John F. Kennedy, hold out for the best word. As Arthur Schlesinger reports in his book *A Thousand Days*, Kennedy worked on his inaugural speech until the last possible moment. On the morning of the inauguration, while reading over his text, Kennedy scratched out "will" and replaced it by "can."[3] "Ask not what your

[3] Arthur M. Schlesinger, Jr., *A Thousand Days* (Boston: Houghton Mifflin, 1965), p. 4.

JOHN FITZGERALD KENNEDY, thirty-fifth U.S. president, was born in Brookline, Massachusetts, on May 29, 1917. A war hero, he was elected to Congress in 1946 and to the Senate in 1952. In the presidential elections of 1960, Kennedy trounced former Vice-President Nixon in a series of televised debates and became the youngest man elected President. Kennedy's speeches and public remarks were characterized by wit and love of language. His inaugural address has become a classic of American rhetoric. His assassination in Dallas, November 22, 1963, caused worldwide grief.

UPI

country can do for you—ask what you can do for your country." Would this sentence have been as memorable if Kennedy had left the word "will"?

4. *To avoid confusion and misunderstanding, it is a good idea to define what you mean whenever possible.* Sometimes, even the simplest term can be confusing. The word "bad," for example, means wrong or evil. We all agree on that meaning. But to a young black man in Harlem, "bad" can mean "good." "That is a bad suit you have on" is a compliment to someone's clothing. Imagine the confusion that "bad" used to mean "good" could cause among people who had never heard the word used that way.

Vague concepts, such as "aid to needy children" and "environmental protection," become much clearer when they are explained. A listing of the various types of aid available to children in need, such as Federal Funding for School Lunches and Community Immunization Programs, eliminates the confusion over what the speaker means. No matter how you choose to explain your terminology, through a description, by using an example, through the use of a synonym or an analogy, remember that your motivation is to make the message clear. One rule is always to define acronyms. These are words, like NATO, formed from the first letter of a series of words—<u>N</u>orth <u>At</u>lantic <u>T</u>reaty <u>O</u>rganization. Never assume that the audience knows what UNESCO is, for example, or PLO, or AAA. If your use of language is ambiguous or confused, the chances that an audience will understand what you have to say are exceedingly slim.

Making It Interesting.   Of almost equal importance to language clarity is the need to make a speech interesting. A message can be crystal clear but if the audience finds the presentation dull, they are simply not going to listen attentively. As we all know from our day-to-day, nonpublic speaking situations, being interesting is not easy. It takes energy and effort to devise new and different ways of expressing ourselves. In public speaking, the task of being fresh and exciting is magnified by the size of the audience and the formality of the situation.

One way to make a speech more interesting is to vary the speaking pattern. Consider this example, from a speech made by Winston Churchill during the Second World War:

Do not let us speak of darker days; let us speak rather of sterner days. These are not dark days; these are great days—the greatest days our country has ever lived; and we must all thank God that we have been allowed to play a part in making these days memorable in the history of our race.

Rather than beginning each sentence with the subject followed by a verb and ending with the direct object, Churchill experimented with word order. When preparing your own speeches, start some sentences with prepositional phrases. Ask rhetorical questions. Use action words and words that will evoke images to your listeners. Even the dullest subject can be given vitality and zest with an energetic and imaginative choice or words:

> Some Americans do not have a very happy opinion about the ability of educational leadership to guide our schools and colleges. Some think that our schools and colleges have been under the dominion of the "administrative mind." Their vision of the administrative mind, however, is not very flattering. It is a vision of men and women who have learned to discount principle in favor of expediency, to subordinate ideas to utility, to equivocate while critical issues swarm about them, to vacillate while decisions need to be made, to shrink into anonymity while leadership is needed to define purpose, to nurture community, and to cultivate standards.[4]

The final section of this chapter offers several stylistic devices which you will find helpful in making your speeches more vivid and interesting. The intelligent use of figures of speech, particularly metaphors, and similes, will add life to your presentation and help keep your audience interested.

Making It Relevant to the Audience. The goal of the public speaker is to use language that listeners can understand. Franklin Roosevelt, an extremely able speaker, tailored his language to fit whatever audience he happened to be addressing. In a speech delivered to a working class audience in Brooklyn on November 1, 1940, Roosevelt spoke intimately as though he were talking "man to man" with his friends.

> It is an unfortunate human failing that a full pocketbook often groans more loudly than an empty stomach.

The most important rule to remember in trying to make your language relevant is to be appropriate. Misjudging the level of your audience can either bore or offend them. A wise speaker would use a different level of language when speaking before a committee at the

---

[4] E. Grady Bogue, "The Hazards of Mediocrity," *Vital Speeches of the Day*, December 15, 1979, p. 148.

Ford Foundation than he or she would use to address a group of school children on a tour of the zoo.

The topic and the occasion determine the language of a speech.

Making It Relate to the Occasion.   The topic under discussion also determines the type of language to be used. For example, the language one uses at a funeral is much more serious and formal than that used at a wedding reception. Although the audience at both functions may be made up of the same kinds of people, the context of the message calls for different language usage.

As you saw in the previous section, Franklin Roosevelt was able to fit the language he used in his speeches to the people he was trying to reach. Roosevelt also fit the language in his speeches to reflect the tone of the messages he wanted to convey. In a speech accepting renomination to run for the presidency, he chose words that conveyed a challenge and were designed to enlist his audience in his bid for reelection:

This generation of Americans has a rendezvous with destiny.

To find the appropriate words, be flexible. Experiment. The more experience you have with a variety of public speaking situations, the easier it will be for you to decide which type of language works best.

USING STYLE IN PUBLIC SPEAKING

The successful public speaker knows not only *what* to say, but also *how* to say it. It is not enough merely to present the facts of an argument and expect an audience to be impressed. How a speaker explains his or her position can be as important as the position itself. For example, Richard was recently invited to a fund raising dinner for the college he had attended. Usually, he avoids such functions. He thanks the person for the invitation, then sends a note of regret with a small donation. This time, however, he chose to attend. The person who called described the dinner as more of a party than a business affair. After talking with her on the phone, Richard was convinced that he would have a wonderful time if he went. The difference between this year's invitation and those from other years was in the style with which the invitation was conveyed. This year's caller worded the invitation in a much livelier and more imaginative manner than those in previous years. In short, this year's caller enhanced her message with an attractive style.

What Is Style?

Style in public speaking is manner, how we express ourselves. We can alter or develop a *particular* style, but every act of communication—whether verbal or nonverbal—by its very nature has some style. A speech, for example, may be pompous or dull, down-to-earth or exhilarating, but it would not be possible to give a speech that was without style.

Since style per se is unavoidable, it is the development and use of an effective style that enhances and distinguishes all forms of communication, including public speaking. Dancers like Martha Graham and Fred Astaire, singers like Tom Jones and Barbra Streisand, actors like Katherine Hepburn and Al Pacino, writers like Ernest Hemingway and Erica Jong are all recognized masters of style in their fields.

In public speaking, Winston Churchill, Franklin Roosevelt, John Kennedy, and Martin Luther King were noted orators who developed a unique and effective style of speaking. "I have a dream" is much more powerful than "I've been thinking about the future."

Four Components of Style in Public Speaking

1. *Style is personal.* There are at least as many ways to say something as there are people in the world. Just as each person attaches a personal meaning to every word in the language, so he or she also has a personal way of using those words in communication. Every idea we share is shaped by the words we use to express it. Every message we communicate is influenced by the words we choose to represent it. Every thought we convey, in other words, is affected by our individual style. No other person is exactly like you. To be unique, you have only to be yourself. Your unique style is a direct product of your experience and your understanding of what is happening around you.

But although everyone has an individual style of expressing him or herself, not every individual style is equally effective. How effective our style of public speaking is depends on how well we have developed it by studying how others—speakers, writers, artists, actors—express themselves.

The way to develop and improve your personal style, then, is to observe the people around you. Notice how your friends and associates express themselves. Perhaps one of your friends talks around issues, taking forever to get to the point. Another friend may tell the punch line before he or she sets you up for the joke. Some people wrap their ideas in flowery images. Others give multiple examples

There are times when flowery language works best.

and synonyms for every message they impart. By noticing the speaking styles of others, you can become aware of how your style resembles and differs from theirs. If you are too abrupt in your speeches, for example, by observing someone else with the same problem you can learn to add qualifiers or examples which illustrate and explain what you want to say.

The main thing is not to fall into an habitual way of speaking. Incorporate as many different language techniques into your speech as possible while maintaining clarity of expression. Choose your words carefully. By thinking ahead, you can devise several alternative ways of saying the same thing. You can then choose the phrase that is most appropriate for you, for your message, and for your audience. In other words, work to develop a mode of expression that is consistent with your attitudes about yourself.

Sam Ervin, the former senator from North Carolina who gained prominence during the Watergate hearings, introduced himself as a

Although a recognized expert on constitutional law, former Senator Sam Ervin used a folksy, ''down-home'' style of speaking that earned him national popularity during the Watergate hearings. (UPI)

Both in and out of Congress, Bella Abzug spoke in a direct, forceful idiom that delighted critics of the establishment. (UPI)

"simple country lawyer from the South." In his public speeches, Ervin used words and phrases that reflected this image:

> The president seems to extend executive privilege way out past the atmosphere. What he says is executive privilege is nothing but executive poppycock.[5]

Bella Abzug, the feminist and former congresswoman from New York, projected a fast-talking, flamboyant image that is reflected in her public speaking style.

> They call me battling Bella, Mother Courage, and a Jewish mother with more complaints than Portnoy.[6]

2. *Relate your style to what you are saying.* The essence of public speaking is communication. A good speaker uses style to enhance what he or she has to say, to make the message of the speech more accessible and more interesting to an audience. Style should never be an end in itself. If the content is dull or unimportant, no style, however vivid or poetic, will succeed in disguising that fact from the audience. When preparing a speech, remember first what you want to say and then decide on the best way to say it.

Your language style should be determined by the purpose, or the intent, of what you are saying. Do you want to provide information? Then a simple declarative sentence which states facts, opinions, or judgments is most appropriate.

> The first element of civilization is labour.[7]

Do you want to be forceful, to control a situation or activate an audience? Then ask rhetorical questions or use imperative or exclamatory sentences.

> You might rightfully ask, "What can one individual do to influence these great and international forces?"[8]

[5] Sam Ervin, as quoted in *The Book of Quotes,* ed. by Barbara Rowes (New York: E. P. Dutton, 1979), p. 155.
[6] Bella Abzug, as quoted in *The Book of Quotes,* p. 281.
[7] Victor A. Rice, "The Transnationals' Impact on Host Countries," *Vital Speeches of the Day,* December 15, 1979, p. 133.
[8] George Marotta, "The Third World: Threat or Opportunity?" *Vital Speeches of the Day,* December 1, 1979, p. 126.

Yet who among you would contest that our social ethics today seem dangerously focused on the satisfaction of individual needs and too little concerned with the collectivity?[9]

3. *Use the active voice.* Every speech is intended to affect an audience. If you want listeners to remember the important parts of your speech, you must impress them with your style. Style can highlight a speaker's main points and make them memorable. Making your speeches as personal as possible is one of the best ways to do this. Since the passive voice tends to be impersonal, use the active voice whenever you can. Rather than saying "It is believed by many people . . ." say "Many people believe . . ." The active voice adds immediacy and force to a speech—two elements essential in making a presentation interesting and persuasive. Compare

A stitch in time saves nine

with

Nine stiches are able to be saved by one done on time.

4. *Style is economical.* To make a message easily understood, the style must be logical and to the point. One way to do this is to eliminate all unnecessary words. Adverbs and adjectives which accurately describe something—a "sunny" day, walking "briskly," a "little" dog—are necessary to understand the speaker's intent. There are, after all, many kinds of days—rainy, snowy, gloomy, gray; and there are many ways of walking—slowly, quickly, gracefully, aimlessly. But adjectives and adverbs often serve no useful purpose. They only pad the area around nouns, verbs, and other adjectives. Is something that is "most essentialA any more necessary than something that is "essential"? The use of "most" here clutters the sentence.

Compound prepositions and conjunctions are another source of clutter. How often have you heard a speaker use "with regard to" instead of simply "about," "in order to" instead of "to," and "in the event that" instead of "if"? These words are not only cumbersome, they obscure the argument, wrapping simple ideas in layers of words. Short, simple sentences and recognizable, straightforward words are the best tools to effective communication.

[9] John S. Pustay, "Energy, Defense, and National Resources," *Vital Speeches of the Day,* November 15, 1979, p. 68.

Stylistic Devices for the Public Speaker

There are many ways to make language dynamic and pleasing to the ear. The most common way is to use figurative language. Certain expressions, called "figures of speech," help the speaker add variety to his or her presentation and thereby capture and hold the attention of an audience. The most frequently used figures of speech are the *simile* and the *metaphor*, each of which is used to compare one object with another.

Simile.   When a football player says "My throwing arm feels like a rubber hose waving in the wind," he is using a simile. A simile compares two dissimilar things or ideas using the words "like," "as," or "as if." For example:

Inflation is like a dictatorship—it must be attacked before it has taken root.[10]

Government intervention is like a strong medicine with major side effects: It should be used sparingly and only as a last resort.[11]

Used in public speaking, a smile can liven up the presentation by providing vivid images for the audience to envision.

Metaphor.   Like the simile, a metaphor compares two objects to each other. But rather than say that one object is *like* another object, a metaphor eliminates the qualifier and says the object *is* the other object. "My love is like a red, red rose" is a simile. "My love is a red rose" would be a metaphor. Metaphors are encountered constantly. The old Elvis Presley song "You Ain't Nothin' But a Hound Dog" is a good example.

Perhaps because they are so popular and are used so frequently, metaphors are frequently sorely abused. The major misuse is called a mixed metaphor in which the comparisons are inconsistent: "encountering rough seas on the rocky road to success" or "drowning under an avalanche of problems." To avoid mixing your metaphors be consistent: "Encountering rough seas while sailing to success" or "drowning under a tidal wave of problems" might not be very origi-

---

[10] Julian M. Snyder, "Know the Truth," *Vital Speeches of the Day*, November 1, 1979, p. 38.
[11] Henry Ford II, "One Businessman's View of the State of the Nation," *Vital Speeches of the Day*, October 1, 1979, p. 751.

nal, but at least they would finish the thoughts with appropriate images.

Hyperbole.   Hyperbole is a figure of speech used to deliberately exaggerate what is being represented. Speakers can use this device to arouse listener attention. Sometimes the hyperbole is used for obvious effect, as in "Please accept my infinite apologies" or "These apples taste so good I could eat the entire bushel." These uses of hyperbole are meant to illustrate the intensity of the feeling or experience rather than to give an exact assessment of the facts. The use of hyperbole was to make a point through exaggeration. A good public speaker will utilize this device in his or her speeches to add vitality to the presentation and diversity to his or her delivery.

Now, however, a vast matrix of incipient technologies promises not just a few new wrinkles in television but the possibility it will become a whole new medium—The Hope of all Humanity?[12]

Understatement.   Understatement is the opposite of hyperbole. Rather than exaggerate, understatement presents a situation as less than is actually the case. "Muhammed Ali was a pretty good fighter." "It's chilly outside" (when the temperature is forty below). By understating the obvious, a speaker calls attention to his or her remark and gives it added emphasis. As with hyperbole, understatement helps to achieve a dramatic effect within a speech. The wider the gap between the truth of the situation and the degree of understatement, the more intense the effect will be and the more exciting the result.

Producing a whole child is a lot more exciting than producing a plastic pitcher.[13]

There are times when I would like to see the press go away.[14]

Personification.   "Sometimes my typewriter gets so tired out from writing term papers, that he just jams up his keys and takes a rest." "God bless this ship and all who sail in *her.*"
These are examples of personification, a figure of speech which endows inanimate objects, such as a typewriter and a ship, with

---

[12] Tom Shales, "The Rebirth of Television," *Current*, September, 1978, p. 17.
[13] Margaret Mead, "Notes on Corporate Culture," *Current*, March 1978, p. 33.
[14] George Meany, as quoted in *Forbes*, August 6, 1979, p. 20.

human characteristics. Personification is useful for adding power to the presentation of an idea:

> If the American people choose to turn their backs, History would not forgive us.[15]

Irony.   Irony is the use of words to express something other than, and especially the opposite of, the literal meaning of a situation, action, or word. For example, a man has just walked into his house after sitting in rush hour traffic for two hours in 98-degree heat. His wife greets him with: "Don't we look cool and rested?"

> When working toward the solution, it always helps if you know the answer.[16]

> One wonders if we will be allowed to eat anything that exists or grows on the earth.[17]

> Always try to do the right thing. It will please your friends and surprise your enemies.[18]

Climax.   Many public speakers use climactic order to maintain listener attention. The word climax is derived from a Greek word meaning "ladder," and in public speaking refers to a buildup of points, images, or ideas each of which is more important or striking than the one which preceded it until the final culmination. Churchill was a master at achieving this kind of effect:

> To die at the height of a man's career, the highest moment of his effort here in the world, universally honored and admired; to die while great issues are still commanding the whole of his interest; to be taken from us at a moment when he could already see ultimate success in view—is not the most unenviable of fates.[19]

---

[15] James R. Schlesinger, "Energy Risks and Energy Futures," *Vital Speeches of the Day*, September 15, 1979, p. 712.
[16] John Ralph Pisapia, "Living With Reality-Centered Leaders and Followers," *Vital Speeches of the Day*, November 1, 1979, p. 56.
[17] John W. Megown, "Topsy Turvy Times for Agriculture," *Vital Speeches of the Day*, October 15, 1979, p. 18.
[18] Harry S. Truman, as quoted by David S. Brown, "An *Amicus Curiae* Speaks Up," *Vital Speeches of the Day*, September 15, 1979, p. 722
[19] *Report on the War*, House of Commons, December 19, 1940.

Alliteration. Alliteration is the use of two or more words in a row that start with the same letter or sound, as in "plodding platoons" and "Peter Piper picked a peck of pickled peppers." One might expect alliteration to be used only in humorous contexts or in tongue twisters. But most skilled public speakers incorporate alliteration into their speeches to convey a sense of rhythm and vitality which might be lacking in an expression similar in meaning but totally different in style. Consider "Peter Flautist grabbed a basketful of marinated vegetables" as an alternative to the tongue-twister quoted above.

Almost daily, our nation's soul is searched, its psyche probed, and its anatomy dissected as seldom before.[20]

First, a world community requires the curbing of conflict.[21]

[20] David Rockefeller, "The Values by Which We Live," *Vital Speeches of the Day,* December 1, 1979.
[21] Henry Kissinger, "Long-Range Problems," *Vital Speeches of the Day,* October 15, 1973, p. 1.

Summary

People study language from many different perspectives. To the linguist, the basic element of language is sound. When we hear "language," we really hear a series of sounds strung together. By themselves sounds mean nothing to us. It is the structure and meanings we attach to them that make sounds intelligible.

Our ability to use language develops through our experience. As we travel, interact with people from varied backgrounds, attend classes, and listen to experts, we develop language skills. In public speaking, these skills are used to inform and influence an audience. The public speaker is constantly challenged to use language in creative and interesting ways.

Language must be clear, interesting, relevant, and related to the topic being discussed. It is not enough merely to present the facts of an argument and expect an audience to be impressed. The successful public speaker knows not only what to say, but also how to say it.

How a person expresses him or herself is known as style. It is the flavoring we give to the language that we use. There are four major components of style. It is personal, purposeful, impressive, and clear. In developing an individual style, a public speaker should use figurative language. Certain expressions, called "figures of speech," enable the speaker to add variety to his or her presentation and capture and hold the attention of the audience. Although there are seventy-three figures of speech to choose from, the most important ones are simile, metaphor, hyperbole, understatement, personification, irony, climactic order, and alliteration.

Exercises

1. On paper, give an example of the following:
   a. comparison
   b. contrast
   c. metaphor
   d. simile
2. Go to the library to read some copies of <u>Vital Speeches</u>. From the publication, get an example of the following kinds of style:
   a. functional
   b. appropriate
   c. flowery
   d. straightforward
3. Record a tape of yourself giving a speech and then a tape of yourself in social conversation. Compare your style and language in each of the two situations. Are the styles similar or different?
4. Develop a brief argument about the need to show tolerance for all people. In the first case state the argument in a very functional style, and in the second state it in an impassioned style. Which do you think is more effective? Why?

deliVERING
The
speech

Tips for Speakers

1. Plan and control your physical behavior as thoroughly as you plan your speech.
2. Dress appropriately for the speaking occasion.
3. Avoid all unplanned vocalizers, such as ''um,'' ''er,'' ''you know,'' and ''and-um.''
4. Maintain eye contact with the audience at least 75 percent of the time.
5. Make your rate of delivery consistent with the normal rate of everyday conversation.
6. Speak at a volume loud enough to be heard and understood by your entire audience.

NONVERBAL COMMUNICATION

There is an American Indian saying that reflects on the often inconsistent relationship between a person's stated values and his or her actions: "What you do speaks so loudly, I can't hear what you say." This adage suggests to us a dimension of communication we have considered only briefly: nonverbal communication.

The Nonverbal Message

As we saw in the last chapter, language is a medium of communication that has developed a particularly high degree of complexity, efficiency, and expressiveness. Its use by human beings is all pervasive, its role in society essential.

But, as important as language is, it is not the exclusive means of human communication. Whenever people assemble, they also transmit nonverbal messages to each other. These messages may or may not be deliberate, but they can be as effective and significant as any which are expressed in words.

Consider what can be communicated by how a person enters a room, or shuffles cards, or shifts nervously before an audience. Many elements apart from our words transmit messages: our dress, our posture, how we "come across" as we talk, our vocal quality, and the extent to which we establish eye contact with our listeners. These elements all affect our success in being understood by others.

A speech is not merely "said" before an audience. It is delivered. In this chapter, we will identify some of the nonverbal signals that people transmit, consciously and unconsciously, to others. Our goal is to understand these important variables of speech delivery, and to learn to use them to our advantage.

The Quantity of Nonverbal Communication.   Most people speak words for only about 10 to 11 minutes a day. Most spoken sentences take only about 2.5 seconds to deliver. Moreover, in the average two-person conversation, "the verbal components carry less than 35 percent of the social meaning of the situation; more than 65 percent is carried on the nonverbal band."[1] Thus, despite the importance of words, most communication is nonverbal.

This becomes more evident if we think of nonverbal communication as including all aspects of the communicative situation except for words themselves. We would thus define certain sounds that are not words, such as grunts or throat clearings, as nonverbal. In a tele-

[1] Mark Knapp, *Nonverbal Communication in Human Interaction* (New York: Holt, Rinehart, and Winston, 1972), p. 12.

phone conversation, for example, many messages are transmitted that are not put into words. Silences and the general timing of word delivery, plus all personal vocal qualities such as accents and diction, are nonverbal. They have to do with the "how" rather than the "what" of communication.

As we have remarked, people receive information through all of their senses—taste, smell, touch, sight, and hearing—which work singly or in combination. To understand how explicit and abundant nonverbal messages can be, consider the measures a host might take to insure the pleasure of dinner guests. Care is put into the choice of foods, their preparation, and their appearance. Special china, glassware, silver, and linen could be brought out for the occasion. Perhaps music will be played softly during the meal. If not one word were spoken at the dinner table, our host would, nevertheless, surely have communicated something to his dinner guests. To prove the point, we have only to consider what their reaction would be (what would have been communicated to them) if stale bread and water were the main course, served on dirty plates in a dark, messy room with a radio blaring.

As we saw in Chapter 8, sight is perhaps the most extensive medium for communication. People react strongly to what they see. Another person's facial expressions, clothes, body type, and posture immediately make an impression on a viewer. It can, in fact, convey a message as explicit as any conveyed verbally in speech. From artist to aristocrat, car mechanic to cowboy, a person's appearance is a veritable signpost of messeges. Most aspects of our appearance and movements can "say" something about us to those who happen to be "listening."

A gesture can mean success or failure.

The Quality of Nonverbal Communication. We mentioned earlier that the use of words, verbal language, combines the highest levels of complexity, efficiency, and expressiveness in a single medium of communication. It is invaluable. Yet people seldom make a judgment based solely on what they are told verbally. This is true in both conversation and in formal public speaking. Our reactions are based on many factors; but an important one is that while someone is talking to us, we are also receiving messages nonverbally. Like words, these messages may be explicit—a warm smile and a hug to indicate welcome, a sneer and an obscene gesture to express contempt. Nonverbal messages convey a definite meaning in the context in which they are used. In fact, certain gestures—the "Vee" symbol for victory popularized by Churchill during the Second World War, a thumb extended up or down to indicate success or failure—have acquired a specific verbal referent. They are literally sign language. Because

SIR WINSTON CHURCHILL, Britain's leader during World War II, was one of the most famous orators of our time. He had several early careers—soldier, journalist, politician—but did not come into his own until the bleak days of World War II when he rallied Britain during what he called its "finest hour." Churchill's ability as a public speaker was one of his major assets as a leader. His powerful, emotional oratory inspired millions in Britain and across the world to fight on to victory.

UPI

these signs have an almost exact equivalent in words, they have more to do with verbal than with nonverbal communication.

More often, however, nonverbal communication is implicit—a shrug, a stutter, one's body stance—and is open to a wide range of interpretations. For this reason, nonverbal messages are sometimes called "cues" because they suggest the meaning in a person's behavior. The broadest dictionary definition of the word "cue" is "anything that excites to action." It can also mean a hint or intimation.

A nonverbal cue, in other words, is not a form of complete communication. A cue is a stimulus—a smell, a taste, a sound, a touch, a gesture—that must prompt a response (an interpretation) from another person to acquire meaning. This means, of course, that nonverbal cues can be interpreted differently by different people. The possible interpretations depend for their meaning on the many things that affect each person's response at a given moment. Consider, for example, how two different listeners might react to a speaker who shifted nervously on her feet. One listener might find this annoying and be unable to pay any attention to what the speaker was saying. A second listener, on the other hand, might react sympathetically and warmly to both the speaker and her message. Both listeners are reacting differently to the same nonverbal cues.

Moreover, a person can display a number of cues at a particular time, and all or a combination of several can provide information for interpreting his or her actions. Picture, for example, a speaker who has come as an expert to address an audience on the subject "Good Health through Proper Diet." He himself is alert, confident, and radiates good health. But during the lecture, he chain smokes and drinks soda. The audience is apt to be confused. The verbal message is clear enough—good health depends on proper diet. But the nonverbal clues are contradictory. True, the speaker looks and acts healthy, but he also indulges a taste for clearly unhealthy substances—tobacco and sugar. Again, the interpretation placed on these nonverbal messages will probably vary from one person in the audience to another.

Verbal and Nonverbal Message Consistency. All of us can probably remember a person with eyebrows drawn together, lips pursed, and facial veins protruding, who barked, "I'm not angry!" This is an example of contradictory verbal and nonverbal messages. The speaker on health described above provides another example.

For the student of public speaking, the coordination of verbal and nonverbal messages is of key importance. When listeners perceive that verbal and nonverbal messages contradict each other, they are likely to trust and believe the nonverbal message. People assume that nonverbal messages are more spontaneous and harder to manipulate, that they are truer indicators of human feeling. Ideally, all speakers would match their verbal message perfectly with their nonverbal behavior. (If this were true, one would also have to hope for the best in human character, since lies and fraud would be even harder to detect.)

An important goal of the good communicator, therefore, is to make his or her verbal and nonverbal messages agree. When preparing a speech, we should decide which aspects need to be emphasized through voice, tone, and gesture. We should consider what to wear and how to carry ourselves. We should know our material well enough to be able to maintain ample eye contact with our listeners. Coordination of verbal and nonverbal messages is at the heart of successful public speaking. We shall discuss some of the ways to achieve this coordination later in the chapter.

Examining Nonverbal Communication

As we suggested in the previous section, nonverbal communication has a broad definition. It includes all "extra-verbal" aspects of our communication—such things as dress, posture, grooming, and gestures. It includes *how* we say something—for example, the quality of our voice presentation—not *what* we say. And it includes the way in which we use our immediate physical and spatial environment to communicate—that is, the way we use body motions to establish a rapport with the audience.

When we look at other people, or listen to them speak, we receive a general and total impression, not a diffuse collection of cues and words. We undoubtedly oversimplify, and perhaps misrepresent, the communication process by attempting to divorce verbal from nonverbal communication. In this chapter we only do so to analyze public speaking.

When people communicate, many stimuli interact to determine the message that passes between them. Only if we remember the complexity of human communication and the wonder of it, is it productive to isolate the nonverbal aspect for study.

Types of Nonverbal Communication. There are seven ways of expressing nonverbal communication: through body motion (kinesic behavior), physiological characteristics, touching, vocal characteristics (paralanguage), proxemics (the use of space), chronemics (the use of time), and artifacts or objects. As each method is discussed, we will consider how it can be significant in public speaking.

Body Motion—Kinesic Behavior. Kinesics is the study of body movement as a method of communication. When people talk, they display a number of physical mannerisms that are part of their communication. All movements of the body, limbs, facial expressions, and eyes are included in kinesic behavior. Some kinesic behavior is deliberately intended to communicate, as when we move a hand forward to indicate passage of time. Other behavior is equally expressive, but often unintentional—a furrowed brow or pursed lips.

Specific kinds of kinesic behavior have been identified. "Courtship readiness," for example, is signaled by preening and adjusting one's clothing. "Positioning" is another source of cues that indicates attraction between people. For example, pairs of people will sometimes sit side by side with their torsos turned in an open position, as if to welcome a third into their conversation. When "threatened" by an "intruder" couples' legs will often close in an arc to exclude the newcomer.

In speech making, we should attempt to use body movement to support our verbal message. This means eliminating all unplanned, disrupting mannerisms (fiddling with things, pacing, flourishing the hands) that block the flow of our message. The goal is to replace random movements with those calculated to make the speech more effective and understandable to the audience. Our physical behavior should be as planned and controlled as is our speech outline and supporting information.

Physiological Characteristics. While the previous category dealt with elements in motion, physiological characteristics remain relatively unchanged during an interaction. These include such influential nonverbal cues as one's physique or figure, general attractiveness, personal hygiene, body odors, hair, and skin tone. All of these are important and affect how listeners will receive our presentation.

Speakers who are physically imposing, strong and large, generally impress an audience more than those who are small and passive. Physically larger speakers thus have an advantage over their smaller colleagues.

But size alone is not decisive. Audiences are affected by a speaker's overall physical appearance, of which size is only one element. We cannot make ourselves taller or bigger, but we can insure that we are as presentable—neat, clean, and attractive—as possible.

Moreover, physical "presence" is also an abstract quality that one projects through self-confidence and self-knowledge. In public speaking, it is certainly important to be aware of the effect of one's body. But speakers are most effective—and attractive—when they radiate the self-confidence that comes from confidence in their ability to speak well and knowledgeably.

Touching. Touching behavior is in many ways culturally regulated. It ranges from the physical relationship of mother and child (breast feeding, for example) to that of adult men (characterized by handshaking and slaps on the back in our society). Political campaigns are noted for the abundance of handshaking and babykissing that occurs during them. Physical contact of this sort is a ritual that seems important both to politicians and the public.

Physical contact can sway an audience.

Touch, then, is an important element of nonverbal communication. Obviously, however, it is of limited application to public speaking. Unless addressing a very small and informal audience, it is impossible for a speaker to make physical contact with most of the audience. When the occasion lends itself to it—at a political rally or in a speech of introduction, for example—speakers will go out of their way to be seen making physical contact with someone on the platform—a member of the audience, the guest of honor, a fellow speaker. This sort of contact is symbolic and demonstrates the speaker's warmth and affability.

Vocal Characteristics—Paralanguage. Paralanguage deals with how something is said as opposed to the words that are spoken. "Para" is the Greek word for beside, near, or beyond. On the telephone, since you cannot see the person to whom you are talking, paralanguage qualifies one's verbal message to a particularly high degree. "Oh, I love it!"—these words can be said to show delight, or in a very different way to express sarcastic disgust. The verbal message remains the same; it is the *vocal* message, a nonverbal message, that is altered.

A speaker's vocal qualities include pitch, volume, rate, and vocalizers, which are the various sounds—"um," "er," "heh," and so forth—with which a person surrounds words. Vocalizers can also be words, such as "you know," that are interjected in speech. Parts of the United States have unique paralanguage characteristics. The throaty "ay-ya" of people in the state of Maine is interspersed through sentences the way "you know" is in other parts of the country. "And-um" is another familiar vocalizer, half word and half utterance.

Extraneous sounds and words are often used to fill up pauses between important words. Using these unplanned vocalizers suggests that the speaker has not much confidence or knowledge. This type of mumbling clots many people's sentences. Like random motions of the body, unplanned vocalizers should be shunned.

Use of Space—Proxemics. Proxemics is the study of physical space in interpersonal relations. Like touching, it is a nonverbal "language" that is observably related to the norms, or rules about behavior, of a particular society. The culture in which a person grows up has a particularly subtle and pervasive influence on how he or she deals with interpersonal space. The sense of what constitutes crowding varies from one country to country.

It can be observed, for example, that in different cultures people of similar acquaintance and in similar situations will talk from varying physical distances—8 inches, 14 inches, 3 feet, and so on. A Latin American or a Frenchman is likely to stand closer to another person when conversing than an Anglo-Saxon would in the same situation. Americans addressed from this closer distance are likely to become aggressive or sexually aroused. Studies show that Americans, unlike many other nationalities, try very hard to avoid close contact with one another in public places.[2]

Kinesic behavior and proxemics overlap when we consider a speaker's manipulation of the distance between him- or herself and the audience. Coming around from behind a desk, and perhaps sitting on the front of it, brings one closer to the listeners and gives the impression of friendliness and warmth. This can be desirable in an intimate or casual setting. In general, the more distance that a speaker places between him- or herself and the audience, the colder and more formal he or she will appear.

Use of Time—Chronemics. Chronemics is the study of how human beings communicate through their use of time. When you ask a question, what is communicated when the initial response is silence? It can mean any number of things, and the other person's kinesic behavior (rolling the eyes, shrugging the shoulders) or paralanguage (a sigh) may well provide some clues.

The communication that occurs between people is directly affected

---

[2] Stewart Tubbs and Sylvia Moss, *Interpersonal Communication* (New York: Random House, 1978), p. 186.

by their use of time. How far in advance should invitations to a dinner party be sent? Is a week too little notice and a month too much? And if the invitation is for 7:30, can a guest arrive at 7:15 or 8:00?

Chronemics is, like proxemics, culture specific. In Latin countries meetings usually begin well after their appointed time. Everyone knows this. It is customary, and no one is offended by lateness. In Scandinavia or Germany, on the other hand, strict punctuality is the rule, and tardiness is frowned upon.

To many foreigners Americans appear to be very time conscious, people who live by their wristwatches. Conversely, the notion of a midday siesta and *mañana* seems as distant to us as the Latin countries themselves.

As speakers, our awareness of schedules is a chronemic element. Have you ever listened to a speaker who said there would be time for questions at the end of the presentation, but then spoke so long that there was no time for the audience to respond? Such a speaker will probably annoy an audience, as will anyone who talks longer than is appropriate for a given situation.

Artifacts.   The term artifacts designates all objects in contact with the speaker that may serve as nonverbal stimuli. Clothing, jewelry, makeup, eyeglasses, and all other personal accessories, are artifacts which tell others much about us and about our attitude toward the speaking situation. Dress and physical characteristics typically dominate a person's first, and longest lasting, impression of another. It is often immediately possible to deduce someone's social position, the type of activity he or she is engaged in, and numerous other personal pieces of information from cues provided by artifacts. The role a person plays in society sometimes strictly dictates his or her clothing (the banker with a pinstripe suit, the nurse in a white uniform, the student in jeans and a tee shirt).

In public speaking situations, the artifacts chosen by the speaker need to be appropriate for the occasion. The formality or casualness of an event largely determines what a speaker will wear. Overdressing is usually wiser than to risk appearing careless about or disrespectful of a particular occasion. Sometimes we see speakers remove their jackets or roll up their sleeves to achieve a more informal appearance before an audience. The underdressed speaker has no such trick available.

A speaker's dress tells an audience a great deal.

Nonverbal Communication in Public Speaking

In all communication, people have an intentional message that they want to transmit. By now, having considered the various types of nonverbal communication, we can see that much unintentional information is also conveyed. Our ultimate impact as speakers is determined both by what we intentionally and unintentionally communicate.

When we talk to an audience, our intentional message should be well-planned and well-organized. It is the backbone of our presentation and should contain everything that we want the audience to assimilate. Our nonverbal messages should complement, not contradict, the intent of the speech. To repeat, a unified message through both verbal and nonverbal communication should be the goal of every public speaker. Through conscious control, the nonverbal variables can be made to act as stimuli that are consistent with, and supportive of, a speaker's spoken ideas.

DELIVERY

If all speeches were silently read by audiences, speech delivery would not exist. By definition, however, speeches are spoken, that is they are physically and vocally delivered to an audience. The quality of a speaker's delivery is determined by the unintentional messages and the intentional messages that he or she conveys.

One who is extremely skilled at delivering a speech can disguise ideas that are neither logical nor worthwhile. A demagogue is "an agitator who plays on the passions and prejudices of the masses." Demagogues—Hitler was a notable example—usually have dramatic and effective delivery styles that gain them attention and win support for their ideas. A less "loaded" or derogatory word to describe speakers whose success is largely determined by their delivery is "charismatic."

Conversely, there are speakers whose delivery is so poor that they cannot communicate even worthwhile ideas. If demagogues betray their audiences by substituting style for substance, poor speakers deprive their listeners of the chance to hear what may be worthwhile and beneficial. Speakers have a responsibility to give worthwhile speeches. But they have a parallel responsibility to deliver those speeches as effectively as possible. Speakers must not allow their ideas to be blocked or obscured by poor delivery.

Important Components of Speech Delivery

In this chapter, we have sought to increase the potential speaker's awareness of how nonverbal stimuli can determine what is communicated to an audience. We have examined some nonverbal behaviors, or "languages." Now we need to apply this knowledge to the actual delivery of a speech.

Eye contact helps hold listener interest.

Eye Contact.

Eye contact is a nonverbal technique that helps the speaker "sell" his or her ideas to an audience. Besides its persuasive powers, eye contact helps hold listener interest. A successful speaker must maintain eye contact with an audience. To have good rapport with listeners, a speaker should maintain direct eye contact for at least 75 percent of the time. Some speakers focus exclusively on their notes. Others gaze over the heads of their listeners. Both are likely to lose audience interest and esteem. People who maintain eye contact while speaking, whether from a podium or from across the table, are "regarded not only as exceptionally well-disposed by their target but also as more believable and earnest."[3]

To show the potency of eye contact in daily life, we have only to consider how passers-by behave when their glances happen to meet on the street. At one extreme are those people who feel obliged to smile when they make eye contact. At the other extreme are those who feel awkward and immediately look away. To make eye contact, it seems, is to make a certain link with someone.

Eye contact with an audience also lets a speaker know and monitor them. It is, in fact, essential for analyzing an audience during a speech. Visual cues from audience members can indicate that a speech is dragging, that the speaker is dwelling on a particular point for too long, or that a particular point requires further explanation. As we have pointed out, visual feedback from listeners should play an important role in shaping a speech as it is delivered. This is a unique advantage of the extemporaneous model of speech delivery, which we will discuss at the end of this chapter.

Paralinguistic Components.

Rate. Rate refers to the tempo of a speech. A smooth, even-paced rate of speech comes readily for some people. Others, often because they are nervous, talk too fast to be easily understood. Still others speak at a ponderous rate that smothers their listeners' interest. The best guide is to make the rate of your speech delivery consistent with the normal rate of everyday conversation.

Pitch. Most of us have seen comedy routines where bashful characters are summoned before an audience. Their eyes bulge in terror. They fidget. When they do speak, their voices are an octave higher than normal. By contrast, if you listen to professional broadcasters, both male and female, you will notice that their vocal pitches are in the very low to moderate range. This probably reflects both listenability and increased authority accorded to lower pitched voices.

---

[3] Tubbs and Moss, *Interpersonal Communication*, p. 197.

The normal pitch of your voice is that pitch at which you are most comfortable speaking. This pitch often does heighten when one speaks before an audience. Public speaking students should keep this in mind and learn to control their vocal pitch.

Volume.   Very simply, good speech volume is that which can be heard comfortably by all listeners. As with speech rate and pitch, volume should be geared to comfortable listening levels.

Changing the volume, pitch, and rate helps make a speech interesting to hear. Avoid monotony of vocal delivery, but don't try changes for their own sakes. Change the vocal quality of your delivery when it is appropriate to what you are saying at that point in the speech. Always emphasize key words and phrases in your delivery.

Vocalizers.   Using unplanned vocalizers while speaking is a common bad habit. It must be corrected by students of public speaking. Good speech delivery eliminates random and idiosyncratic elements. Vocalizers clutter a speech. They can make listeners feel that a speaker is uneasy or uninformed. Try reading aloud this transcription of a student's speech delivery:

As-uh World War II ended and-uh Harry S. Truman-ummm succeeded-uhh Roosevelt, like—you know—the-uh great question in the-uh world-uh seemed to be: Would history repeat itself?

Dependence on vocalizers is often very strong. Some people are literally unable to communicate their ideas without vocalizers. Checking the vocalizer habit thus can be grueling work. It can be very frustrating to be corrected every time you fall back on a vocalizer.

To overcome this problem, train your own ear to identify vocalizers whenever you hear them. Try listening to yourself on tape. You might be shocked at how often they will show up, even in casual conversation. When you have trained yourself to recognize vocalizers, eliminating them from your language is comparatively easy.

Appropriateness.   Speech delivery, like the content of the speech itself, must be tailored to the speaking occasion. Our dress, movements, and all other elements of delivery, will vary according to different situations—a pep rally, a business meeting, a classroom debate.

Some situations call for a very informal, relaxed delivery. Perhaps a speaker has prepared a speech to be delivered from a podium in an auditorium. At the last minute, however, she learns that the meeting is to be held in a lounge. The listeners will be scattered about on sofas, chairs, and the floor. In this more informal setting, relying heavily on her notes and not maintaining ample eye contact would be a serious mistake. Moreover, instead of facing an audience seated in formal rows, the speaker will have listeners on three sides of her. To establish a rapport with all of them, she should often glance around her.

Other speaking occasions would call for a formal, official delivery style. Experienced speakers know that etiquette and delivery have much in common: "When in Rome, do as the Romans do."

Content also determines what delivery is appropriate. Most of us have probably heard a clergyman tell an anecdote during a rather solemn sermon. His style of delivery should have altered during the anecdote; perhaps his face and voice became theatrical and animated. If his delivery did not change, chances are that most of the congregation missed the humor.

Besides the occasion and the topic, delivery should also be influenced by what a group of listeners expects to hear from a speaker. This does not mean that one should say only what an audience wants to hear. But it is to a speaker's advantage to know how certain ideas should be presented to a particular group of listeners. After all, some ideas are likely to be generally accepted. Others will be opposed. In other words, it is prudent to know when you are on firm ground with an audience and when you may be on thin ice. In this context, appropriate delivery means that ideas are delivered in a strategic manner, that is, in a manner that gives them the best chance of being grasped by the audience. As we have reiterated throughout this book, you speak to communicate. To communicate effectively is to get your message across. Whatever helps you to do this is an aid to good communication.

The volume of a speech should be comfortable to hear.

Planning. The key to good strategy, of course, is planning. Think about the topic, yourself, and the speaking situation. Then plan the delivery that can best transmit your ideas to an audience. Important points in a speech need to be emphasized. Using gestures and vocal intensity (altered volume, pitch, and rate) an effective speaker can take key phrases and imprint them in capital letters on the listeners' memories.

Planned speech delivery reduces the number of random elements. These include nervous vocalizers, jingling of change, pacing about, and unrehearsed removing and replacing eyeglasses. There are times when any of these gestures might be effective. For example, Robespierre, the French Revolutionary orator, always began a speech with his glasses off, although he was very nearsighted. Then, at a strategic point in his address, he would replace his glasses and look carefully at his audience, making eye contact with as many as possible. This tactic never failed to capture their almost hypnotic attention even when the subject matter was not especially arresting. Careful planning of one's delivery can thus be as important to the speaker as determining what to say.

In summary, good speech delivery has much eye contact, is well paced, is comfortably audible, is appropriate, and is well planned.

Delivery Models

There are four basic ways of delivering a speech—from memory, off the cuff, by reading, and extemporaneously. Each of these has its place, but the extemporaneous model, as we mentioned earlier, is generally the most effective. First, we will briefly examine the three limited models of delivery before discussing extemporaneous speaking.

From Memory.   Some people feel most confident writing out an entire speech ahead of time and then memorizing it. The speaker then simply "gives back" the memorized text to the audience. Memorized speeches can be effective, but they sacrifice a great deal of freedom and freshness. When reciting by rote, it is possible to say words without even thinking about their meaning. Good acting on the part of the speaker can compensate for this, but good actors are rarer than good speakers. Morever, a speaker who has memorized a speech risks getting blocked on a particular word. The whole delivery can then stop dead. You should always have an outline to fall back on in case you become badly lost.

The most serious drawback to delivering a memorized speech, however, is that it is difficult for a speaker to adapt to the unexpected. It is possible that the speaking situation will be different from what was expected when the speech was written. Adding new ideas and opinions to a memorized speech is a very tricky business. The speaker may have to discard much of the memorized text, or he may deliver the speech as planned and then add new elements at the end.

Off the Cuff.   Off-the-cuff or impromptu speaking violates most of the rules of good speech making discussed in this book. One speaks "off the cuff" when addressing an audience without having any opportunity to prepare. Impromptu speaking guarantees freshness of delivery. By definition, it is unrehearsed. But it can also hamstring an inexperienced speaker. Nonetheless, sooner or later most of us have to talk at a moment's notice. When your time comes, it will help if you are brief, talk as generally as possible, and try to connect the topic in some way to your own experience. Finally, if you really have nothing to say, then say nothing. Silence at least is safe. It is better to say nothing than to prattle like a fool.

Reading.   Reading from manuscript and intermittently looking up at the listeners is probably the most common way to deliver a speech. When accuracy is crucial, a speech maker can sometimes not afford to risk the slightest improvisation. Politicians and press secretaries issue public statements, and often their speeches demand the precision that can only be insured by reading a text. These are public figures, by the way, who often do not write their own speeches. They depend on speech writers, "ghosts," or assistants to put together ideas in an intelligible form. Since the speech may not be their own, they often have to read it because they may never have seen it before! Reading from a manuscript, however, has many of the drawbacks of memorizing a text, plus an additional problem: the inability of a reader to maintain eye contact with an audience.

Extemporaneous.   Extemporaneous speaking is the most versatile and expressive method of delivery. Speakers who have done their research and know what they want to say can, by only referring to an outline, speak extemporaneously. Selecting key words ahead of time is often very helpful, but generally the speaker waits until the actual presentation to choose his or her exact words.

The extemporaneous model has many advantages. It helps the speaker be spontaneous while addressing the audience. The speaker can also adapt to topics and situations for which he or she had not planned. The extemporaneous speaker can establish the best possible rapport with the audience. He or she can respond to cues from the audience for further explanation of a particular issue or cues indicating that the delivery is too slow. Finally, the extemporaneous speaker can maintain the eye contact with the audience that helps keep their interest and personalizes the address.

All of these advantages, however, depend, on the speaker's having done his or her homework thoroughly. As we saw in Part II of this book, preparing a speech properly is hard work. The reward comes when the speaker actually delivers the speech. Extemporaneous speaking is generally the most effective speaking; but it is only possible when the speaker has mastered the material, developed a working outline and a logical organization, and worked out an effective introduction and conclusion. It is thorough preparation that distinguishes extemporaneous speaking from the much less effective impromptu model.

Summary

The term "nonverbal" describes all forms of communication that do not use spoken or written words. Nonverbal cues are stimuli for interpreting human behavior and are found in our dress, our posture and body, physical movements, and vocal qualities.

Nonverbal communication can be broken down into the following seven areas: (1) body motion or kinesics, (2) physical characteristics, (3) touching behavior, (4) paralanguage, (5) proxemics, (6) chronemics, and (7) artifacts. Nonverbal communication is important because of the quantity of informational cues it provides and because of the essential role communication plays in our society. Nonverbal communication can be extremely helpful to the public speaker in conveying information, but if uncontrolled can obscure and contradict a speaker's intended message. Consistency of nonverbal and verbal information is, therefore, a major goal.

A speech, we noted, is not merely "said" before an audience, it is delivered. Important components of speech delivery include generous eye contact with listeners (75 percent of the time), and intelligible rate and volume of speech. It is the public speaker's task to control the variable meaning of words and their delivery so that both match his or her ideas and the communicative situation.

Finally, we examined the four basic models of delivery that a speaker can use in presenting a speech. They are memorized, "off the cuff," reading, and extemporaneous. The extemporaneous model was judged superior to the other three because of its combination of good organization and flexibility.

Exercises

1. Identify five factors of nonverbal communication that are highly supportive to the speaking situation.
2. Identify five factors of nonverbal communication that can be distracting to the speaking situation
3. List several speakers you consider to be the best, in terms of delivery, that you have heard. How would you characterize their individual delivery?
4. In this chapter, it was suggested that a speaker's delivery ought to be appropriate to the audience and the topic of the presentation. Describe the kind of delivery that would probably work best with the following speech topics:
   a. ending capital punishment for good
   b. closing income tax loopholes
   c. darning your socks
   d. developing good golf shots off the tee
   e. the greatest American president

PART III: SUGGESTIONS FOR FURTHER READING

Anderson, K., and T. Clevenger. "A Summary of the Experimental Research on Ethos," *Speech Monographs*, 30 (1968), 59–78.

Birdwhistell, R. *Kinesics and Context.* Philadelphia: University of Pennsylvania Press, 1970.

DeVito, J., ed. *Language Concepts and Processes.* Englewood Cliffs, N.J.: Prentice-Hall, 1972.

Ekman, P. "Differential Communication of Affect by Head and Body Cues," *Journal of Personality and Social Psychology* 2 (1965), 726–735.

Giffin, K. "Interpersonal Trust in Small Group Communication," *Quarterly Journal of Speech*, 53 (1967), 224–234.

Giffin, K. "The Contribution of Studies in Source Credibility to a Theory of Interpersonal Trust," *Psychological Bulletin*, 68 (1967), 104–120.

Johnson, W. "The Fateful Process of Mr. A Talking to Mr. B," *Harvard Business Review*, 31 (1953), 49–56.

Knapp, M. *Nonverbal Communication in Human Interaction.* New York: Holt, Rinehart, and Winston, 1972.

Loflund, J. *Analyzing Social Settings.* Belmont, Cal.: Wadsworth, 1971.

Miller, G. "Speech and Language" in S. Stevens, (ed.) *Handbook of Experimental Psychology.* New York: Wiley and Sons, 1951.

Smith, A., and A. Rich. *Language and Communication in Black America.* New York: Harper and Row, 1972.

Types of Speeches

PART **IV**

iNFORMiNG AN AUdiENCE

Tips for Speakers

1. Avoid overloading your audience with too much information.
2. To help your audience absorb new information, repeat, illustrate, and restate your point.
3. Be thorough in your research but selective in the data you decide to transmit.
4. When deciding what to exclude from your speech, ask yourself: What am I really trying to say?
5. To explain basic information, provide details that answer the question how, what, and why.
6. In order to transmit information successfully, use some or all of the nine technical skills.

In the next three chapters, we shall examine the two basic types of public speeches, informational and persuasive. This chapter deals with the first type, informational speeches. An informational speaker does not seek to change the audience's attitudes or opinions. His or her chief aims is to inform. Persuasive speakers, on the other hand, may also offer information to their listeners. But their main goal is to persuade the audience to act or think as they themselves do. The essential difference, therefore, between speeches of information and those of persuasion is one of speaker intent.

Transmitting information—telling something to someone—is a primary function of communication. As students, in our everyday lives, at work, we are constantly required to give and receive information. In public speaking, success is often determined by the speaker's ability to convey information to an audience clearly, accurately, and in a manner that will hold their interest and attention. This is not easy to do. The major problem lies in the failure of public speakers to understand how an audience goes about receiving information.

HOW LISTENERS RECEIVE INFORMATION

In many respects, the human mind is like a computer that stores, assimilates, and produces data. But human beings are not machines, and our minds do not function with the systematized efficiency of sophisticated technology. Audiences, in other words, will not absorb information automatically. Much, therefore, of what we need to know about how to give a successful informative speech is related to communication theory.

Communication Theory

Communication theory is the study of how people interact. One aspect of communication theory, how people receive information, concerns us here. An audience's absorption of the information contained in a speech is affected by five factors: the fact that communication is an ongoing process; filtering; distortion; communication overload; and redundancy. Let us discuss each in turn.

Communication as an Ongoing Process. Human interaction—communication—is continuous. The mind is constantly active, and many different thought processes occur simultaneously. For example, while listening to a speech you may also be noticing the weather, worrying about an interview, or looking forward to the evening's entertainment. Moreover, you are also more or less concerned with what happened yesterday or last week and with what may happen tomorrow or next year. All of these strains of thought coexist with the attention you are paying to the speech and influence what you get from it. As a result, you will probably not pick up all that the speaker has to say.

Suppose, for example, that you are listening to a speech about tax reform. You have just spent the past week struggling with your income tax forms. It is April 14. The deadline for filing is the next day. When the speaker is talking about tax loopholes, you may find yourself thinking only of those which you wish applied to you. The speaker's discussion of a possible Internal Revenue Service crackdown on tax evaders may simply lead you to imagine an IRS audit on your own tax returns.

Similarly, information which you may have heard in the speech, yet not consciously absorbed, might find its way into a conversation the following day. You suddenly find yourself heatedly arguing for a national sales tax as the only sane method of taxation, when previously you had not felt strongly about this issue. The mind is continually cycling and recycling the information it receives in the communication process.

Filtering. Because of these many other concerns which constantly influence our ability to concentrate on what we hear, the average listener will normally "filter out" certain things that he or she hears. This is not altogether a conscious process, although it can be deliberate. Frequently, for example, statements or points of view that are alien to the listener will be dismissed or filtered out. He or she will simply ignore a point made by the speaker, as though it had never been presented. In effect, listeners hear what they want to hear in many public speaking situations.

For instance, your family owns a big American car, has always owned one, and wouldn't be without one. During a speech about the bad energy habits of American consumers, you might well find yourself "tuning out" a statement such as this: "Those Americans who continue to purchase and drive gas-guzzling automobiles should be penalized with higher fuel taxes." It is unlikely that you will agree with that statement. You may act as if the speaker never expressed that point of view.

Distortion. For much the same reason, the human mind also "distorts" what it hears. This, however, is an entirely unconscious process. It arises simply because every person tends to remember best what agrees with his or her own values. An excellent way to observe this in action is to select five students and ask them to leave the room. While they are outside, make a statement to the class which you intend to make (in exactly the same words) to the first of the five people outside. He or she will then tell it to the second person, who will tell it to the third, and so on. It will be instructive to see how the original statement will have changed when the fifth person returns with the final version of the story.

Communication Overload.   Let us return to our earlier comparison between machines and the mind. If too much strain is placed on a machine, its electrical circuits will blow a fuse, and the machine shuts down. This is a defensive reaction. It protects the machine and warns the operator that he or she has overtaxed the machine's mechanical or electrical capacity.

Similarly, our minds can only receive and retain a limited amount of new information without showing strain. Communication theorists call the amount of information that we can handle without developing problems our *channel capacity*. In other words, as a public speaker, there is only so much that you can expect your audience to absorb. The ability to handle new data will vary from audience to audience, but every group of listeners will have a limit. If a speaker goes beyond that limit, if he or she overloads the system, the audience will cease to listen. It will, in effect, blow a mental fuse and defensively shut down the communication process. This may occur either when too mch information is poured out or when the new material is emotionally unacceptable.

Suppose that you are speaking to a high school economics club about our economic system. If your speech is well planned and well delivered, you might be able to inform them in a broad way of how the system works. If, however, you go into great detail about the complexities and various theories of the American economy, the chances are that you will have lost your audience. They are simply unable to digest this kind of high-level data. You will have overloaded their capacity to understand and even to listen.

An audience will react to communication overload in any of three ways: by withdrawing, by becoming anxious, or by getting frustrated. Withdrawal is the most obvious form of tuning out a public speaker because it is often manifested physically. Members of the audience fall asleep, get up and leave, daydream, or become absorbed with someone or something around them—anything to avoid concentrating on what is being said.

Anxiety occurs when listeners cannot cope comfortably with what is being presented. Most students have had anxious periods during a lecture when they were trying to take notes about something that they

Try not to drown your audience in a sea of complex detail.

did not fully understand. Their anxiety about a particular point tends to prevent their concentrating on the remainder of the lecture.

Frustration is a more overt way of coping with excess or unacceptable information. It can lead to a form of the physical withdrawal discussed above, or it can produce a "simmering" effect in which listeners nurture their resentment instead of concentrating on what the speaker is saying.

Take, for example, a speaker at an antinuclear energy rally. The rally is one of those huge outdoor events that includes musicians and other performers to entertain the crowd. Although the audience is theoretically opposed to nuclear power, many of them may have come just to hear certain performers or to be part of a crowd. If a speaker takes too seriously his or her duty to discuss nuclear power, the audience may become restless and bored. If the speaker delivers a long, factual analysis—no matter how informative or even persuasive the speech may be—the audience may well become frustrated, possibly even booing the speaker. In this instance, the speaker has ignored the emotional flavor of the event. Instead of communicating with the audience, he or she alienated them.

Repetition.   Each of the concepts that we have discussed so far in this section helps explain why audiences have difficulty with informative speeches. Repetition, on the other hand, can help a speaker overcome these difficult reactions. Even under the best conditions an audience often has problems grasping or fully appreciating the significance of something new. By repeating it, by illustrating it, by restating the same point in different ways, however, a speaker can make it much easier for an audience to understand and retain what he or she is trying to say. For example, as we saw in Chapter 8, visual aids repeat visually the same point that the speaker has made verbally, thereby reinforcing it in the listener's minds. Because of the problems that audiences have receiving new information, some planned repetition should be included in any informational speech.

> What the country needs is a "plan-and-act" policy. But instead . . . we have a "wait-and-see" policy.
>
> America waits for news from the dozen or so foreign countries whose decisions will determine whether we have enough energy for our homes, cars, and factories.
>
> America waits to see how much oil Saudi Arabia will produce.
>
> America waits to see how much crude oil Libya will shift to the spot market.
>
> America waits for the latest word on production cutbacks in Nigeria, Algeria, Kuwait, Venezuela. . . .[1]

[1] Charles J. Dibona, "Dreams and Illusions," *Vital Speeches of the Day*, January 1, 1980, p. 187.

Depending on us are those black people who have no hope nor hope of hope. Depending on us are those black people who cry out today not for freedom and equality but for a crust of bread and a morsel of meat. Depending on us are little black children who cry out . . . for medicine for their festering sores and protection from the rats and roaches. Depending on us are black people . . . who can't deal with the issues that galvanize those more fortunate than they. . . . The issues for these black folk boil down to one big issue—survival.[2]

We should be zealous in our protection of all citizens in their right to a public trial by an impartial jury. That means we should take care that nothing we do prejudices the minds of those who will be called upon to give judgment on a person accused.

That also means, surely, that we should uphold the right of an accused to obtain witnesses in his favor. . . . And we should remember that the First Amendment protects the freedom of all citizens, not just our own voices.

That is where we should stand our ground, defending the rights of all. Beyond that, I think we must *stand our ground, defending the rights of all.*[3]

TRANSMITTING INFORMATION

Selecting and Limiting

We can now look at how to prepare for an informative speech. The first step is selecting and limiting what to transmit. It is related both to selecting and organizing a topic that we discussed in Chapters 4 and 5 and to the methods of audience analysis that we discussed in Chapter 3. For an informative speech, you should select the best and most appropriate information available on the topic. This requires thorough research. Initially, you should include *all* the material on the subject that you can find. Use this data to become as knowledgable and expert as time will allow. This first step in the research process not only provides the raw material for your speech but should also let you familiarize yourself with the topic in a broad way.

Once this has been achieved, you are ready to analyze the material and decide what to exclude from your speech. Obviously, not all the data can or should be included. As we discussed above, most listeners have difficulty absorbing new information. It is the speaker's task to

[2] Vernon Jordan, "End of the Second Reconstruction," *Vital Speeches of the Day,* July 1, 1972, p. 535.
[3] Vermont Royster, "Freedom of the Press," *Vital Speeches of the Day,* March 15, 1979, p. 346.

As a first step, gather as much data about your topic as possible.

make it easier for the audience to receive this information by narrowing the material in the speech.

This process is exactly the opposite of what was required in the first stage. When gathering data, the object was to be as *inclusive* as possible. When selecting which material to transmit, you should be as *exclusive* as possible. You should analyze and judge each piece of information according to both the scope of your speech and the nature of your audience.

- What are you really trying to say?
- What do you want your audience to remember?
- How does the information relate to the listener's needs, interests, and expectations?

Let us suppose, for example, that you are asked to give two speeches about the effects of inflation—one to consumers and the other to a group of retailing executives. Your research produces a mass of data about how inflation affects all sectors of the economy. Since there is too much material to be included in any speech, a great deal has to be discarded. Having decided to talk to the consumers about how inflation affects the cost of feeding a family and to the retailers about how inflation may affect sales, you can select the material for each speech accordingly.

The Techniques

To make an effective informative speech, a speaker should develop nine technical skills: explaining, defining, reporting, describing, demonstrating, comparing and contrasting, narrating, applying, and quantifying. Each of these are "tools of the trade" which enable a speaker to present information clearly and proficiently. Each, moreover, is designed to help the audience understand and retain what they are being told. Never forget that the goal of public speaking is communication. In informative speeches this goal cannot be reached unless the audience absorbs the information that the speaker is presenting.

Explaining. Explanations provide the details to basic information. An informative speech introduces certain new material which needs to be explained to be clearly understood. The more difficult the material, the more a speaker should explain it. Remember that new information is hard to digest. Additional details help a listener to grasp and remember it. A good explanation should answer three questions: how, what, and why? If these questions are answered, then the speaker has probably explained his or her material adequately.

As we all know, proteins are essential for good nutrition because their specific roles are to build new muscle tissue and to maintain tissue already formed. In addition, proteins form nitrogen-containing substances essential to body functions, such as enzymes, antibodies, and some of the hormones.[4]

The experiments in question consist in joining together fragments of DNA from bacteria with fragments of DNA from cells of more complex organisms, plants or animals. The joint fragments can then be introduced into bacteria, grown in large amounts, and studied in a variety of ways to investigate the properties and functions of specific genes and groups of genes. This technology makes available a powerful tool....[5]

Defining. To convey information about something—particularly about an abstract idea—we first have to let our listeners know what we mean. In other words, we have to give them a definition to clarify the precise meaning of the term or idea that we are discussing. A good definition should be as exact as possible. It should make our meaning perfectly clear—both to ourselves and to our listeners. We do this in our social lives every day. For example, we may say to someone in conversation, "No, that is not what I meant when I said that Paul acted peculiarly today. I meant that he seemed uncomfortable." Defining, in other words, sharpens our focus, so that both we and the listener can understand what we mean.

[4] A. Richard Baldwin, "Increasing Protein in the Diet," *Vital Speeches of the Day,* January 15, 1979, p. 194.
[5] Salvador E. Luria, "The Goals of Science," *The Bulletin of Atomic Scientists,* May, 1977, p. 31.

There are two basic types of definitions: those that classify and those that stipulate. Classification defines by putting a thing or an idea into a class or category. A Frank Lloyd Wright-type house; MacIntosh apples; a thoroughbred horse—are all examples of definitions of classification:

There are two kinds of people . . . one kind is gossipers, and the other kind is gossipees.[6]

Stipulating, on the other hand, puts the word or concept we are trying to define into a context that is applicable for the particular situation in which we intend to use it. For example, a speaker might say, "To me patriotism is loyalty to the principles of individual freedom and diversity from which the United States was founded." To *you* it might mean something entirely different, but because the speaker has stipulated a meaning for the term, you can understand what he or she is talking about.

In this sense, moreover, definitions can do more than facilitate clear communication between the speaker and the audience. By defining a term like patriotism that can lend itself to many meanings, a speaker can use his or her definition to help evoke a particular audience response. During the Vietnam war, for example, antiwar speakers frequently cited Dr. Johnson, the eighteenth-century English scholar, who defined patriotism as "the last refuge of a scoundrel." By using an overtly subjective definition, these speakers were both expressing their own point of view (that patriotism used as an argument for the war was chauvinism) and were appealing to the presumed antiwar sympathies of their listeners.

Definitions of stipulation, thus, may be used to reflect the speaker's opinions; that is, they can be a means of persuasion as well as a tool for providing information. The effectiveness of definitions used in this way will depend on the makeup of the audience and also on how idiosyncratic the speaker's definition is. Thus, a prowar audience would probably have been alienated by the definition of patriotism given above and might have treated the speaker and the speech with hostility.

Similarly, a speaker who defines in unprecedented or highly eccentric terms risks losing his or her audience. A speaker who defines a good person as one who is law abiding and respectful of the rights of others, for example, is certainly offering a subjective definition. It will not be shared by every listener. The definition is reasonable enough, however, to be the basis for a serious, objective discussion. If, on the

[6] Ogden Nash, "I'm a Stranger Here Myself," in *I Have It on Good Authority* (Boston: Little, Brown, 1938).

other hand, a speaker defined a good person as someone who agreed with him or herself, the audience could be excused for not taking either the definition or the speech seriously.

Reporting. Reporting is a form of sharing experience. The reporter tries to tell the audience exactly what took place in a given situation at which the audience was not present. Reporting should be objective. Good, objective reporting is vivid, thorough, and exact. An effective reporter should use graphic and consistent terminology. He or she should make the report as complete as possible, and should ensure above all that the facts are correct.

On Thursday, June 3, 1976, the dam's engineers noticed two small streams of water coming out of the rocks slightly downstream of the dam.... On Saturday, at 8:30 AM, two large leaks sprang from the juncture of the north wall of the canyon and the base of the dam itself.... At 10:45 AM, a warning went out to the downstream population. Then, at 11:57, the north end of the dam collapsed. The 80 billion gallons of water surged through the opening and across the peaceful countryside. Rushing like a 10-foot tidal wave, it took the lives of 11 people, ripped topsoil from 10,000 acres of fertile farm land, drowned 13,000 head of cattle and destroyed thousands of homes. In all, it caused a billion dollars worth of damage.[7]

Describing. Describing is much like reporting. The speaker uses detail to recreate an event for the audience. A description is much less objective than a report, however, because it allows the public speaker to relate events according to his or her own point of view. For example, suppose you were asked to give a speech about a trip you took abroad. Some of it might be objective reporting. However, you would probably also want to describe what you saw and experienced, the foreign sights and smells of people. At this point your speech would become more personal and subjective. Chances are that your description of Paris or Mexico or Japan would be different from the descriptions of another traveler, although both of you might agree about the basic facts.

Saigon ... is a filthy cesspool of a city. Garbage is uncollected, rats are in evidence.... It seems that in Saigon, every other store is a bar.... Near An Khe, I beheld what is meant by defoliation. Miles, length and width of what had been beautiful green forestland, ... are being defoliated, as

---

[7] Dorothy Gallagher, "The Collapse of the Great Teton Dam," *New York Times Magazine Section*, September 19, 1976, p. 62.

our forces have burned, destroyed, and poisoned the trees and foliage in the entire area.[8]

Demonstrating. Some informative speeches require the speaker to show his or her audience how to do something, how to tune an automobile engine, for example, or how to make a soufflé. The best approach is to break the demonstration down into its major parts and go over each of them with the audiences step by step. The demonstrator can be either an authority figure, who shows the audience how an expert does the job, or a coach, who assists the audience to learn to do it for themselves. Depending on the size of the audience and the nature of the demonstrations, either approach can be successful.

For example, if you are speaking to a hobby club about building ships in a bottle, you might well present yourself as an authority. You would tell the audience step by step how you have refined the process in your years of creating these unique models. If, on the other hand, you are speaking to a group of job-seekers about how to prepare a resumé, you would probably find it more helpful to combine your expertise with the role of coach, exhorting members of the audience to prepare the best possible resumé for themselves.

Comparing and Contrasting. Public speakers compare and contrast to make their audiences aware of similarities and differences between two things or situations. For, example, you might tell an audience that Paris is like New York except that the inhabitants speak French. You are asking the audience to compare and contrast New York, which presumably they have some actual or second-hand experience of, to Paris which most may never have seen. This is an effective means of helping to transmit information. It only works, however, when the items being compared and contrasted are similar in important respects. Paris and New York are huge cities of international importance. If you had compared Paris with a small town in Kansas or Vermont, for example, the comparison would not have worked.

Similarly, if you are speaking about decision making in a large corporation, you might find it effective to compare and contrast the inner workings of this corporation with those of the state or federal government. Most people who have at least a vague understanding of how the government is run know very little about large corporations.

Another example of this method would be the contrasting of daily life in say, Iran, with the daily life in America. Here, the differences are greater than the similarities, and pointing out these dif-

Comparing and contrasting helps to transmit information.

[8] Stephen M. Young, "South Vietnam: A Recent Trip," *Vital Speeches of the Day,* March 1, 1968, p. 293.

ferences would illuminate the subject far more than pointing out the similarities.

Narrating. In speeches of information, a narrative is really an elaborate example that clarifies the details of a particular concept or idea. The speaker uses the narrative not to prove a point but to make an idea more concrete and easier for the listener to understand. Narrative is thus not an end in itself but a help in transmitting information to the audience. Suppose, to return to our example of a speech about a trip abroad, that you wanted to tell your audience that French food can be simple and uncomplicated, as well as elaborate and refined. After reporting on menus and describing your impressions, you might find it effective to narrate one or two accounts of meals in France that illustrate your point.

Applying. Applying occurs when the speaker makes an abstract idea personally meaningful to his or her listeners by applying it to them as individuals. Let us say that to extol the benefits of foreign travel, you cited the opportunity it provided to discover one's roots. You could apply this to almost everyone in your audience by pointing out that most Americans had roots in foreign countries.

Quantifying. In many speeches, information becomes more relevant to an audience if it can be put into numerical terms. It is more effective, for example, to say that "the United States spends sixty cents out of every dollar on defense" than to say that the United States spends a lot—or even most of its tax revenue—on defense. The point is made. Even if the audience forgets the exact figures, they are more likely to remember the thrust of the argument.

We are talking now about inflated inventory valuations which have a significant impact on the bottom line. From 1945 through 1973, corporate profits in America were approximately $73 billion higher as a direct result of inventory inflation. This meant an added tax bite of about $31 billion, of which more than half fell due between 1969 and 1973. By any measure, this represents a big drain in profits.[9]

Take the Ford Motor Company, for example. Here is a corporation whose dividend was 50¢ per quarter ten years ago; in 1970, the rate was raised to 60¢ per quarter, and in 1973 to 80¢ per quarter. Now, in the 4th quarter of 1974, following their worst 3rd quarter in 5 years, the dividend

[9] Walter E. Hanson, "America's New Economic Frontier," *Vital Speeches of the Day,* January 1, 1975, pp. 182–183.

momentum continues at 80¢ and this despite the fact their working capital declined by over half a billion from June 30, 1973 to June 30, 1974.[10]

Summary

Transmitting information is a major function of public speaking. Informative speeches convey information. Persuasive speakers want to change an audience's opinion or get them to act. An informative speech has only reached its goal if the audience grasps the new information that the speaker is presenting. However, public speakers need to be aware that audiences have difficulty absorbing new material. According to communication theory, which is the study of how people interact, an audience's understanding of new information is affected by five factors: (1) communication as an ongoing process; (2) filtering; (3) distortion; (4) communication overload; and (5) repetition. The first two steps in preparing for an informative speech are selecting and limiting what to transmit and developing a thesis statement. Research for an informative speech should begin by being all-inclusive, but only data that relates directly to what the speech is about and what the speaker wants the audience to retain should be included in the speech itself. The thesis statement briefly and clearly spells out exactly what the speech is about. There are nine techniques which a speaker can use to make the transmission and retention of new information easier. They are: explaining, defining, reporting, describing, demonstrating, comparing and contrasting, narrating, applying, and quantifying.

Exercises

1. As a hypothetical speech, for practice, develop a three-minute presentation to tell someone how to:
   a. tie a shoestring
   b. check the oil level in their car
   c. change a lightbulb
2. Read an interview story in a popular newsmagazine (e.g. **Newsweek**, **Time**). Summarize the interview in a three- or four-minute presentation.
3. Develop a two- or three-minute informative speech using at least four of the following technical skills: explaining, defining, reporting, describing, demonstrating, comparing and contrasting, narrating, applying, and quantifying.

[10] Walter E. Hanson, "America's New Economic Frontier," p. 183.

INFORMATIONAL SPEECH

The following student speech is a good example of how one's personal experience can provide an excellent topic for an interesting informational speech.

Behind the Scenes in a Political Campaign*
Randy Everett

In this drawn-out introduction, the speaker uses the listeners' general knowledge to develop the theme of the specific presentation, the political campaign.

Probably for most of you the closest that you have ever been to a political campaign is watching the voting returns on television each November. I suppose to most Americans, the election process is something to be taken for granted. We may vote for our candidate with little or no real understanding of where he or she stands on the issues. Since so many elections take place during our life, we may give hardly a second thought to any political campaign.

By demonstrating his expertise on the topic, the speaker is giving his listeners a reason to pay attention.

Like some of you, I was totally uninvolved in politics up until three years ago. I really knew very little about political affairs and, what was worse, I cared less. But about three years ago I noticed that in our neighborhood, some of the essential services such as street cleaning and animal control were being neglected. To find out more I went down to City Hall to ask some questions. During this period, I became convinced that the problem in my neighborhood really started with the city council people. The more I visited the city council, the more I became convinced that at least three of the members were, in my judgment, totally incompetent and had no business serving on the council.

Since that time I have become active in three different campaigns, two direct elections, and one recall election, aimed at driving what I consider to be incompetence off the city council. I would like to share with you what I learned during my three years' experience as a campaign worker.

The important phases of the speaker's topic are organized chronologically.

For my speech, I will talk about political campaigns in four separate chronological phases: determining the issues, selecting the candidate, reaching the voters, and rounding up the votes.

Before anyone becomes involved in a campaign, he or she must feel very strongly about the issues. I realize that many of you would say that people get involved with a campaign because of a candidate they believe in. However, at the professional and volunteer level, most people get involved because of an issue. The determination of the

---

* Speech given in an oral communications class, April 14, 1979, California State University, Los Angeles. Reprinted by permission of Randy Everett.

The speaker
makes a clear
transition from
one
chronological
phase to the
next.

issues may be at the most basic level, Republican or Democrat. Or, it could be about a very specific topic such as abortion, a balanced budget, or as in my case, incompetence on the city council. During this phase, the individual decides what the issues are and tries to join with those people who believe in the issues like he or she does. If you believe in the issues strongly, you will work hard on the campaign. At least this has been my experience. Now let us turn our attention to the next phase.

Once you have affiliated with an issue-oriented group you are now able to participate in the selection process for the candidate, and, of course, the particular position the candidate will run for. If you have reached a position of influence within the issue-oriented group, you will be able to exert a greater influence in the selection of the candidate. There are all kinds of ways to select the candidate. Most of the techniques center around some form of a caucus or primary. As an individual, in a caucus, you can have a great deal of influence. At a primary, the person can help a particular candidate sweep a primary. After the candidate has been selected, we can now help our person reach the voters.

Throughout the
speech, as in this
passage, the
speaker is
attacking myths
that the listeners
may believe
about
campaigns.

There now comes a period of time when the candidate and his or her issue-oriented group must reach the voters. Perhaps you have thought that this period was really *the campaign* but much has already gone on beforehand. This phase may well last up to six months. The candidate will use advertising and public speaking to reach as many people as possible. If you are working for a candidate, you will do such things as ringing doorbells to talk to people about the candidate, addressing envelopes, writing press releases, and organizing neighborhood meetings. The entire effort during this phase is aimed at getting the candidate and his or her ideas before the voters. Now we are ready for the "last lap."

The final phase of a campaign is likely to take place just before or on election day. The individual's effort is on getting as many people to the voting place as possible to vote for your candidate and his or her platform. This means that you might make telephone calls, pick up voters, and drive around the precinct. The volunteer wants to get as many people to vote as possible.

Notice that the
speaker tries to
"personalize"
the speech by
referring to the
listeners as
"you."

If you are successful in your campaign efforts, you will meet at your headquarters on election night to celebrate. If your candidate does not win, then you will be crying with the other losers at your headquarters. But, regardless, whether you win or lose, the campaign is an exciting and lively time. If you are one who likes politics and believes in some issue or movement, I would urge you to get involved in the political process.

PERSUADING AN AUDIENCE, I

Tips for Speakers

1. Convince your audience, never try to coerce them.
2. Use evidence, logic, and argument to persuade your listeners; but appeal to their emotions, too.
3. Avoid the techniques of propaganda, such as preying on your listeners' fears and weaknesses.
4. Every element in your presentation—including appearance, tone, and gesture—should reinforce your argument.
5. Initially, at least, attempt to influence your listeners' attitudes and opinions rather than their beliefs.
6. Take into account basic human needs and common cultural dispositions to help you prepare an effective persuasive speech.

PERSUASION: WHAT IS IT?

Persuasion: An Oral Process

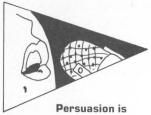

Persuasion is usually considered an oral process.

Persuasion is the process by which a speaker (or writer) changes the attitudes, beliefs, or actions of others. Persuasive arguments can be written as well as oral, but persuasion is usually considered an oral process. There are several reasons for this. First, although some writing—for example, parts of the Bible or the *Declaration of Independence*—may be more persuasive than most speeches, few writings can be as effective as a speech delivered before a live audience. Even a live television address will usually be more persuasive than the transcript reprinted in the morning paper. A speaker is much more likely than a writer to be persuasive because a speaker has direct personal contact with his or her audience. Public discussion itself impresses most listeners, especially if they have freely chosen to listen.

Persuasion: An Action Process

Persuasion is an active process, not a static one. It involves a series of attempts to alter the listener's state of mind. No single appeal or single element of a speaker's presentation can be depended on to carry the whole weight of his or her argument or to achieve the desired effect with every listener. Therefore, more than one approach is necessary in a given speech if the speaker is to succeed in persuading an audience. Furthermore, every speaker should remember that even a logical argument depends on more than the text of the speech. Every element in a persuasive speaker's presentation, including appearance, tone, and gesture, should reinforce the argument and help change the listener's attitudes or actions.

Every persuasive speaker has two purposes in making a speech. He or she wants to reinforce the beliefs of those listeners who already agree with his or her position and to alter the convictions of those who oppose it. Planning a persuasive speech, therefore, is simple in one respect. Every element in the speech should serve to reinforce agreement, weaken opposition, or encourage undecided listeners to share the speaker's point of view. This is not always easy. But a speaker should be able to judge the potential effect of each element that he or she wants to include in a speech.

Persuasion Involves Argument

Whenever possible, speakers should use evidence, argument, and logic to persuade their listeners. They should avoid preying upon their fears, weaknesses, and ignorance, even though these are often effective, as we can readily see from advertising and propaganda. For example, an automobile salesman wants to convince potential customers to purchase new cars of certain makes and models. Moreover, he wants people to buy them from his dealership, not from a dealer in the next town. We should not expect this salesman to follow the highest ideals of persuasion. It is not his business to help us decide to buy the best car. Rather, we can expect him to appeal to our vanity and greed. He will assure us that the new car will "hold its price" better than our old one. He will also argue that our present car is "over the hill." It will need expensive repairs if we keep it much longer. It may, in fact, be dangerous to drive. Automobile salesmen—whose jobs, after all, depend on selling cars and not on advising car owners—may ignore the facts to make a sale.

We would be surprised and angry, however, if a surgeon advised a patient to have a serious operation without being certain that the operation was necessary or even knowing that it was not! Speakers are not surgeons. But they, too, have an obligation to be well informed about their subjects, to respect the facts, and to make a rational appeal to the audience.

Persuasion: Convincing, not Coercing

The absence of coercion distinguishes persuasion from other attempts to affect the thinking and behavior of an audience. Having heard and considered the speaker's arguments, each listener may decide for him or herself whether to adopt the beliefs or to perform the actions that have been urged. A skillful speaker, of course, will try to be as persuasive as possible; but each listener is, nonetheless, free to reflect on the arguments and to change his or her mind at will. Members of the audience will often question speakers and oppose their point of view. This freedom to choose, even to make the wrong choices, distinguishes true persuasion from the more coercive methods used in totalitarian societies. Our democracy values freedom of expression and belief. It uses persuasion, as we have defined it here, as the preferred means of shaping opinion. Inevitably, not all listeners will be persuaded. But no punishment threatens a dissenter. No retribution menaces those who refuse to conform. Although it is expected that once the majority adopts a course of action, the minority will not prevent them from following it by unlawful or violent means, even active dissent is protected in our society. Listeners know that they cannot be compelled to submit to a different point of view. And a minority view can become the majority if enough people can be persuaded to adopt it. Persuasive speech, therefore, must be skillful if it is to succeed.

Nonpersuasive Techniques of Change

Threats.   One very effective technique is to threaten. Kidnappers often demand a ransom by threatening to harm their victims. Strong nations threaten their weaker neighbors with invasion or economic hardship if they fail to cooperate. Gangsters extort "protection" money by threatening to ruin merchants. Threat implies the use of force. It seeks to intimidate the weaker party. As long as it succeeds, force is not actually used.

Coercion.   Coercion, on the other hand, is applied force. The weaker party has no choice. There is an aggressor and a victim. The victim of a holdup is forced at gunpoint to empty a cash register or surrender a wallet. The political prisoner is tortured to make a statement dictated by his or her captors. The rapist threatens his victim with injury or even death if she resists. Although some cases of threat may seem close to coercion and vice versa, coercion is much more violent.

Brainwashing.   Brainwashing is a covert psychological technique. It may be accomplished without the conscious knowledge of the victim. Once brainwashed, a person will behave differently from his or her normal pattern. Brainwashing was a term coined to describe the indoctrination of war prisoners. Contemporary brainwashing victims, however, are more likely to be young members of radical groups or religious cults who have been convinced by various techniques to repudiate their past values and even their families. These people are often unable to extricate themselves from the new group and can return to their former lives only after being "deprogrammed." Brainwashing is psychological force.

True persuasion does not involve force.

PERSUASION IN AMERICAN SOCIETY

Persuasion, properly and expertly practiced, is the most effective means of getting others to change their beliefs, attitudes, and actions. This is especially true in today's mass society, in which people consider themselves well informed and yet remain ignorant of many things that lie outside their experience. Moreover, people are often skeptical of the values and actions that are preached at them by authority. Presenting the facts; making a strong pitch for what the speaker stands for; but finally letting the listener make up his or her own mind is more likely to succeed in the long run than the more coercive techniques first discussed. Americans are comfortable with rhetorical persuasion. Key issues in American history—independence, slavery, labor unionism, civil rights—have usually been fought as much on the speaker's podium as on the battlefield. Listeners who decide on an issue for themselves will also usually become firmer supporters of the side they choose than those who act without conviction.

A Barrage of Persuasive Appeals

Television is the most persuasive medium.

Our society is crowded with attempts to influence the way we think, act, and feel. We are daily advised about what food to eat, which books to read, how to exercise, where to take vacations, how to travel, what clothing to wear, whom to vote for, which foreign countries to visit, how to spend our leisure time, whether to live in the city or the suburbs, which job to apply or train for, or even whether to chuck the whole thing and go homesteading in Alaska.

Television is the most powerful and pervasive of the media which urge us to embrace an idea or product. The average American spends more time watching television than the average college student spends attending classes. The commercials on television can be dramatic, forceful, clever, and convincing. Between plays of a ball game or parts of a movie, we are shown why drinking a certain soft drink, using the latest toothpaste, or owning a "dream" car will make us happier and more popular. Liquor and tobacco are presented not just as sources of pleasure—though why else would one drink or smoke?—but for the status or image associated with Brand X beer or Brand X cigarettes. Every advertisement is a persuasive message, and the best advertisements are seductively persuasive indeed.

In recent years, politicians have learned to borrow from the techniques of persuasion associated with advertising. Now, all major candidates have public-relations advisors who use modern market analysis and opinion molding to gain the widest possible appeal for their candidate. As a result, issues and convictions are often pushed far into the background. The opinions of the voters are constantly being solicited, analyzed, and reported by polling organizations. This lets a candidate decide whether it is wise to support or oppose ERA or SALT II, to praise or to criticize the president or governor, or to try to get a professional football team or new factory for his or her home state. To get elected, a candidate may do—or promise to do—any number of things that he or she does not really believe in. To convince the voters that a policy is right and ought to be supported, politicians will look for noble slogans: "The New Frontier," "The Great Society," "The Great Leap Forward," or "the moral equivalent of war." The people hearing them may not have a clear idea what these phrases mean—or remember for long who coined them—but they sound good. They can also be persuasive. Often, in fact, people with completely different values support them because they are broad and undefined.

On the personal level, we also constantly try to persuade others. In turn, we ourselves are persuaded by other people. A girl who wants a bigger allowance tries to persuade her parents to give her more money. Her parents may counter by trying to persuade her to earn the money by doing more chores. A group of friends trying to decide which movie to see will listen to various persuasive efforts before choosing. An applicant for a job will have to persuade a potential employer to hire him or her.

Some Typical Persuasive Situations

In one form or another, persuasion, then, is universal. In nearly every social or personal setting, one or more "speakers" will try to influence the beliefs or actions of "listeners." These listeners use formal techniques, even in brief, casual conversations between friends or relatives. Let us consider several examples of persuasive situations to see how common and pervasive they are.

Situation No. 1:   You have been out of high school for several years when you receive a telephone call from Jean, an old friend whom you have not seen since you graduated. She invites you to meet her for dinner; you accept and talk over old times at a local restaurant. You fill each other in on what you have done since high school, with Jean asking a number of questions about your family, career, whether you plan to have children, and the like. It turns out that she now works for an insurance company. Eventually, she advises you to arrange for life insurance now, while you are young and eligible for low premiums. You listen with interest, but get suspicious when she takes a policy out of her pocket and tries to convince you to buy it on the spot.

Situation No. 2:   You decide not to spend Thanksgiving at home with your family. You are hundreds of miles from home, have only four days off for the holidays, have work to do, and have been invited to spend Thanksgiving with a friend. Nevertheless, a week before the holiday your mother calls to tell you that you will be the only family member absent. She urges you to reconsider your plans.

Situation No. 3:   You are about to get into your car in the local shopping center parking lot when a young, neatly dressed man approaches you. He is carrying a clipboard, and asks whether you care about the welfare of children. You tell him that of course you care. He thrusts the clipboard under your nose and asks you to sign a petition against nuclear power plants.

Situation No. 4:   Your car has been running well, but the brakes seem a bit sluggish. You therefore take you car to a nearby mechanic and ask him to check the brakes and to adjust them if necessary. The mechanic puts the car on the lift, looks at its underside and pokes at something near the front wheels. He then informs you that your car needs a new set of ball joints and warns you that it would not be safe to drive the car unless they are replaced.

Situation No. 5:   Your younger brother has led his high school basketball team to two successive state championships. He wants to play basketball in college but is determined to attend a good school. For the past several days, the coach of the basketball team at a big state university has been trying to convince your brother and your parents that your brother will get the best possible education if he attends the state university.

HOW PERSUASION WORKS

To understand how persuasion works, we must examine some of the key elements of the persuasive process. These include the listener's beliefs and attitudes; the interaction of the speaker with the audience; the nature of the speech itself and its function in persuasion; and the psychological makeup of the audience. Listeners' beliefs are often strongly held. They may not yield to any attempts to question or to change them, let alone to a single persuasive speech. Attitudes, on the other hand, are often less firm, and the effective speaker can hope to have some impact on them. To do so, however, the speaker will have to appear both credible and to have the best interests of the listener at heart. The speech itself will also have to show concern for the listener and dispose of the uncertainties that prevented him or her from forming strong beliefs about the subject. Moreover, listeners are guided by other rational and emotional factors. A speech that appeals exclusively to the rational side of the personality may strike an audience as too dry, and it may not reach some listeners at all. On the other hand, a speech that is too emotional may fail just because it does not appeal to reason, or because the speaker's passion alienates the audience. The effective persuasive speech has to reach both elements of an audience.

Belief

Our basic beliefs are deeply ingrained and very resistant to change. Beliefs of this type should not be confused with knowledge. What we *know* changes much more easily than what we *believe*. We may think we know, for example, that the distance from New York City to Greenwich, Connecticut, is forty miles. One day, however, someone tells us that Greenwich is only 39 miles from New York and proves it with an atlas. People will usually accept new data about things when they discover that they are wrong, even if the correct information is unpleasant, or they are stubborn by nature.

Belief is quite different. For example, we know that the United States is a democracy. But it may be pointed out that it is not a *pure* democracy because its citizens do not participate directly in the process of government. Therefore, we can refine our statement of what we know. The United States is a *representative* democracy because its citizens elect representatives who conduct the business of government in their name. But if we assert that democracy—whether a specific form of it or not—is the ideal form of government, we enter the realm of belief. Belief may be based on knowledge, but ultimately a particular belief depends on the faith of the believer. It is not usually possible to prove or disprove a belief. A biologist, for example, may say that he *knows* that life forms evolved on earth, although he or she might be unable to convince a skeptic that evolution has in fact occurred.

We should be careful to distinguish between strongly held beliefs and opinions, even though we often use the same language to describe both of them. For a belief is something which we hold strongly and which, as we said earlier, we will not abandon easily. Religious and moral values are examples of beliefs of this kind. On the other hand, we may "believe" that Bradshaw is the best active professional quarterback or that Meryl Streep is the finest actress in the movies, without placing much value on that belief (which is really an opinion) or caring whether we are correct or not.

Beliefs, then, are convictions that certain things are true without proof, especially things to which we ascribe value. Examples of beliefs include many of the principles we live by. A person may believe in the existence of a single god—or in many gods; in the importance of family ties—or in the necessity for each individual to strike out on his or her own; in the virtue of a democratic system—or in the evil of all governments; in the principle that all men are equal before the law—or in a system based on inherited privilege.

Listener Attitudes

Attitudes are our feelings and judgments about what we know or believe in. You may know, for example, that you are in a speech class at a university, but you may wish that you were lying on a tropical beach watching the tide roll in. Or you may believe that deciding to major in marketing was a wise career choice, but you may suspect that you might have been happier if you had studied music. Attitudes, then, are our responses to knowledge and beliefs, our opinions about them. They are similar to beliefs in some ways, but they are much less intense and represent more transient ideas and values.

It should not be supposed, however, that attitudes are insignificant. They are not passing fancies or mental tantrums. On the contrary, they can faithfully reflect a person's personality or deepest feelings. Many attitudes persist for a long time, perhaps even for an entire lifetime, without changing. Some may never even be seriously challenged. In general, however, they can be challenged and may be abandoned or changed with relative ease. The persuasive speaker should therefore attempt to change the attitudes of listeners rather than their beliefs, at least initially.

To illustrate this point, let us suppose that you are enrolled in a course in contemporary ethics. The instructor has invited the Protestant chaplain to address the class. You consider yourself a moral person, but you don't believe in participating in organized religion. Because you expect the speaker to recommend joining a church, you approach the speech with a certain unease. To your surprise, however, the minister does not suggest that a moral person must follow any kind of formal religious routine. Instead, he discusses the importance and difficulty of leading a life that is consistent with one's beliefs. He gives examples that show his tolerance of a broad range of life-styles and systems of belief. You abandon your old attitude about clergymen even before the speech is over. It may be some time before you adopt a new one. When you do, it may not be one recommended by this speaker, but he has succeeded in getting you to change one of your attitudes.

Credibility of Communicator

We discussed the importance of credibility to a speaker in Chapter 8. To a persuasive speaker, credibility is essential. No speaker can expect to persuade an audience unless they find him or her to be reliable and well informed and unless they believe the speech to be forceful, consistent, and truthful. They must also perceive the speaker to be sincere. They must be convinced that he or she cares about both the subject and about them. They must find him or her personally, even physically, attractive.

Every speaker must establish his or her expertise and qualifications to speak as an authority on a topic. Often, the speaker has done this long before he or she stands before an audience. But even these speakers must establish themselves as experts within the speech. For example, many Americans today are concerned about diet and physical fitness. They would have receptive, serious attitudes to a speaker on this topic. No matter how lofty the speaker's qualifications, however, he or she would have to demonstrate expertise within the speech by showing broad and accurate knowledge. Someone who endorses fad diets, who recommends the use of drugs as part of a program of long-term weight loss, who seems ignorant of basic facts about nutrition, or who dismisses the idea that people with severe weight problems should diet under a doctor's supervision would probably arouse the suspicion of any audience regardless of his or her claims to expertise.

The Persuasive Speech

An effective persuasive speech should be finely attuned to the nature of both the subject and the audience. The speaker must consider how to present the topic and how to invite the listeners to change their attitudes. If a speaker is confident of his or her credibility with the audience, he or she can consider a bold approach, one which challenges the listeners to rethink their positions immediately. If a speaker is not familiar with the audience, is uncertain of their trust, or considers the subject too controversial, he or she will have to build the audience's confidence in him or herself before asking them to change their beliefs or attitudes toward the subject.

When Martin Luther King addressed college audiences in the 1960s, he would begin his speeches by stressing what he and his listeners shared: an urban, academic background and liberal beliefs. He knew that the majority of this audience respected him, but he did not assume that they all shared his belief in equality and integration pursued by peaceful means. During his talk, however, Dr. King often succeeded in weaning his listeners away from any skepticism they might have had about his goals or techniques. He would shift from the urbane, analytic nature of his opening remarks to the impassionate gestures and phrases of an Evangelical preacher. His audiences responded in kind, often clasping hands or applauding rhythmically as Dr. King chanted "We Shall Overcome," the theme of the integra-

MARTIN LUTHER KING, America's greatest civil rights leader, was born in Atlanta, on January 15, 1929. Ordained as a minister, King became active in the NAACP. In 1955, he helped organize the successful bus boycott against segregation in Montgomery, Alabama. In 1958, King traveled throughout the country, speaking out for racial justice. His passionate oratory and insistence on nonviolence gained him a large following. At the 1963 civil rights rally in Washington, King delivered his powerful speech "Let Freedom Ring." He was awarded the Nobel Prize in 1964. In 1968, he was assassinated in Memphis.

tion movement. Had he begun his speech at so high an emotional pitch, he might have left many of his listeners cold. The effective speaker should always link up with his or her audience.

The Listener

The example of Martin Luther King's speech also emphasizes that most people have both a rational and an emotional side. A speaker must consider both. One technique is to begin a speech by appealing to reason and move gradually toward emotional appeals as the audience increases its identification with and acceptance of the speaker. But the speaker should always realize that some in the audience will reject approaches that are either too rational or too emotional. Others will respond affirmatively to a speech only if it is either highly emotional or highly rational. A speaker can seldom persuade everyone. But he or she must try to reach as much of the audience as possible. To do this, a speech should be composed with the nature of the audience in mind.

For example, a financially burdened city decides to cut the budget of its public school system. Among the cuts is part of the program for disabled children. The superintendent must justify this cut to two different audiences: a committee representing the teachers' union and a group of parents of disabled children. The two talks would have to be different if they were to be effective. The first might stress the importance of spreading the cuts evenly through the system and the efforts to retain as many jobs as possible for teachers despite the cuts. The second might reassure the parents that the quality of education and services to their children would be maintained in some way even though economies were necessary. By anticipating the concerns of each group, the superintendent would enhance her chances of convincing them of her sympathies. To win them to her point of view, she must also try to anticipate how they feel about the subject.

Typical Listener Needs

To persuade audiences, we must know something about both the makeup of their members and how they feel about the topic under discussion. Everyone has needs. Most theorists agree that the drive to satisfy those needs is among the strongest in human behavior. Motivation theory, as this area of psychology is called, maintains that individuals will do what they have to in order to satisfy their most important needs.

There are several theories of motivation, each stressing a different aspect of human behavior or character. No single theory explains all of human behavior, but the theory of Abraham Maslow is straightforward, easy to understand, and comprehensive. We will therefore use Maslow's theory as our model of human motivation and apply its insights in planning our speeches. (See the following figure.)

Maslow theorizes that there are five basic needs that motivate each

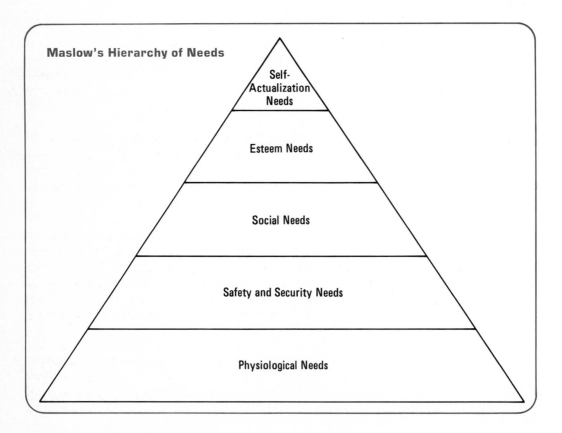

Maslow's Hierarchy of Needs

Self-Actualization Needs

Esteem Needs

Social Needs

Safety and Security Needs

Physiological Needs

From: A. Maslow, <u>Motivation and Personality</u> (New York: Harper and Row, 1954).

person and that it is possible to list them from most primitive to most complex: physiological, safety and security, social, self-esteem, and self-actualization.[1] Before one can move from a lower to a higher need, a person must satisfy the previous set. For example, physiological needs must be satisfied before someone can meet his or her security needs. Everyone moves up and down this scale of needs, driven by what is perceived as crucial from one situation to another. A brief examination will clarify the specific components of Maslow's hierarchy.

People must satisfy certain basic needs.

Physiological Needs.   These are the lowest or most basic level of need. They include what is necessary for survival: food, shelter, sex, and the like. Most Americans meet these needs with little or no effort, but situations do arise (natural or emotional disasters) which threaten them. In such crises, we will always revert to this lowest point of the hierarchy.

Safety and Security.   The safety and security of ourselves and our families is the next level of need. To protect either of these, we may behave in a way that would seem extreme at other times, even to ourselves. An entire group or nation may band together to protect itself from threatened violence or conquest. The rise of patriotism in wartime may express this basic need for security.

Social.   Once the basic physiological and safety needs are met, we are driven to form friendships and to establish ourselves as members of social groups. Some of these are one-to-one associations as in close friendships. Others are related more to our natures as social animals and involve our joining groups or organizations.

Esteem.   Two general traits identify esteem needs: the feeling of accomplishment that arises when a person reaches or nears a significant goal, and the satisfaction that follows that accomplishment. This satisfaction may be an inner feeling or may be expressed in the approval shown by others. This last element connects with the previous level of need, since giving and receiving approval and encouragement is a key function of friendship.

Self-Actualization.   The most abstract of Maslow's categories, self-actualization may often not be expressed externally. Having reached a level of accomplishment, and enjoying the esteem that this brings, a person may perceive him or herself as "self-actualized." But

[1] A. H. Maslow, *Motivation and Personality* (New York: Harper and Row, 1954).

this feeling does not last long. New needs always arise. New goals upset the temporary balance and force a person to return to a lower stage of need. Except for very complacent persons, new accomplishment is necessary before one again feels self-actualized. Thus, the drive for new goals is renewed.

Maslow and Persuasion

Since the drives at the bottom of the scale are stronger and more pressing than those higher up, an audience will be more easily persuaded by what promises to satisfy one of these basic needs. The higher up the scale a speaker ascends, the less crucial his or her proposals will appear. It might seem that listeners would be more responsive to a suggestion that could enhance their self-esteem or social status than to one that offers to fulfill a basic need that is probably already taken care of. This seems not to be the case, however. Again, advertising provides useful examples. Many advertisements make what seem like sensible appeals to our desire for safety and security (like advertisements for smoke detectors or seat belts). Others prey on our fears—a certain traveler's check as protection against being robbed on vacation. Many other advertisements promote products that promise to satisfy our appetite or make us sexy or popular.

Typical Listener Dispositions

Although there may not be a "typical" American, there are nevertheless some commonly held "dispositions" in our culture. When a speaker can assume that a sizable portion of his or her audience holds one of these dispositions, he or she can use that knowledge when preparing a persuasive speech. These beliefs will not be held by every member of every audience, but the brief list that follows is a useful starting point for many speeches.

The Flag. Patriotism still appeals strongly to many Americans. It tends to solidify in a crisis, and it may surface in many people at any time. Without considering themselves chauvinists, many Americans believe that their country's political system is superior to any other; that America has earned its riches; that Americans are the nicest folks on earth; that all truly civilized people speak English and use dollars; and that football and basketball are superior to soccer and ping-pong.

Right Will Triumph in the End. People sympathize with underdogs. Popular literature and folklore are filled with characters who overcome great obstacles to triumph in the nick of time. Everyone loves a winner, but those who are too successful may become remote from the common people. During the years of the great Yankee-Dodger baseball rivalry in New York, for example, baseball fans may have admired the Yankees' endless stream of pennants and all-stars, but their deeper affection probably went to the Dodgers, the annual also-rans. When the Dodgers finally won a World Series, it seemed that virtue had triumphed. The underdog image has such great appeal that even political candidates often court it to rally support. A candidate who is assumed to be a sure winner can inspire apathy rather than enthusiasm.

The Work Ethic.   A belief in hard work and a suspicion of anyone who loafs are the hallmarks of the work ethic. Wealth is often admired in America. But most Americans reject both the idle rich and the idle poor and suspect anyone who was paid more than he or she was worth. People who are willing to take something for nothing are considered almost thieves, whatever their reasons for not working. This attitude can often be seen during protests against welfare and systems of public assistance. "Nobody ever gave me anything" is often the cry of those who embrace the work ethic. They believe that anything gained through one's own efforts is more gratifying and valuable than something gotten for nothing.

A Man's Home Is His Castle.   The right to privacy and the sacredness of private property are widely supported in our society. This is perhaps the most widely believed of all the dispositions we are discussing. The right of people to enjoy the privacy of their homes is an almost universal value. The resistance to intrusion into that privacy is enormous. We demand that the police produce a warrant before we allow them into our house. We are shocked by those societies that do not guarantee their citizens privacy. Burglary, which violates that right, is often considered as serious as a crime of violence. A person who protects his or her home and family against intruders is usually thought to be within his or her rights no matter how violent the defense.

Blondes Have More Fun.   This may be a less clear or conscious disposition in the minds of many, but it has considerable currency. It is not simply blondes who have more fun (although the number of women—and men—who do dye their hair blonde is an important signal), but the young, fit, attractive, and sexy are believed to get more out of life. They seem to enjoy themselves more, to succeed more easily, to take liberties that are denied to plain people, and in general to have a better deal. American advertising puts great emphasis on these qualities and implies—as do the movies—that unattractive people play less important roles in life than the beautiful people. It may be noted that this disposition conflicts with much of the work ethic; but, of course, not all of these dispositions will be held by the same person at once.

Cleanliness Is Next to Godliness.   Perhaps this is a stronger than necessary statement (or one now considered old fashioned), but Americans do emphasize cleanliness and personal hygiene. It is not at all unusual to hear a hotel condemned for being "dirty" by someone who gives no weight at all to the design of the building, the furnishings, the quality of the service or the courtesy of the staff. Its failure to pass the cleanliness test alone disqualifies it.

We apply similar standards to people. We expect them to look and smell clean. We buy a vast assortment of products to achieve both ends. We fuss about rings around the collars on shirts. We want laundry products that smell nice as well as clean thoroughly. Occasionally, we may forgive a poor person or a laborer for not meeting these standards, but even then we expect to see proof of maximum effort: "His clothes are dirty but his hands are clean" runs a line in "Lay Lady Lay," by Bob Dylan.

An Eye for an Eye.   We don't like people to "get away with murder." We expect just punishment to follow swiftly whenever rules are broken or crimes are committed. We are pleased when the guilty are brought to jutice and we want fitting punishment to be inflicted. If a guilty person escapes detection and punishment, we feel that the scales of justice have been upset. This view, also, is not always consistently held. When a wrongdoer is ourself or a close friend or relative, we may prefer leniency or no punishment at all.

Big Is Better than Small.   Despite some changes in recent years, there are still more who subscribe to this slogan than to one that declared that "small is beautiful." A big (expensive) car will seem preferable to a small (cheap) one, even with expensive gasoline. Big implies wealth. Everything else being equal, a 10-room house will seem preferable to a little cottage, a case of champagne to a bottle, a banquet for a thousand guests to a small cocktail party.

To most Americans, big is more impressive than small.

Don't Meddle in My Affairs.   Most people who see a door marked *private* will not walk through it without being invited by someone in authority. This principle is widely followed and respected. We want our own privacy respected and believe that we should respect that of others. It is usually enough to be told that something—information, the contents of a drawer, a telephone conversation—is private to discourage our questions. We refrain from opening other people's mail, prying into their private lives, or trying to force them to reveal their secrets. Paradoxically, perhaps, we are often terribly curious to know the latest gossip about friends and the famous; read magazines devoted to exposés of the romances and scandals of the rich and famous; and are not always above eavesdropping in a public place or at a party.

Winning Is Everything.   We may sympathize with the underdog, but a constant underdog becomes a loser. Losers tend to invite contempt or pity. Although the remark "Winning Is the Only Thing" was made by a football coach, the attitude that the ends justify the means can be seen in most facets of American life. Even in sports contests, where some have to win and others lose, we have grown tolerant of "bad sports" and unsportsmanlike conduct to a degree that would surprise athletes of any earlier age. Even in a sport like tennis that boasts a patrician background, the popularity of certain players depends in part on their "bad boy" image. They throw tantrums, argue with fans and officials, taunt their opponents when they lose—in short, pride themselves on winning and not on sportsmanship.

Needs, Dispositions, and Appeals

The beliefs of audiences will vary according to their age, class, wealth, level of education, experience, geographical location, and other factors. It is wise not to make too many generalizations about what opinions a given audience will hold unless a great deal is known about it. Nevertheless, the dispositions that we have just examined are widespread in our society. Speakers should take them into account when planning persuasive speeches.

A speaker should be especially wary of espousing a proposition that runs counter to the values stated or implied in these dispositions. Not all of them are equally prevalent or held with equal tenacity. But some, like the belief that a person's home is his or her castle and the right to defend it is sacred, are basic to the American conscience. A speaker who argues against certain private property and privacy rights will face an uphill struggle with an unfriendly audience no matter what its makeup. In contrast, the proposition that blondes have more fun, though it may be widely believed, is not so passionately held and could be opposed by a speaker without much risk.

A speaker who knows something about his prospective audience can calculate which are their most cherished beliefs. He or she should avoid stirring up controversy in areas closely connected to them if it is possible to do so. Audience analysis was discussed in detail in Chapter 3, and should be consulted by speakers who wish to refresh their knowledge of the relevant techniques.

Summary

Persuasion is the process by which a speaker (or writer) attempts to reinforce or to change the beliefs or actions of an audience. It involves argument, presenting facts, and appeals to an audience that is free to make up its own mind. Persuasion that is free of coercion is the most effective long-term means of changing attitudes.

Attempts to persuade Americans to change their tastes and practices are numerous and cover every area of life. Candidates have borrowed advertising techniques to help in election campaigns. Personal encounters, both formal and informal, are likewise frequently persuasive in nature.

To become an effective persuader, a speaker must learn to recognize and understand the beliefs and attitudes of audiences, the natures and makeup of listeners, and the ways in which speakers and what they say affect those who hear them. They must learn to appeal both to the rational and emotional sides of their listeners and to understand the role that basic needs play in human thought and action. Besides these basic needs, many people also cling to beliefs or dispositions that are likely to affect their response to a speech. An effective persuasive speaker will take these needs and dispositions into account when planning a speech.

Exercises

1. Visit your city council meeting to study the persuasive techniques being used. Write a brief paper on the persuasive strategies used by:
   a. members of the public
   b. the city staff
   c. the mayor
   d. council members
2. Analyze the persuasive techniques used by the president of the United States. In a brief oral discussion in class, compare the present president to previous ones. Is he more or less persuasive? Why?
3. Consider your favorite and least favorite television commercials. Make a tape of each. Why does your favorite appeal to you? What is the problem with your least favorite? What type of persuasive techniques does each use?
4. Cut out an editorial from today's newspaper. Analyze it in some detail. How is it as a model of persuasion? Did it persuade you? Why? Or why not?

TWO PERSUASIVE SPEECHES

The following are two persuasive speeches. In the first, Ms. Deubler's arguments about the benefits of exercise offer a good example of persuasion based on Maslow's hierarchy of needs. Notice how she appeals to each of the five levels. This, of course, makes her argument much stronger. The second speech by Jonathan Hunt is persuasion based on a combination of arguments from personal experience, reason, and the self-interest of the audience.

The Need to Exercise as a College Student*

Marilyn Deubler

In her introduction, the speaker tries to relate "feeling good" to the topic of her speech, the need to exercise.

Good morning on this lovely spring day. I hope that you are all feeling fine, ready to face the day with enthusiasm. If you are feeling a little sluggish, not quite with it, a bit lazy, or even sleepy, you may have a problem—premature old age from lack of exercise.

As I was walking out of campus about a week ago, I noticed that a number of my young and supposedly "in shape" peers were having trouble managing the short walk up the hill in front of the Administration Building. Some 18- and 19-year-olds were huffing and puffing after that little exertion. A couple of the students were appreciably overweight and some others were smoking cigarettes.

The speaker's credibiliy is being established here.

Since I am a physical education major and hope someday to teach conditioning to adults, I was really saddened to see some of my friends have such a difficult time with what should be a very easy physical task. It was this experience that gave me the idea for this speech. Since I saw the students, I have done some research on the topic and I am convinced that many 18- and 19-year-old college students are hopelessly out of shape.

This is the statement of the speaker's thesis.

As I talk with you, I hope that my remarks will lead you to initiate a regular program of physical conditioning. I feel that the reasons for such a program fall into three categories: physical, recreational, and psychological. I would like to talk with you about each of these.

The physical, recreational, and pyschological reasons for exercise are really the main points of the speaker's outline.

I am sure that all of us want to feel better. Young people, especially college students, should be in the prime of life. But such is not the case for many students. A recent study of students in a junior college in Kansas found that nearly 75 percent were unable to complete a simple agility test. Another research project studying college age young people determined that 62 percent were unable to complete a very low-level obstacle course. Still another study found that 90 percent of the entering class of freshmen at a midwestern college could not run a complete mile.

---

* Speech given to class in persuasion, May 11, 1978, California State University, Los Angeles.

Some
supplemental
material is given
here to support
the speaker's
position.

Most of you, I am sure, have been exposed to the statistics that indicate active people have far fewer health problems than inactive ones. I will not try to summarize all of that here except the few following highlights:

Stating ideas in
a list makes it
easy for the
listener to
remember them.

(1)   People who exercise have been found to work better, sleep better, and have better nutritional habits than people who don't.

(2)   People who exercise are much less likely to have heart attacks and cancer than people who do not.

(3)   People who exercise are less likely to be overweight than people who don't.

The evidence is overwhelming indeed and it increases everyday. Regular exercise leads to better physical condition.

This is an
appeal to unite
the intellectual
and the physical.

I have heard more than one of my friends say something like: "I don't have time to exercise." My response is that they should try to make time. I know that many of you are very busy and you really do not have much time for recreation. But I hope you will remember that we are in college to get a total education. We should leave this place better socially and spiritually, as well as better intellectually, than when we came. College should educate the whole man or woman. The proper program of recreation enhances rather than detracts from our other pursuits.

The most simple and easily accomplished recreational program is exercise. Exercise such as daily swimming, running, and/or racquet ball is cheap, fun, and offers many payoffs. The next time you are slaving over the books or working hard at your part-time job, give some thought to the rest of your life. Are you really doing what is best for you? If you are not engaged in some positive recreation, especially exercise, I would submit that you are not treating yourself well.

The first two sets of reasons were straightforward and easily understood. However, there are some other kinds of reasons to exercise that are more spiritual. If you exercise regularly, you begin to experience psychological benefits not produced elsewhere. Let's look at an example. Runners sometimes say that they experience something called a "runner's high." It comes after the runner has completed a few miles. He or she is feeling good, and the body seems to be moving almost effortlessly. It is during this runner's high that the runner is really "in touch" with himself and his body. It doesn't happen often but when it does, it is a rare moment.

Other sports, in addition to running, have psyche rewards similar to a runner's high. I urge you to talk with any person who is in a regular exercise program. I would bet that most of them report that they are psychologically better off after exercising than they were before. I would urge you to see if you aren't more "in touch with yourself" after exercising.

The speaker gives a summary here and makes a final appeal.

I have already taken up a good deal of your time. Let me urge you to seriously consider exercise as a way to improve your life. In review, let me restate that there are strong physical, recreational, and psychological reasons for exercise. I hope that you will consider my words and that they make you want to get off that duff and out into the active, dynamic game of life.

Riding the Bus*

Jonathan A. Hunt

A strong rhetorical question is used both as an introduction and to give the thesis of the speech.

As I walked on campus today, I noticed that just about every car that entered the parking lot was occupied by a single driver.

Did you know that of every two gallons of gasoline that you buy, one of these comes from a foreign country that does not have the best interests of the United States at heart?

The speaker states an important theme here: "Everybody must do his or her share." In the next paragraph, the speaker establishes expertise on the subject.

Over the past few years we have heard a number of appeals directed toward us to use alternative forms of transportation. Yet the automobile is still the most widely used transportation alternative for students at this university. We must face the fact that the single person riding in a single automobile is creating a tremendous waste of natural resources.

For the past four years, while I have been attending this school and holding down a part-time job downtown, I have been riding the bus. In this speech I would like to present a number of reasons why you should do the same. If we were all to ride the bus, we would be saving millions of barrels of oil daily. With every barrel of oil saved, the likelihood is improved that inflation can be slowed. So let's look at four very good reasons why you should consider the bus as your primary method of transportation:

The four reasons for riding the bus provide an excellent organizational technique for the speech. They are used to build the speech's basic structure.

(1)   The bus is convenient. I realize that the public transportation system in our city has been heavily criticized as being inefficient and incapable of handling the task of getting large groups of people around. Perhaps, in the past, this criticism is justified. But not anymore! If the people who criticize our bus system would ride our buses, I think they would find a modern, clean, efficient means of transportation.

In my car it takes me roughly 25 minutes to make the trip from campus to my home. If you add the time it takes to find a parking place and walk to class, from the time I leave my front door, I am in class 40 minutes later. All of this is based on the assumption that I can find a parking place.

Notice the speaker's transitions from one point to the next.

With the bus, I walk two blocks to the line and it delivers me right to the Student Union about 30 minutes later, and I don't have to look for a parking space. Roughly the bus takes 10 minutes longer than the car, but I use the time on the bus to read and study, so the longer time does not bother me. Now, let's go on to the second reason.

* Speech given in an oral communications class, California State University, Los Angeles.

(2) The bus is generally less expensive than the car. During the bus strike last year, I was forced to drive my car to school; I calculated the cost. It costs me roughly $3.50 a day to drive and that was when gasoline was $1.00 a gallon. Today the cost would be even higher. For $22.00 a month, I can buy a bus pass that allows me to use the bus for the entire month. In terms of coming to school, the bus is much cheaper than my car. If I didn't need my car for an occasional week-end trip, I might even consider selling it and using the bus for all my transportation needs. Okay, number three.

(3) You meet new friends on the bus. When I started taking the bus, I pretty much kept to myself. I would not get into any conversations with the other passengers. To be honest, I suppose I was a little frightened. But as I became more familiar with the bus system, I became more outgoing. Now on my basic line, I know maybe 15 people by name who ride the bus regularly. There are certain people I sit next to. A couple of people have even invited me into their home. There is a great deal of camaraderie on the bus. It is certainly a lot more friendly than being closed up in your car on the freeway. Now, for the final reason.

(4) We have a social responsibility to ride public transportation. We have to face facts. There is only a limited amount of natural resources available. Oil is a consumable natural resource. When it is gone, it is gone. Conservation will be a policy for the rest of our lives. That's the way it's going to be. So we might as well get with it. We all need to conserve. Although it sounds like flag waving, we do have a responsibility to be as frugal with our natural resources as we possibly can. Which is better: one person or 40 persons traveling 10 miles on a gallon of gasoline? Obviously, the 40. The bus enables us to travel in much larger numbers. I don't want to come across as a preacher, because that is not my intent. What I do want you to consider are the opportunities that will be available for your children. Don't you want them to have the same chance at a future as you?

The first three reasons were specific. This final one is much more general. Recognizing this, the speaker almost apologizes for it to the audience. This is a way of heightening speaker-audience rapport.

Our future does depend on having, at least, some natural resources. And, one small way that each of you can help the future generations is to take the bus today.

This is a strong statement reinforcing the reasons for using a bus. The four reasons are repeated here as a summary.

In a final appeal, the speaker uses an emotional argument (guilt) to suggest that the listener should reorder his or her priorities.

Let me quickly review my four reasons for using the bus for transportation. First, the bus is efficient; second, the bus is cheaper than the automobile; third, you are able to meet new friends on the bus; and finally, we all have a social responsibility to conserve. I would hope that you would think about these reasons as you walk down to your car when you leave class. Consider for a moment the amount of gasoline you are wasting when you and you alone drive that automobile home. Perhaps tomorrow, you will consider taking the bus.

PERSUADING AN AUDIENCE, II

Tips for Speakers

1. When presenting a speech of persuasion, use one of the three strategies: association, balance, or rein-forcement.
2. Conduct a detailed audience analysis to enable you to choose the most appropriate strategy.
3. In planning a persuasive speech, first decide what ac-tion you want your audience to take.
4. When delivering your speech, you must capture the au-dience's attention; present your proposal in an under-standable manner; induce the audience to act on the proposal.
5. Be ethical in both content and tactics.

> He, from whose lips divine persuasion flows.
>
> —Homer, Iliad, Book VII, line 143

Men and women have always used the art of persuasion to get other people to do their bidding. Persuasion takes many forms. As we saw, one way to persuade people is to threaten or coerce them into doing as you demand. Another way is to offer people incentives or rewards—to buy their cooperation. Bribery is one example of this form of persuasion; salary increases, pension plans, paid vacations, company cars, and expense accounts are other, more socially accept-able, examples of persuasion incentives.

For centuries, scholars have been concerned with how people change other people's attitudes. One ancient technique is to persuade by giving a speech. For centuries, speakers have tried to persuade listeners to do everything from throwing off their chains and walking into the Red Sea to buying a bottle of elixir guaranteed to cure "what ails 'em." Great speakers have been acknowledged as major influences on history. Moses, Pericles, Cicero, Lincoln, Lenin, Churchill, Franklin D. Roosevelt, Adolf Hitler, and Martin Luther King have used their eloquence to inspire whole nations to undertake great tasks and to change their lives for both good and ill.

As we saw in the last chapter, the enormous persuasive power of speech makes it important for all students of public speaking to develop a solid understanding of how persuasion works. Students must also be able to give an effective speech that can change people's attitudes.

STRATEGIES OF PERSUASION

There are three general strategies that a speaker may use to persuade: association, balance, and reinforcement. Each suggests ways in which a speaker can get listeners to understand his or her argument and apply it to their own situation or experience. When examining these three strategies, remember that the ultimate goal of the persuader is to convince. People are persuaded when they perceive a relationship between two stimuli, between one that they feel neutral about and one that they react to strongly. The persuader must connect the two stimuli in the listeners' minds, so that they react as strongly to the first, neutral stimulus as they do to the second. Each of the three strategies of persuasion is designed to make this connection. Consider the following examples:

1. In certain ads rugged men smoke cigarettes while riding horses. In others attractive men and women smoke cigarettes while walking arm in arm on the beach, or through a field. The advertisers are trying to make the consumer associate his or her feeling about masculinity or being with a lover with the action of smoking a brand of cigarettes. The more closely the two stimuli are connected in the listener's mind, the more effective will be the persuasion to buy the cigarettes.

2. A pacifist who believes very strongly that nonviolence is a moral truth, wakes up to find that his country has been innocently attacked by an invader who should be resisted. He is thrown into a state of imbalance, uncertain which "truth" to believe and act on—nonviolence or the moral duty to resist evil. To retain a sense of equilibrium, or emotional balance, he will have to choose between these two conflicting "truths." At this point, an effective persuasive speaker who advocates resistance can induce this person to relinquish his own prior belief and accept the necessity for war.

3. A banker speaking before the local chamber of commerce advocates tax breaks for business as a remedy to the nations' economic woes. The audience, already on the speaker's side, does not need to question its opinions. The speaker merely strengthens, or "reinforces," their current attitude.

The strategy that a persuasive speaker uses depends on the audience and on the speech.

Obviously, the particular strategy that a speaker uses will depend on the nature of the audience and of the speech. A strategy guides the speaker and gives him or her a firm foundation from which to launch an effective persuasive attack. To help you select the proper strategy for your own public speeches, let us discuss these strategies of persuasion in more detail.

Association

People value certain ideas, concepts, causes, and individuals very highly. Some people respect men and women like Ronald Reagan, Shirley Temple Black, and Billy Graham; other people prefer Jerry Brown, Gloria Steinem, and Cesar Chavez. Some people think war is hell; others consider it a necessary aspect of international relations. In using the strategy of association, the prospective persuader must first find out which ideas, concepts, causes, and individuals are regarded favorably and unfavorably by an audience. The speaker will then design the speech to associate every point he or she wants the audience to favor with an idea, concept, cause, or individual that the audience likes. Every point the speaker wants the audience to reject will be associated with an idea, concept, cause, or individual that the speaker knows the audience dislikes.

For example, one of the heroes of the United States space program is Neil Armstrong, the first American to walk on the moon. After Armstrong retired, he became a professor of engineering at a quiet, respected midwestern university. He did not try to capitalize on his fame, and his credibility in the eyes of the American public remained high. Because Armstrong is considered a man that people can trust, Chrysler Corporation, in the late 1970s, approached him with an offer to endorse the engineering principles demonstrated in its automobiles. Armstrong accepted the offer and made several commercials for the product. Chrysler's strategy was to induce the car-buying public to associate their feelings of trust and integrity for Armstrong with the performance capability of Chrysler cars.

Balance

Most people have a primary need to maintain a condition of cognitive balance. In other words, we prefer things to be in their place. If faced either with two incompatible beliefs or with a new fact that is inconsistent with what we already believe, we can become acutely uncomfortable. This discomfort produces a state of psychological tension or imbalance called cognitive dissonance.[1] To resolve this tension, we

---

[1] See Leon A. Festinger, *A Theory of Cognitive Dissonance* (Evanston, Ill.: Row, Peterson, 1957); and Charles Kiesler et al, *Attitude Change: A Critical Analysis of Theoretical Approaches* (New York: John Wiley and Sons, 1969), pp. 190–195.

need to restore our sense of balance. People react to cognitive dissonance in several ways: They can discount the source of the tension ("He doesn't know what he's talking about anyway."). They can abandon their original opinion ("I didn't *really* believe that."). They can refuse to deal with the situation ("Don't bother me with that stuff."). Or, they can play down its importance ("It really doesn't matter to me one way or the other.").

In all of these behaviors people attempt to regain their equilibrium by putting distance between themselves and whatever threatens them. The balance strategy helps public speakers profit from this situation. The speaker would first create a state of cognitive dissonance by saying something that upsets the audience's equilibrium. He or she should then offer a vehicle through which the listeners could regain the balance that was lost in the jolt caused by the speaker's initial argument. The remedy suggested by the speaker, of course, is to accept or adopt his or her proposal. The speaker's goal is to change the listeners' attitudes. That goal will only be won when the listeners accept the speaker's argument. Consider the following example of a speech using the balance strategy. Ths speaker is President Herbert R. Coursen of Bowdoin College. He is speaking to an audience of Maine businessmen and community leaders who are disposed to support the United States involvement in Vietnam. Professor Coursen wants to change that attitude:

> *Why are we in Vietnam? We have been given several reasons by our president and secretary of state. . . . First, we are in Vietnam because of treaty obligations. Dean Rusk . . . . has asked many times, "If we pull out now, who will believe our promises?" In his Thanksgiving 1967 message, President Johnson told us that "we are involved in fidelity to a sacred promise." What are our promises?*
>
> *First, we signed the U.N. Charter and promised to abide by Article 33: The parties to any dispute, the continuance of which is likely to endanger the maintenance of international peace and security, shall, first of all, seek a solution by negotiation, enquiry, mediation, conciliation, arbitration, judicial settlement, resort to regional agencies or arrangements, or other peaceful means of their own choice.*
>
> *Second, we made a unilateral declaration on the Geneva Agreements of 1954, which formally ended the French-Indochinese War. We promised to "refrain from the threat or the use of force to disturb the provisions of the Geneva Agreements in accordance with Article 2 (Section 4) of the Charter of the United Nations." Article 2 (Section 4) says, "All members shall refrain in their international relations from the threat or use of force against the territorial integrity of any state. . . ." The Geneva Agreements, contrary to popular belief, did not create two separate Vietnams, North and South. . . . It was the United States which created South Vietnam—a fictitious state created in clear violation of international agreements—the United States which placed Diem in power, the United*

States which prevented the elections for which the Geneva Agreements called. Thus, even if we accept Mr. Rusk's highly dubious assertion that the United States is now "combating aggression from the north," the argument stands only if we first accept the fact of separate Vietnams, a fact on which we have insisted unilaterally in defiance of our solemn pledges.[2]

In the above example, the speaker first created a condition of imbalance in the minds of the audience and then suggested how the lost balance could be restored. Both elements—the creation of imbalance and its remedy—are essential for a successful balance strategy. If a speaker creates imbalance but fails to reduce it or restore equilibrium, he or she will not succeed. Unless the speaker can get the audience to associate a sense of balance with accepting his or her argument, then the speaker will have failed to persuade them. The audience must be dominated by the speaker and led from uncertainty to certainty—that is, to adopt the speaker's ideas. The persuasive speaker wants the listener to feel better, to be comfortable, and to achieve a sense of equilibrium and consistency—so long as this sense of well-being entails accepting the speaker's ideas.

Reinforcement

The reinforcement strategy seeks to identify the speaker's proposal with what the listener already believes. This strategy does not require that a speaker draw the listener into virgin attitudinal territory. Instead, it reinforces what is already inside the listener's mind.[3]

For example, let us assume that your listeners tend to be conservative, middle of the road, and family-oriented. If you are speaking about the need to maintain the neighborhood school and resist the busing of school children, you should have little trouble gaining support for your ideas. All you have to do is design your speech to reinforce the idea that neighborhood schools are traditional and keep families together. If, however, you believed in the need for forced busing, your task would be more difficult. You would have to find those elements of busing which are compatible with or enhance attitudes held by conservative, middle-of-the-road, family-oriented listeners. If no such elements exist—and the fact that busing is such a volatile issue suggests that they do not—the reinforcement strategy

[2] Herbert R. Coursen, Jr. "Why Are We in Vietnam?" *Vital Speeches of the Day*, March 1, 1968, p. 305.
[3] For a complete treatment of the theory of reinforcement see Charles Osgood and Percy Tannenbaum, "The Principles of Congruity in the Prediction of Attitude Change," *Psychological Review* 62 (1955): 42–55.

would not work. You might be more successful with the balance strategy.

It should be apparent that the reinforcement strategy works only when the opinions of the audience and those of the speaker are already closely allied. An address to a hostile crowd should reflect a different approach. The reinforcement strategy is the easiest of the three strategies to implement because it does not force the listener to stretch his or her beliefs, attitudes, wants, or opinions very far. As such, it is only successful when what the speaker has to propose is generally consistent with what the listener already wants or accepts. If a speaker's task is to sell ice to the Eskimos, he or she would be well advised to try an alternate strategy of persuasion. For selling air conditioning units at the equator, on the other hand, the reinforcement strategy would be ideal. The reinforcement strategy, in other words, is for preaching to the already converted.

The following speech is an example of the reinforcement strategy. Senator James A. McClure of Idaho, a proponent of nuclear energy, is speaking before the National Conference on Energy Advocacy, a pronuclear organization:

> *The proponents of nuclear energy have surrendered the moral issues involved; the opponents have wrapped themselves in the invisible emperor's cloak of righteousness. They have assumed the role of good while casting the proponents as evil. . . . When you debate the issue of nuclear energy, you are actually debating the issue of growth. . . . It is useful to take a look at who these opponents of growth are.*
>
> *Tom Wolfe has called them the "Me Generation" and Herman Kahn termed them "the new class." They often call themselves consumerists or environmentalists. What this group represents is an affluent, politically active, college educated minority whose influence is far out of proportion to its numbers. . . . One of the characteristics of this "new class" is to want to limit growth so that no one else's enjoyment of the goods of society will infringe on their own.*
>
> *Hypocritically, the members of this new class choose to couch their selfish desires . . . in moral terms.*[4]

The Need for Audience Analysis

Basic to the successful use of any of the three strategies of persuasion mentioned above is the thorough knowledge and understanding of an audience—the ideas, concepts, causes, and individuals that they like and dislike. Imagine, for example, telling a group of Richard Nixon

[4] Senator James A. McClure, "Nuclear Energy: The Moral Issue," *Vital Speeches of the Day*, March 15, 1979, pp. 325–326.

supporters that they will be certain to love your proposal because Alger Hiss and Jane Fonda thought it was terrific. Imagine trying to set an audience of antifeminists off balance by telling them that a woman's place is in the home. Or consider the speaker who thinks he or she is using the reinforcement strategy when exhorting a group of "Right-to-Lifers" to vote for more liberal abortion laws.

As Professor Harold Hill said in Meredith Wilson's musical comedy *The Music Man*: "Ya gotta know the territory." The same is true for the speaker in real life whose intention is to persuade. The only way to "know the territory" is to implement the techniques outlined in Chapter 3. Before a speaker can plan a persuasive presentation, he or she must determine what the physical and psychological needs of the audience are; who the people are that the audience likes and dislikes; what the various ways are in which he or she can get the audience to like and believe in him or her; and which words and phrases are most like to affect them, both positively and negatively. Only after these factors have been determined can a speaker select a strategy of persuasion with any expectation of success.

PLANNING AND PRESENTING THE PERSUASIVE PRESENTATION

Planning

The first part of planning a persuasive speech is deciding what you want your audience to do. Do you want them to change their attitudes or opinions? Do you want them to believe what you will tell them to believe? Do you want them to identify with a situation you will be describing? Do you want them to sign a petition, donate to charity, or walk out of the room? Before selecting which strategy of persuasion to use, you must first determine what response you want from your audience.

Next, once you have determined the action you want, you have to emphasize audience commitment to that action or to specify in explicit terms what you want them to do. Since most speeches of persuasion imply or demand a call to action, words and techniques which direct or encourage an audience to answer that call should be emphasized. For example, in the following lines from Shakespeare's *Julius Caesar*, Brutus is trying to justify to the Romans his involvement in the murder of Caesar. Note the skillful choice of words:

Had you rather Caesar were living, and die all slaves, than that Caesar was dead, to live all free men? As Caesar loved me, I weep for him; as he was fortunate, I rejoice at it; as he was valiant, I honor him; but, as he

*was ambitious, I slew him. There are tears for his love; justice for his
fortune; honor for his valor; and death for his ambition. Who is here so
base that would be a bond man? If any, speak, for him have I offended.
Who is here so rude that would not be a Roman? If any, speak, for him
have I offended. Who is here so vile that will not love his country? If
any, speak, for him have I offended. I pause for a reply.*[5]

Compare this to Antony's lines to the same audience, in which he
hoped to persuade the Romans to avenge Caesar's murder:

*If you have tears, prepare to shed them now.
You all do know this mantle . . .
Look, in this place ran Cassius' dagger through;
See what a rent the envious Casca made;
Through this the well-beloved Brutus stabb'd,
And as he pluck'd his cursed steel away,
Mark how the blood of Caesar followed it . . .
For Brutus, as you know, was Caesar's angel.
Judge, O you gods, how dearly Caesar lov'd him!
This was the most unkindest cut of all;
For when the noble Caesar saw him stab . . .
. . . great Caesar fell.
O, what a fall was there, my countrymen!
Then I, and you, and all of us fell down,
Whilst bloody treason flourish'd over us.
O now you weep, and I perceive you feel
The dint of pity. These are gracious drops.*[6]

The truly effective persuasive speaker can direct his or her audience to act in completely predetermined ways. Audiences can be
controlled; listeners can be led. The greater the commitment called
for by the speaker and the more specific the behavior demanded
from the audience, the better. To demand that the audience act gives
the speaker a goal and provides him or her with a standard against
which to measure the success of the speech. For example, the audience response to Antony's speech was to cry: "Mutiny!" And a mutiny
was just what Antony wanted. When the audience was moved to
behave in exactly the way, to the exact degree, that Antony specified,
he knew that his speech had worked, had *persuaded.* If Antony had
been less specific, it would have been more difficult for the audience.
They would have been unclear as to what kind of response was expected from them. It would also have been harder for Antony to
control the crowd. By structuring his speech as he did, Antony was

[5] *Julius Caesar,* Act III, Sc. 2; ll. 13–33.
[6] *Julius Caesar,* Act III, Sc. 2; ll. 211–230.

able both to stir up the crowd and to persuade them to his desired end.

Steps in Presenting the Speech

Getting Audience Attention.   The first step in presenting a speech of persuasion is to *grab the attention of the audience.* If a listener is not tuned in to what the speaker is saying, the speech holds little hope of success. There are several ways to gain an audience's attention. One way is to begin the speech with a startling statement as FDR did in his war speech to Congress on December 8, 1941:

Yesterday, December 7, 1941—a date which will live in infamy—the United States of America was suddenly and deliberately attacked by naval and air forces of the Empire of Japan.

The United States was at peace with that nation and, at the solicitation of Japan, was still in conversation with its government and its Emperor, looking toward the maintenance of peace in the Pacific. Indeed, one hour after Japanese air squadrons had commenced bombing in Oahu, the Japanese Ambassador to the United States and his colleague delivered to the Secretary of State a formal reply to a recent American message. While this reply stated that it seemed useless to continue the existing diplomatic negotiations, it contained no threat or hint of war or armed attack.

It will be recorded that the distance of Hawaii from Japan makes it obvious that the attack was deliberately planned many days or even weeks ago. During the intervening time the Japanese government had deliberately sought to deceive the United States by false statements and expressions of hope for continued peace.

The attack yesterday on the Hawaiian Islands has caused severe damage to American naval and military forces. Very many American lives have been lost. In addition, American ships have been reported torpedoed on the high seas between San Francisco and Honolulu.

Yesterday the Japanese government also launched an attack against Malaya.

Last night Japanese forces attacked Hong Kong.

Last night Japanese forces attacked Guam.

Last night Japanese forces attacked the Philippine Islands.

Last night the Japanese attacked Wake Island.

This morning the Japanese attacked Midway Island.

Japan has, therefore, undertaken a surprise offensive extending throughout the Pacific area. The facts of yesterday speak for themselves. The people of the United States have already formed their opinions and well understand the implications to the very life and safety of our nation.

As Commander-in-Chief of the Army and Navy I have directed that all measures be taken for our defense.

Always will we remember the character of the onslaught against us.

No matter how long it may take us to overcome this premeditated in-

vasion, the American people in their righteous might will win through to
absolute victory.

I believe I interpret the will of the Congress and of the people when I
assert that we will not only defend ourselves to the uttermost but will
make very certain that this form of treachery shall never endanger us
again.

Hostilities exist. There is no blinking at the fact that our people, our
territory, and our interests are in grave danger.

With confidence in our armed forces—with the unbounded determina-
tion of our people—we will gain the inevitable triumph—so help us God.

I ask that the Congress declare that since the unprovoked and das-
tardly attack by Japan on Sunday, December 7, a state of war has existed
between the United States and the Japanese Empire.[7]

Another way is to challenge an audience, as Simon Bolivar did in 1819:

LEGISLATORS! I deposit in your hands the supreme command of Vene-
zuela. Yours is now the august duty of devoting yourselves to achieving
the happiness of the Republic; you hold in your hands the scales of our
destinies, the measure of our glory; your hands will seal the decrees in-
suring our Liberty. At this moment the Supreme Chief of the Republic is
nothing but a plain citizen, and such he wishes to remain until death.[8]

A third way is to illustrate the speech with relevant pictures or displays. This is particularly effective when a speaker's argument is highly technical or somewhat routine. Illustrations help to clarify difficult points and enliven an otherwise bland presentation.

Presenting the Proposal Understandably.   The second step is to *present the proposal in an understandable manner.* Some persuaders become so caught up in the process of persuasion that they forget the point that they are trying to make. Occasionally a speaker will withhold his or her specific proposal from the audience as part of a creative or narrative technique. In this case, the speaker tells a story in which the "hook," or persuasive purpose, comes at the end. Consider the following speech in which Charles DeGaulle called on the French to continue to fight in 1940:

The leaders who, for many years past, have been at the head of the
French armed forces have set up a government.

Alleging the defeat of our armies, this government has entered into ne-

[7] *Congressional Record*, 77 Congress, 1st Session, Volume 87, Part 9, pp. 9504–9505, December 8, 1941.
[8] Louis Copeland, ed., *The World's Great Speeches* (New York: Dover, 1958), p. 386.

gotiations with the enemy with a view to bringing about a cessation of hostilities. It is quite true that we were, and still are, overwhelmed by enemy mechanized forces, both on the ground and in the air.

But has the last word been said? Must we abandon all hope? Is our defeat final and irremediable? To those questions I answer—No!

Speaking in full knowledge of the facts, I ask you to believe me when I say that the cause of France is not lost.

For, remember this, France does not stand alone. She is not isolated. Behind her is a vast empire, and she can make common cause with the British Empire, which commands the seas and is continuing the struggle. Like England, she can draw unreservedly on the immense industrial resources of the United States.[9]

Although this technique can be effective, the inexperienced public speaker should avoid it. Far more reliable is the speech in which the purpose is stated simply and straightforwardly at the beginning, as in the following example from a speech by Susan B. Anthony.

Friends and fellow citizens—I stand before you tonight under indictment for the alleged crime of having voted at the last presidential election, without having a lawful right to vote. It shall be my work this evening to prove to you that in thus voting, I not only committed no crime, but instead, simply exercised my citizen's rights, *guaranteed to me and all United States citizens by the National Constitution, beyond the power of any State to deny.*[10]

Inducing the Audience to Identify with the Speech. The third step in presenting a persuasive speech is to *induce the audience to apply the speaker's idea or proposal to themselves.* The speaker does that by personalizing his or her message. This can involve using words such

[9] Houston Peterson, ed., *A Treasury of the World's Great Speeches* (New York: Simon and Schuster, 1965), p. 783.
[10] Copeland, ed., *The World's Great Speeches*, p. 321.

New York Public Library

SUSAN B. ANTHONY, abolitionist and leader of the women's suffrage movement, was born in Adams, Massachusetts, February 15, 1820. Influenced by feminist Elizabeth Cady Staton, Anthony campaigned vigorously for women's right to vote. She organized the National Woman Suffrage Association, edited the influential New York weekly *The Revolution,* and crisscrossed the country lecturing on women's rights. She attended her last suffrage convention in 1906, one month before her death. A powerful speaker, she ended her final speech with the stirring words: "Failure is impossible."

as "you," and "your," "my friends," or "my fellow classmates." President Lyndon Johnson, for example, used to pepper his speeches with the phrase "my fellow Americans." Other orators, such as Dwight Eisenhower, have used similar expressions in their speeches:

> Now, my friends, before giving you the last few words that I have written down, I want to tell you I am forever ... sensible to the great honor that was twice bestowed upon me by a body such as this. It is the highest ambition that any American can have and by your generosity and by your action, I was permitted—a poor farmer boy from Kansas—to enjoy it.[11]

The use of personalizing words and phrases may not be enough to allow an audience to identify with a speech. A speaker should also use stories, anecdotes, and illustrations which link the proposal to the lives of the listeners. For example, when addressing a group of fire fighters, the speaker should use illustrations that relate to them. When speaking to soldiers, one should tell stories accessible to soldiers. Picture the following speech, delivered before a group of academics and students. How effective would the same speech have been before a different audience?

> There is a story that Theodore Herzl, the brilliant leader of practical Zionism at the turn of the century, once asked the gardener of an Oxford college how to cultivate and care for beautiful lawns like those that graced the grounds of Oxford College. The gardener replied, "It's very simple, Sir. You sow the grass, you water it, cut it, roll it, and when you have done that for a hundred years, you get a lawn like this."
>
> Similarly, the building and flowering of a liberal arts university of distinction normally requires a century or so of painstaking care, untiring devotion, and sustained commitment to the principles of scholarship and free inquiry.[12]

Actualizing the Proposal.   The fourth step in presenting a persuasive speech is to *actualize the proposal.* If the purpose of the speech is to move an audience to action, the final step in presenting it should be a call to action. Stress the desired behavior, so that the audience knows exactly what is expected of them and how they can most easily fulfill those expectations. The final appeal—the call to action—must not be ambiguous. As we discussed in the planning section of this

[11] Dwight D. Eisenhower, "Address to the Republican National Convention," *Vital Speeches of the Day,* August 15, 1964, p. 647.
[12] Marver H. Bernstein (President of Brandeis), "Learning as Worship—A Jewish Perspective on Higher Education," *Vital Speeches of the Day,* December 1, 1978, p. 117.

chapter, the speaker should direct the audience to a specific course of action. The end of the speech is the time to actualize that call. It is the right moment for eloquence and enthusiasm. Whether the speaker wants to get the audience to vote for a political candidate, buy a product, or go on strike, this is the time to use all of the weapons and techniques in the arsenal. Notice how this is accomplished in the following examples:

> *No, my friends, that will never be the verdict of our people.... If they dare to come out in the open field and defend the gold standard as a good thing, we will fight them to the uttermost.... We will answer their demand for a gold standard by saying to them: You shall not press down upon the brow of labor this crown of thorns! You shall not crucify mankind upon a cross of gold!*[13]

> *When we let freedom ring, when we let it ring from every village and every hamlet, from every state and every city, we will be able to speed up that day when all of God's children, black men and white men, Jews and Gentiles, Protestants and Catholics, will be able to join hands and sing in the words of the old Negro spiritual, "Free at last! Free at last! Thank God almighty, we are free at last!"*[14]

> *Our government should ... end unconditionally all bombing of North Vietnam.... An end to the killing in Vietnam can never by negotiated as long as the bombing of North Vietnam continues.... So, let us resolve that all the sacrifices from our earliest forbears, the young men in the jungles of Vietnam, the presidential candidate who also gave his life—let us take from the meaning of their lives a new courage, a new conviction, a new resolve.*
>
> *That all this shall not have been in vain and that in our firm and unswerving determination, we can yet serve the end Robert Kennedy so tenderly sought for all of us—tame the savageness of man and make gentle the life of the world.*[15]

How to Build a Persuasive Presentation: Tactics

Building Credibility.   In the persuasive presentation, the speaker is trying to give the audience a reason to believe what he or she says about a particular topic. It is essential that the expertise of the

[13] William Jennings Bryan, *A Treasury of Great American Speeches;* ed. by Charles Hurd and Andrew Bauer (New York: Hawthorn Books, 1970), p. 149.
[14] Martin Luther King, *A Treasury of Great American Speeches;* ed. by Hurd and Bauer, p. 371.
[15] Senator Edward M. Kennedy, "Halt the Bombing: Mutual Withdrawal," *Vital Speeches of the Day,* September 15, 1968, p. 719.

speaker be apparent. If the speaker has no expertise, perhaps he or she should not be giving the speech. If the speaker does have expertise, he or she must tell the audience about it. If it is difficult for the speaker to describe his or her own qualifications, he or she can provide the audience with a data sheet or arrange to be introduced by another speaker. (See Chapter 9.)

Since many persuasive speeches are given to in-house audiences of business or professional colleagues, listeners may already know why a speaker is (or is not) qualified to speak on a given topic. But if there is any doubt, the speaker must remind the audience by saying, "You will remember that I have been working in this area for six months"; or "Let me remind you that our recommendations are based on nearly 800 hours of background work." This will show the audience that the speaker has given the presentation a certain amount of thought and is therefore qualified to make it. The importance of credibility to persuasive speaking will be further illustrated later in this chapter, when we discuss the various arguments of persuasion.

Fitting Your Proposal into Audience Range of Acceptance.   People possess a range of acceptance about a specific idea. On any given topic, a person will be open to an argument that falls within this range, but will reject an argument that falls outside it. For example, suppose Jean believes that capital punishment deters crime. Her range of acceptance on capital punishment might look like the continuum represented below:

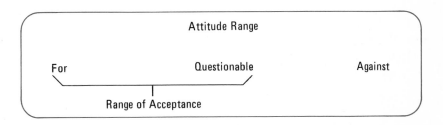

Given this range of acceptance, Jean would probably not accept the argument that capital punishment is morally wrong and should be abolished. Such an argument would fall so far out of range that she would probably turn against whoever advocated it.[16] (See "Balance,"

16 This idea was first developed by C. Sheriff, et al, in *Attitude and Attitude Change: The Social Judgement-Involvement Approach* (Philadelphia: W. B. Saunders, 1965). The authors argue that the width of the attitude range is based on the *ego-involvement* of the individual. Ego-involvement might be thought of as one's commitment to a topic. The theory goes that the more your ego is involved in a particular topic, the more narrow will be your range of acceptance of arguments about that topic.

under Strategies of Persuasion in this chapter.) However, Jean might listen to an argument more to the center of her range of acceptance—for example, that capital punishment has been shown to be ineffective in lowering the homicide rate in states that execute capital offenders.

The persuader who uses arguments that fall outside the listener's range of acceptance is wasting everyone's time. Not even the balance strategy can accomplish attitude changes of extreme dimension. In planning a persuasive presentation, the speaker should calculate his or her audience's acceptance range, based on the results of audience analysis. (See Chapter 3.) It is easier to get the listener to move a little way toward a proposal than a long way. It is probably impossible to move the listener greatly with a single presentation. Chances for such a shift are far greater in a prolonged campaign in which a speaker has the audience's attention for an extended period.

Structuring Arguments for the Specific Audience.

A persuasive speech should be geared to a specific audience. Personalized words and phrases can be effective here. If the audience has any special characteristics—if it is composed entirely of Republican teachers, taxicab drivers, or Chicanos, for example—the speaker may be able to build on that. If the speaker's own background can be closely identified with the audience, he or she should emphasize it. Each argument posited should be structured to appeal to a particular audience. For each argument, the speaker must ask him or herself, "Will it work with this audience?"

On any given topic, most people have some raw nerves—areas where they are particularly open to persuasion. Careful planning and development can help the speaker hit precisely those vulnerable areas.

A persuasive speaker should appeal to the special character of his or her audience.

Dealing with Opposition Arguments.

It is debatable whether a persuasive speaker should try to answer opposition arguments. By giving the opposition the chance to present its case, the speaker may be providing the ammunition for his or her own defeat. On the other hand, it can be argued that persuasion really consists in encouraging rational decision making and that this implies covering all possible alternatives. The speaker who seems to be dealing with every possible counterargument will probably impress the audience with his or her command of the issues. Another reason for dealing with the opposite case is to assist oneself in preparing to give the speech. The mental exercise of developing counterarguments and attempting to refute them strengthens a speaker's grasp of the subject and increases his or her chances for success.

ARGUMENTS OF PERSUASION

In ancient Greece, Aristotle developed a pattern of persuasion that is still applicable today. He stated that a speaker can persuade a listener by means of three different types of arguments: (1) on the basis of the speaker's trustworthiness, which Aristotle termed *ethos;* (2) through the logical appeal of the message, called *logos;* and (3) via the emotional appeal of the message, called *pathos.*[17]

Dealing with opposing arguments can result in defeat.

According to Aristotle's theory, the use of authority figures and trusted personalities—such as Linus Pauling as a spokesman for the health benefits of Vitamin C or, as we saw earlier, Neil Armstrong as a speaker on behalf of the Chrysler Corporation—can be an effective example of the *ethos* argument.

Logos is the use of logical arguments, which appeal primarily to a listener's reasoning ability and skill at analysis: "There is no arguing with the facts."

We all like to think of ourselves as logical, rational beings, who form opinions based on sound reasoning and facts. But, as listeners we respond to many stimuli, most of which are not appeals to logic. *Pathos*, the third type of persuasive argument, seeks to make an audience respond based on how they feel, not on how they think. Let us examine these three arguments of persuasion in detail.

Ethos

How the audience perceives the speaker—whether he or she is smart or stupid, considered trustworthy or a born crook—will affect how the audience responds to the speaker's proposal. A person who has never even looked inside the crankcase of an automobile cannot be regarded with the same degree of trust as someone who has spent his or her entire life as a mechanic in a garage. As we saw in Chapter 9, for an audience to be persuaded by the *ethos* technique, they must be convinced of the speaker's credibility. Remember the old joke: "Would you buy a used car from *this* man?" It may not be as funny as you might think.

A trustworthy speaker will be more persuasive.

Sometimes a speaker with limited background in the area of his or her speech can still make an effective *ethos*-type argument. If he or she is accepted as generally trustworthy, but no expert on that subject, the speaker can strengthen his or her argument with the opinions and recommendations of other authorities. The extent to which these other authorities are respected may govern the response of the

---

[17] *The Rhetoric of Aristotle,* trans. by Lane Cooper (Englewood Cliffs, N. J.: Prentice-Hall, 1960).

listeners to the speech. For example, consumer activist Ralph Nader uses *ethos* arguments with great success. Nader is perceived by many Americans as honest and public spirited. He is not personally expected to be an authority on everything that affects consumers. By drawing on the research and findings of others, however, Nader can present an argument that many people will believe. His credibility, combined with that of his staff, gives force to his arguments.

Logos

The dictionary defines logic as a "method of reasoning, inference, etc.; especially, correct or sound reasoning." Logical arguments, therefore, appeal primarily to our reasoning ability and our skill at analysis. We can be persuaded when we are moved by the evidence and the weight of the facts presented. But logical arguments have limitations. For one thing, they are rarely exciting or vivid. Note the following example: "When selecting a college or university, the prospective student should consider the qualifications of the faculty, the size of the library, the academic programs, the school's financial resources, and its scholarly reputation."

That argument is extremely logical; it makes very good sense. But, really, who cares? Despite its solidity as an argument, it has a "persuasive quotient" of about minus 10. It does not stimulate the listener and does not provide the impact a speaker needs to persuade.

Moreover, logical arguments will not work for every topic. Not every proposal can rest on data, facts, and logical analysis. Sometimes a speaker wants to change how a listener feels, not how he or she thinks. The best way for a speaker to do this is to appeal to a listener's emotions, rather than exclusively, or even primarily, to his or her intellect.

Pathos

Other intelligent people bridle at the suggestion that they can be persuaded by emotional argument. To criticize a speaker for "playing on our emotions" is sometimes cited as reason enough to dismiss the speaker's opinions. We pride ourselves on our basic common sense, our sensitivity to logical persuasion, and our resistance to emotional appeals. In fact, we are fooling ourselves. Most people are moved by emotional arguments—and often.

Emotional arguments appeal to such things as our pride and our vanity, our sense of justice and fair play, as well as to our fears for personal, family, and national security. Perhaps the most vulnerable of these target areas is our sense of fear: "Hey, man, if you expect to appeal to the ladies, you'd better use our skin cream to get rid of that acne. Girls never come on to guys with pimples." "Mary, as your mother I love you, and you know I would never say anything to hurt you. But if you don't circulate more in school and try to make some new friends, you're going to end up an old maid like your Aunt Gladys."

People are particularly vulnerable to frontal attacks on how they look, to threats to their safety and security, and to the suggestion that their futures may lack promise. A skilled speaker will take advantage of this in making a persuasive speech.

Combining the Three Approaches

Not surprisingly, the most effective persuasion uses all three arguments—a mixture of *ethos, logos,* and *pathos* in the same appeal. Whereas individually each approach has limitations, used together they can prove irresistible. Purely logical arguments can be dry and dull. Overly emotional arguments may make audiences feel that they are being manipulated. Combinations and mixtures of the two are much more effective. The exact proportions of emotional and logical elements will vary, depending on the audience and the topic. In planning a speech, the skilled public speaker should be sensitive to the type of arguments that will work best.

In the following three speeches, notice the ratio of emotional to logical elements in each. Remember that each speech was given to a very different audience.

And who is it that deceives the state? Surely, the man who speaks not what he thinks. On whom does the crier pronounce the curse? Surely, on such a man! What greater crime can an orator be charged with than that his opinions and his language are not the same? Such is found to be your character. And yet, you open your mouth and dare to look these men in their faces! Do you think they don't know you? Or are sunk in such slumber and oblivion as not to remember the speeches which you delivered in the assembly, cursing and swearing that you had nothing to do with Philip, and that I brought that charge against you out of personal enmity without foundation? No sooner came the news of the battle than you forget all that; you acknowledge and avow that between Philip and yourself there subsisted a relationship of hospitality and friendship. . . . You were hired to ruin the interests of your countrymen; and yet, though you have been caught yourself in open treason, and informed

New York Public Library

DEMOSTHENES was born in 384 B.C., in Attica. Legend says that he practiced speeches with pebbles in his mouth to cure a stutter. He is considered Greece's greatest orator. More than a master of rhetoric, Demosthenes was a man of great insight. His most famous speeches, the "Philipics," were delivered between 351 and 340 B.C., against the threat of the expanding Macedonian kingdom under Philip. His masterpiece, "On the Crown," is a bitter denunciation of his archrival Aeschines, who supported Philip. Condemned to death under Alexander, Demosthenes fled, and committed suicide in Calauria, in 322 B.C.

against after the fact, you revile and reproach me for things which you will find any man is chargeable with sooner than I.[18]

Why do you not exactly estimate the terrible crisis through which the country is passing? They say that we are the authors of the scandal, that it is lovers of truth and justice who are leading the nation astray, and urging it to riot. Really, this is a mockery! To speak only of General Gillot—was he not warned eighteen months ago? Did not Colonel Picquart insist that he should take in hand the matter of revision, if he did not wish the storm to burst and overturn everything! Did not M. Scheurer-Kestner, with tears in his eyes, beg him to think of France and save her from such a catastrophe? No! Our desire has been to facilitate everything; to allay everything; and if the country is now in trouble, the responsibility lies with the power which, to cover the guilty, and in the furtherance of political interests, had denied everything, hoping to be strong enough to prevent the truth from being shed. It has maneuvered in behalf of darkness, and it alone is responsible for the present distraction of conscience! . . . Dreyfus is innocent. I swear it! I stake my life on it—my honor! At this solemn moment, in the presence of this tribunal, which is the representative of human justice . . . before the whole of France, before the whole world, I swear that Dreyfus is innocent. . . .[19]

We must never forget the solid assurances of sea power and those which belong to air power if they can be locally exercised. I have myself

---

[18] Demosthenes, speaking against Aeschines, "On the Crown," *The World's Great Speeches*, ed. by Lewis Copeland, p. 22.
[19] Emile Zola, "Appeal for Dreyfus," *The World's Great Speeches*, ed. by Copeland, pp. 116–117.

full confidence that if all do their duty and if the best arrangements are made, as they are being made, we shall prove ourselves once again able to defend our island home, ride out the storms of war and outlive the menace of tyranny, if necessary for years, if necessary, alone.

At any rate, that is what we are going to try to do. That is the resolve of His Majesty's Government, every man of them. That is the will of Parliament and the nation. . . . We shall not flag nor fail. We shall go on to the end. We shall fight in France and on the seas and oceans; we shall fight with growing confidence and growing strength in the air.

We shall defend our island whatever the cost may be; we shall fight on beaches, landing grounds, in fields, in streets, and on the hills. We shall never surrender and even if, which I do not for a moment believe, this island or a large part of it were subjugated and starving, then our empire beyond the seas, armed and guarded by the British Fleet, will carry on the struggle until in God's good time the New World, with all its power and might, sets forth to the liberation and rescue of the Old.[20]

ETHICS OF PERSUASION

Does one person have the *right* to persuade another person to act or think differently? Does anyone have the right to ask someone to accept something which may or may not be in his or her best interest? Persuasion is a fact of life. It is also a means to rational decision making. But there is a question as to the ethics of persuasion.

Take the case of Jim Jones, who began as a fairly traditional clergyman, became the leader of a radical cult, and eventually became a murderous demagogue. He was extremely successful in persuading people to join his congregation; to sell their homes and give him the money; to move to Jonestown, Guyana; to abandon their family and friends; and, eventually, even to kill themselves. Jones used the techniques of persuasion for deadly ends. Hitler is another example, perhaps the most notorious in history, of an evil genius in the art of persuasion.

It is easy to repudiate the insane ethics of a Jim Jones or a Hitler who persuaded people to go to their deaths. But closer to home and on an infinitely less significant scale, we encounter various attempts at persuasion everyday and seldom question the ethics behind them. On Saturday morning television, for example, advertisers sell breakfast food. The market they want to reach consists, for the most part, of children. But many of these cereals are nearly one-third sugar, which has been called a harmful product for all people, and particularly for children, who tend to consume too much of it. The media blitz, however, emphasizes everything about the cereal to the child—

---

[20] Winston Churchill, "Dunkirk," *The World's Great Speeches*, ed. by Copeland, p. 439.

taste, packaging, color, cartoon romance—except the possible tooth decay and poor nutritional habits that come from eating unnecessarily highly sweetened foods.

Is it ethical for persuaders to use the principles, the techniques, and the arguments of persuasion in this manner? Many people would think not. Within the past five years, legislation has been enacted to curtail the number of commercials televised during children's programming hours. Citizens groups have lobbied to keep favorite television characters, such as the Muppets and Superman, from endorsing commercial products.

Obviously, the ethical issue is very important—to advertisers, politicians, consumers—to all of us. It is a larger issue than we can deal with in a textbook on public speaking. But when it comes down to planning your own persuasive speeches, it will be for you—the potential persuader—to decide for yourself what is and what is not ethical. This is a personal decision and one that should be given considerable thought. Keep in mind both how the techniques of persuasion are to be used and what the desired result and possible outcome will be.

This book does not presume to dictate a code of ethics. It is possible, however, to suggest guidelines to assist the persuasive speaker to reach responsible conclusions. Here are four broad criteria against which a speaker can judge the morality of his or her persuasive speeches.

The Topic

The speaker should determine whether his or her topic is worthwhile. Is it important enough to present to a group of listeners? Is it informative? Is it educational? If there is some doubt about the topic's worthiness, perhaps it should not be discussed. Topics should have some intrinsic value to be the subject of a speech. They should have consequences in their own right.

The Speaker's Conscience

A speaker should feel comfortable with what he or she is advocating. If you have to speak in favor of a proposal that is repugnant to you—either because an association or a job demands it—then perhaps you should question the agency that is forcing you to violate strong personal beliefs. This is a thorny issue because, for one thing, a person has to earn a living. And it is not easy—it never has been—to say "no" at the risk of one's livelihood. Moreover, it is difficult to be persuasive under these circumstances. Chances are that feeling this way, most speakers would deliver an ineffective speech. Thus, practicality as much as morality would seem to indicate that, in persuasive speaking, you should "let your conscience be your guide."

The Audience

The composition of the audience also plays a role in determining the ethics of a presentation. Speaking before an adult audience raises ethical considerations different from those to be considered when speaking to children. A speaker may be able to give a particular type of speech to an audience of professionals that would not be appropriate before a general audience. A religious audience may be offended by a speech that would have only limited impact on an audience of people without religious convictions. A thorough knowledge of the attitudes and orientation of the listeners—determined through careful audience analysis—will help define the ethical considerations involved in speech making.

Potential Negative Results

The speaker should consider who could possibly be hurt by the long- and short-run consequences of a speech. What are its possible effects on the individual members of the audience? If the audience accepts the speaker's proposal, will they suffer physically, spiritually, or psychologically?

Again, this is very shaky territory. If a speaker is trying to convince someone to give up smoking, the short-term effects can be troublesome. The smoker may be damaged psychologically by the difficulties of withdrawal. Scientific evidence is conclusive, however, in asserting that the addicted smoker will, in the long run, benefit by giving up the habit. In cases like this, judging the potential harm is relatively easy. This particular case, which is based almost completely on a logical means of persuasion, presents only a minimal question of ethics. But what about trying to convince an audience to permit a nuclear power plant to be built in their community? How easy is it to decide the ethics of that? The potential persuader must always ask him or herself: What are the potential negative results of the response I hope to elicit?

Ethical questions are important to the potential speaker in both the classroom and the real world, where one is both the persuader and the persuaded. As both a user and a consumer of persuasion, we must consider the question of ethics each time we encounter a persuasive situation. Otherwise, we can jeopardize our integrity, credibility, and independence.

Summary

There are three general strategies of persuasion: association, balance, and reinforcement. For each of these strategies to work, the speaker must have a thorough understanding of his or her audience's likes and dislikes, attitudes and opinions.

There are two general steps in developing the persuasive speech. The first is to plan the speech. A speaker does this by deciding what he or she wants an audience to do and then selecting words and phrases which emphasize a commitment to that action. The second step is to present the speech persuasively. There are four guidelines to help the speaker persuade: (1) get the attention of the audience; (2) present the proposal in an understandable manner; (3) induce the audience to apply the idea or proposal to themselves; and (4) actualize the proposal. There are also four tactics which help the persuasive speaker build an effective presentation: (1) establish credibility; (2) fit the proposal into the audience's range of acceptance; (3) structure arguments geared to the specific audience; and (4) deal with opposing opinions.

Aristotle identified three types of persuasive arguments: (1) ethos, in which a speaker persuades on the basis of trustworthiness or expertise; (2) logos, based on the logical appeal of the message; and (3) pathos, based on the emotional appeal of the message. Each argument can be effective in and of itself, but for maximum effect a combination of the three approaches is best.

In every persuasive presentation there is a question of ethics. The speaker must decide for him or herself what is ethical. There are four general criteria against which the speaker can judge the ethics of his or her behavior: (1) the topic of the speech; (2) the speaker's conscience; (3) the audience; and (4) the potential negative results of the speech.

Exercises

1. Using one of the three strategies of persuasion—association, balance, or reinforcement—develop a five-minute speech to convince your classmates to:
   a. eat more / less meat
   b. vacation in your hometown
   c. donate to your favorite charity
   d. learn a foreign language
   e. join your political party

2. Take as many of the following emotions as you can and develop an argument for or against nuclear power. Appeal to:
   a. pride
   b. justice
   c. vanity
   d. love for the underdog
   e. freedom
   f. nationalism
   Remember to present the proposal understandably, induce the audience to identify with your ideas, and actualize your proposal.
3. What persuasive appeals seem to work best on you: ethos, logos, or pathos? If a person wanted to move you to "do something," what appeal should he or she emphasize? Why?
4. Analyze four advertisements in a national magazine. What appeals did the writers try to use? Did the ads appeal to you? Why? Why not? Do you think these ads were ethical in what they said and the way they said it? Why, or why not?

TWO PERSUASIVE SPEECHES

The following two persuasive speeches offer two contrasting types of argument. The first speech by Mark Jolley attempts to persuade using logos or rational argument. The topic of his speech, an attack on a scientific theory, makes a logos-type argument both essential and effective. An emotional, or pathos-type, argument would be out of place here. The second speech by Mary Jean Parsons appeals as much to emotion as to logic. Again, her topic lends itself to this combination and makes it potentially effective for an audience.

A Look At Evolution*
Mark C. Jolley

This is both the speaker's introduction and thesis. The lack of scientific evidence to support evolution will be a continual theme throughout the speech.

In 1859, Charles Darwin published his well-known work, *The Origin of the Species.* His work was only meant to be a simple study on the variations of kinds of species. But with the onslaught of humanism, scientism, and liberalism, this scientific investigation helped alter society's beliefs about creation vs. evolution and has provoked public debate, as demonstrated by the Scopes trial in 1925. Evolution has become the most widely held belief as to the origin of man. Although evolution is referred to by many as a theory, I will argue that the social or intellectual acceptance of the theory of evolution is not an accurate judgment of scientific data. Evolution is widely accepted as the true origin of man and is even taught as fact in the schools today.

* Speech given by student in argumentation class, February 20, 1979, California State University, Los Angeles.

The speaker cites the counter arguments to his position. Evolution is defined.

Professor Dobzhansky, geneticist and widely known evolutionist, professor of zoology at the University of Davis, states that "the occurrence of the evolution of life in the history of the earth is established about as well as events not witnessed by human observers can be." The late Richard B. Goldschmidt, a professor at the University of California, before his death stated, "Evolution of the animal and plant world is considered by all those entitled to judgment to be a fact for which no further proof is needed."

The speakers "signposts" the presentation to let the audience know what is coming. In this passage the speaker makes it clear that the speech gives his opinion, not objective fact.

In order to properly address myself to these claims I will define the term evolution, discuss the aspects and qualifications of theory itself, and discuss the theory of evolution in reference to the fossil record. Lastly, I will discuss some of the important archeological finds supporting the theory of evolution. All these areas will be discussed in light of my belief that the scientific data available to us all has not been judged accurately by the evolution theorists.

What is evolution? The scientific definition follows as such: All living things have arisen by a materialistic, naturalistic, evolutionary process from a source which itself arose by a similar process from a dead, inanimate world. This theory may also be called the molecule-to-man theory of evolution.

The first area in which the theory of evolution falls short is its own name. The theory of evolution does not even qualify as a theory. A theory, according to scientific method, is a hypothesis which is able to be proved or disproved, observed, and capable of falsification. Obviously evolution cannot meet any one of these demands. We are not capable of repeating the experiment to observe it or to be able to falsify it. Evolution has been postulated, but never observed. Scientists can only hypothesize what happened in the beginning. Evolution may serve as a model which certain events may be compared to, but evolution does not scientifically qualify as a theory.

Here, the speaker uses questions to demonstrate his position.

Experts are cited to support his opinion.

Evolution requires a transition, a succession of events. These events are recorded in the history of earth—namely the fossil record. Estimates are given by evolutionists as to how long it took us to evolve, using the fossil record. The oldest fossils known to man are found in the Cambrian period rock, which is estimated to be six-hundred million years old. Every major invertebrate form of life has been found in Cambrian rocks. What kinds of fossils are found in Pre-Cambrian rocks? None! This leaves a gap of 1.2 billion years from the single-celled microscopic life forms to the multicellular, highly complex and highly diverse forms found in the Cambrian Period rocks. Preston Cloud, an evolutionary geologist, states that "there are as yet no records of unequivocal metozos (multicellular forms of life) found in undoubted Cambrian rocks." Axelrod, a biological scientist, is quoted as saying, "When we turn to examine the Pre-Cambrian rocks for the forerunners of these early Cambrian fossils—they are nowhere to be found." According to Duane Gish, biochemistry Ph.D. at the University of California, "Strata of sedimentary rock, some over five-thousand feet thick, lies in unbroken succession below the strata containing the earliest Cambrian fossils. The fossil record does not give any evidence of Pre-Cambrian ancestral forms. Furthermore, not a single fossil that has been found can be considered a transitional form." Also found in the fossil record is the origin of flight. Almost every structure in a nonflying animal would require modification for flight. The resultant transitional forms should be detectable in the fossil record. Flight supposedly evolved four separate times, independent of each other—insects, reptiles, birds, and mammals. E. C. Olson, evolutionist and geologist, states that "as far as flight is concerned there are some very big gaps in the record." He goes on to say that "there is almost nothing to give any information about the history of the origin of flight in insects." As for reptiles, Pterosaurs are found in the Jurassic period (one-hundred million years ago) with no ancestors. Flying bats (mammals) are found in the Eocene period, supposedly fifty-million years old, fully grown, all bat with no ancestors or transitional forms. The first bird found on the fossil record is the archeopteryx. W. E. Swinton, an evolutionist and an expert in birds, explains that "the origin of birds is largely a matter of deduction. There is no fossil evidence of the stages through which the remarkable change from reptile to bird was achieved." Actually the first bird found already had wings and feathers. No transitional forms have been found. All of these finds have shown fully equipped winged animals with no ancestral or transitional forms found.

Again, the speaker uses scientific evidence to question the validity of evolution.

The origin of man is also explained by using transitional forms. The evolutionists depend upon archeological finds to substantiate their claims. These finds are often, if not always, considered in an evolutionary sense, attempting to link man to the ape. Along with this attempt to link man with apes comes doubt and unsurety. As Elwyn Simons, world expert in primates, says, "The time and place of the origin of the primates remains shrouded in mystery." A. S. Romer, paleontologist, states that "as for early primates, no ancestral transitional forms are found." Romer continues, "Little is known, unfortunately, of the fossil history of the South African monkeys." Unfortunate indeed since they are our supposed ancestors. The categorical term used for our ancestors is "catarrhine," denoting monkeys, apes, and man. Simons tells us that "although the word has been used, there is actually no such thing as a protocatarrhine known from the fossil record." What he is saying is that there are no ancestors. Duane Fish, Ph.D. at Berkeley, informs us that "evolutionists believe man's ancestors branched off from apes about thirty million years ago. The earliest hominid (man) fossils are dated at one to three million years old. This leaves twenty-five million years of evolution from which no hominid fossils have been found."

The speaker repeats his thesis. This can be very effective in influencing listeners.

All of these statements surely give us reason to doubt the credibility of the statements regarding the theory of evolution as fact. I don't deny the variation within kinds, but I doubt the evolutionary origin of animals from common ancestors. In 1973, Richard Leakey, world renowned anthropologist and archeologist, gave a lecture in San Diego describing his latest results. He states his convictions that these findings simply eliminate everything we have been taught about human origins. He went on to say that he had nothing to offer in its place.

The speaker begins his final appeal by reviewing previous evidence.

In reviewing the above information I find a great lacking in all three general areas. Not only does evolution fail to validate itself, it also falls short as a theory. The transitional animals needed to link the species have never been found in fossil record and it is admittedly a matter of deduction in reference to flight in birds. The fossil record has not produced any substantial evidence supporting the origin of man as the evolutionists would like us to believe. Neither Professor Dobzhansky nor Professor Goldschmidt had access to any enlightening findings or information which were not accessible to the scientific community. What it comes down to is that it takes a great deal of faith to believe in the "theory" of evolution. Therefore, I believe, from the material presented, that the social or intellectual acceptance of the theory of evolution is not an accurate judgment of scientific data.

In this passage, the speaker returns to his thesis and then makes a strong concluding statement.

Idealism: What's Wrong With It*

Mary Jean Parson

The title of my talk today is probably guaranteed to fill the golf course before lunch. Because *of course* we're all idealists. Pragmatic idealists, many of us. Idealistic pragmatists, many more. But like patriotism and motherhood, idealism just isn't talked about much any more. We talk about sex a good deal—even teach it in the schools. And I've not heard anybody knock apple pie lately. But we don't talk about idealism much anymore.

In a long but revealing introduction, the speaker sets the stage for the speech. She recalls previous meetings with her audience. But she indicates that she will not be talking about her established area of expertise, Affirmative Action.

I don't think I'm betraying a trust when I give you a brief rundown of how this title evolved. I was called and invited to speak to you again this year, and in the course of the conversation I was told, "We'd rather you didn't talk about Affirmative Action this year. We all know our legal obligations and we don't need to hear about it again."

In truth, I suppose I could let your employment numbers speak for themselves, and let *you* decide if there's a need to talk about Affirmative Action anymore.

However, I said, "What *would* you like me to talk about?"

I was told, "Try to do something thought provoking, not just a presentation. Give us something with an unusual perspective on life. Enlarge our horizons. What do you think?"

My first thought was, "At 10:30 in the morning?!" But my *response* was, "You sound like an idealist."

Quick as a wink, he came back, "What's wrong with idealism?"

Well, I allowed as how nothing was wrong with it, and I'd get back to him with my answer.

And then I began to think, what *is* wrong with idealism? Nothing. Except we don't hear much about it anymore.

* Delivered to the New York State Broadcasters Association Annual Executive Conference, New York, July 14, 1975. Quoted by permission of Ms. Parson, former national vice-president, American Women in Radio and Television.

*She makes a
good attempt to
identify with the
needs of her
listeners. A
recurring theme
throughout the
speech is the
broadcasters'
responsibility.*

And in this industry, in this time in our lives, as a people and as individuals, perhaps we'd *better* start talking about it again. Exploring it. Weighing it. *Is* it, like some folks say about God, dead? Or is it somewhere around the corner, waiting to be invited again, into our homes, into the boardrooms, into the smoke-filled rooms, into our consciousness?

You know how it is when you start thinking about someone, the phone rings and they're on the line? Or you start thinking about an idea and you encounter it in everything you read?

Or you start talking with somebody about something that's been troubling you, and you find out *they've* been thinking about it too?

That's what I hope happens with us today.

*The speaker
uses two major
pieces of
evidence to
support her
case. The
conference cited
here and the
work of
Schwartz cited
later.*

A convocation was held at Yale recently, between alumni and the graduate and professional schools, discussing many areas of society's concerns. One panel discussed professional responsibility and ethics. Charles W. Powers, an associate professor in the Divinity School, Robert Stevens of the Law School, and John E. Smith of the Philosophy Department conducted the forum. There was a consensus of the panel that competition has a correlation with honesty: the more intense the competition in business, in politics, in education, the more likely the breakdown in moral behavior.

*Note this idea of
competition. It
will be
important later
when contrasted
with idealism in
the speaker's
thesis.*

I'll read it again: The more intense the *competition* in business, in politics, in education, the more likely the *breakdown* in *moral* behavior.

That's the most chilling "consensus" I believe I've ever read. Because it strikes at the very heart of American society—competition.

We're taught to compete from the time we're children. In fact, recent social scientists have postulated that one of the reasons men have a better chance than women of succeeding in the business world, is that they play competitive games as little boys, while little girls play supportive games, like dolls and nurse.

And yet a group of respected thinkers, representing religion, philosophy, and law, can blandly say—the more intense the competition in business, in politics, in education, the more likely the breakdown in moral behavior.

Can any one of us here say them nay?

I think not:

—when the number of lawyers involved in that swamp called Watergate is enough to boggle the mind and to make one wonder if *any* ethics courses are taught in law schools anymore.

—when organized crime can publicly, and evidently with impunity, cooperate, and indeed, work *for* a secret agency of the federal government.

*She mentions
some general
breakdowns in
society. Later
she will discuss
more specific
ones dealing
with
broadcasters.*

—when doctors go on strike, endangering the lives of thousands, to protest the bilking they are taking from insurance companies for malpractice insurance premiums, instead of attacking the real problem of an elitist AMA which keeps the *number* of doctors low, the *prices* of medical care high, the hours *long,* and the incidence of *real* medical mistakes growing.

—in our own industry, in the forgettable fifties, when payola for DJs was rampant, and giving answers to quiz-show contestants was practiced, all in the name of the almighty mass audience. Ratings! Shares!

—in your own lives, when you take junkets, complete with family, at the expense of a station advertiser or supplier. Do you ever think twice about it?

—when you turn down a Black or a Puerto Rican for a job at your station because he "wouldn't fit in." Do you ever think about it?

—when you pay a woman less than you'd pay a man for the same job, because "she doesn't need to work." Do you ever think about it?

It appears that, indeed, competition *does* cause a breakdown in moral behavior in our society's business world. And we shrug our shoulders and say, "That's business. What does that dame know about business?"

This a good concise statement of the speaker's thesis.

Again, the speaker tries to identify with the audience.

Let's talk about our personal conduct in the business world for a moment.

If you're the station engineer and you were buying a new piece of equipment this year, how many companies romanced you? How many took you and your wife out to dinner? Which one handed you cash when he shook your hand one day? Who did you buy from?

If you're program director at a radio station, when was the last time a record company representative contacted you to offer you free tickets to a concert, or an invitation to a special party, or a "free-lance promotion fee" for helping raise a record on the charts in your area?

If you're a station manager, have you served with the chamber of commerce, the mayor's council, or on boards of other corporations? When you meet with the "leaders" of the community—the politicians, the bankers, the real estate interests, the union leaders—do you come to understand their point of view? And with that understanding, do you tacitly ignore the graft, the corruption, the deals, which we all know mar the lives of the people in your community, *your* constituency, your *audience*?

These are hard questions. They're not pleasant, and they're not meant to place blame. They're questions we have to ask. Not of each other. But of ourselves.

And it's not enough to accept the panacea that society has gone wrong. We must look at the tools of our trade, to see if we use or abuse their power.

A new theorist has appeared on the scene, to explore the almost Pirandellian influence of television. He explores the question of where does reality end and fantasy begin. Not in the *content* of television programming—although there is an ocean of territory to be explored in that area—but in the *tool* itself.

Schwartz's writings are used to clarify the speaker's position.

Tony Schwartz is the author of the book, *The Responsive Chord.* Mr. Schwartz's insights have peculiar power, because he created the ill-famed political commercials for the 1964 presidential campaign, which showed a child innocently picking daisy petals, one after another, as a countdown for a hydrogen bomb blast. Though there was no mention of the presidential candidate at whom the message was aimed, the effect of the commercial was so unnerving that its sponsoring party withdrew it after a few showings. Schwartz appears then to have some credentials for this theory.

Schwartz believes that the *totality* and *instantaneousness* of television, more than its *program content*, contributes, for instance, to more violence in society.

His premises lead him to the shattering conclusion that *"truth* is a *print* ethic, not a standard for *ethical* behavior in *electronic* communication." We must now be concerned not with Gutenberg-based concepts of *truth,* but with the *effects* of electronic communication.

So perhaps it's a matter that what you see *too much of* is what you *come* to *dislike.* Familiarity breeds contempt. Or, perhaps it's a more fearful conclusion. Perhaps we're becoming observers to life, not participants: the *eternal audience.* We'd rather watch football on Sunday afternoon than go out and get some exercise. We'd rather watch somebody make a statement at the voting booth than go out ourselves and vote.

So it's a fundamental question: Is it real, or is it fiction? Is it truth, or is it the illusion of truth? And make no mistake—if it is illusion, then it certainly isn't truth.

She places the audience in a dilemma that she has created: idealism vs. competition.

So we have two dilemmas—recent theories which offer those of us in broadcasting perplexity. We are told that intense competition—the cornerstone of American society—undoubtedly causes a breakdown in moral behavior. And we are told that at least one of the tools we use in our industry—television—is in and of itself a possible enemy of truth to the audience which views it.

Some of you are now saying, what the hell is she talking about? We're in this business to make money. We operate in the public interest, we keep the community happy, we don't offend the FCC, and we sell as much advertising as we can. And that's *it*!

Well, that's exactly what I'm talking about. We are a *competitive, electronic, communications medium.* What you see—and what you hear—is what you get.

We are the greatest *selling* tool in the history of humanity. We can sell anything: horizon property in the middle of the desert, Preparation H, or a presidential candidate. If this industry decides to sell something, the American public buys it—and ultimately the entire world buys it.

This is the final thrust of the speech, the "declaration of

As we enter our Bicentennial year, I would like to propose a "declaration of independence" for broadcasters.

If as an Association, we can believe in this; if we can cause other colleagues in our industry, to pause, to think, to join us. If we can

*independence"
for broadcasters.
She uses the
Bicentennial as
a background
for this idea.*

dedicate ourselves for one year, as individuals and as a group, to the following propositions, we can change the world. We can sell *anything.* Why not sell *ideas?* Why not make fools of those professors at Yale and prove that the power of broadcasting can alter the ethical and moral behavior of those who hear us and see us. So here goes.

We, the broadcasters of the United States, in order to insure a more perfect society, declare these truths to be self-evident:

(1) That *equality* is an idea worth *selling.* That all persons are entitled to equal treatment under the law, whether it be in job opportunity, housing accommodations, schooling, or equal pay for equal work. And that all citizens are entitled to mutual respect, one of another, and shall be treated that way, and shown that way, by broadcasters.

(2) That *honesty* is an idea worth *selling.* That individual honesty, in word and deed, is the bedrock of corporate honesty, governmental honesty, societal honesty. That "the rules of the game" begin at home, in our day-to-day dealings as individuals, and that as broadcasters we will tell the truth, cut the pay-offs and risk the consequences.

*This is really a
revolutionary
idea for an
audience
composed of
supposedly
practical
business leaders.*

(3) That *duty* is an idea worth *selling.* That all persons are endowed by their Creator with certain inescapable duties and that, among those duties, are work, learning, and the pursuit of responsibility; that our attitude toward work determines our relationships with others; that a willingness to learn, meaning an open mind both to the new and the old, is necessary to keep liberty real; that a sense of responsibility to the future as well as to the present is necessary for real happiness.

(4) That *love* is an idea worth *selling.* That a person need love the earth and all its inhabitants, the Creator of the mystery, and one person more than life itself, to have experienced truly that wonderment called living. And that any program, any station break, any commercial, broadcast without that fullness and wisdom called love, shall be banned from *our* air waves.

We declare these ideas—equality, honesty, duty, and love—to be ideas worth selling, and dedicate ourselves to that effort.

*This is the
speaker's strong
final appeal.*

I invite all of you to join me in this declaration of independence. To adopt it, to mean it, to live it, to broadcast it. If we do, we have the power to change the world.

15

SPEAKING ON SPECIAL OCCASIONS

Tips for Speakers

1. In preparing a speech of praise, research the background of the person or group being honored.
2. Dress and use language appropriate to the occasion.
3. When giving an introductory speech, speak briefly and refrain from stealing the main speaker's "thunder."
4. In presenting an award, be factual about the recipient's accomplishments and merits; avoid exaggeration and excessive emotion.
5. In accepting an award, convey your sense of gratitude and the value you place on the honor.
6. In giving an after-dinner speech, keep your remarks light and maintain a sense of humor.

Most public speeches are either "informational" or "persuasive." In this chapter, we shall discuss a third category, "speeches for special occasions." These are ceremonial speeches whose intent is neither to inform nor persuade. Speeches delivered at Fourth of July celebrations, retirement dinners, funerals, graduations, and awards ceremonies are all examples of speeches made to honor, inspire, or amuse.

FOUR CATEGORIES OF SPECIAL OCCASION SPEECHES

We have divided speeches for special occasions into four categories: (1) speeches of praise; (2) introductory speeches; (3) speeches of presentation and acceptance; and (4) speeches of entertainment. Although all speeches for special occasions share common goals, each category has concerns particular to itself. Let us take each of these categories individually before discussing general guidelines for special occasion speeches.

Speeches of Praise

Speeches from this category honor another person's accomplishments or ideals. The purpose of the speech is to praise the person being honored. This is done by presenting the person's achievements in a way that will engender respect, emulation, and appreciation from the audience.

Kinds of Speeches of Praise.   Anniversary addresses, dedicatory speeches, eulogies, and some nominating speeches are all examples of speeches of praise.

Anniversary Addresses.   Throughout history, men and women have met to mark the anniversary of some important event, either political, historical, or personal. There are rallies to honor America's war dead, to mourn the day President Kennedy was assassinated, and to celebrate the signing of the Declaration of Independence. These are ceremonial commemorations. They emphasize basic values and ideals in the hope that the participants will carry on in the spirit of the occasion. In 1963, Martin Luther King, Jr. spoke before a huge crowd which had gathered in Washington to commemorate the centenary of Lincoln's signing of the Emancipation Proclamation. The following excerpts from his speech that day are an excellent example of an effective anniversary address:

Five score years ago, a great American, in whose symbolic shadow we stand today, signed the Emancipation Proclamation. This momentous decree came as a great beacon of light and hope to millions of Negro slaves who had been seared in the flames of withering injustice. It came as the joyous daybreak to end the long night of captivity.

But one hundred years later, the Negro still is not free. One hundred years later, the life of the Negro is still sadly crippled by the manacle of segregation and the chain of discrimination. One hundred years later, the Negro lives on a lonely island of poverty in the midst of a vast ocean of material prosperity. One hundred years later, the Negro is still languishing in the corner of American society and finds himself an exile in his own land. So we have come here today to dramatize a shameful condition. . . .

In a sense we have come to the capital to cash a check. When the architects of our republic wrote the magnificent words of the Constitution and the Declaration of Independence, they were signing a promissory note to which every American was to fall heir. This note was a promise that all men—black men as well as white men—would be guaranteed the unalienable rights of life, liberty, and the pursuit of happiness.

But it is obvious today that America has defaulted on this promissory note insofar as her citizens of color are concerned. Instead of honoring this sacred obligation, America has given the Negro people a bad check— a check that has come back marked "insufficient funds." But we refuse to believe that the bank of justice is bankrupt. We refuse to believe that there are insufficient funds in the great vaults of opportunity in this Nation.

So we have come to cash this check. A check that will give us the riches of freedom and the security of justice.

We have also come to this hallowed spot to remind America that the fierce urgency is now. There is not time to engage in the luxury of cooling off or to take the tranquilizing drug of gradualism. Now is the time to make real the promise of democracy. Now is the time to rise from the dark and desolate valley of segregation to the sunlit path of racial justice. Now is the time to lift our Nation from the quicksands of racial injustice to the solid rock of brotherhood. Now is the time to make justice a reality for all of God's children. . . .

I say to you today, my friends, even though we face the difficulties of today and tomorrow, I still have a dream. It is a dream deeply rooted in the American dream. I have a dream that one day this Nation will rise up and live out the true meaning of its creeds—"we hold these truths to be self-evident that all men are created equal."

I have a dream that one day on the red hills of Georgia the sons of slaves and the sons of former slave owners will be able to sit down together at the table of brotherhood. I have a dream that one day even the state of Mississippi, sweltering with the heat of injustice, sweltering with the heat of oppression, will be transformed into an oasis of freedom and justice.

I have a dream that my four little children will one day live in a Nation where they will not be judged by the color of their skins, but by the conduct of their character. . . .

I have a dream that one day in Alabama, with this vicious racist, its Governor, having his lips dripping the words of interposition and nullification—one day right there in Alabama, little black boys and black girls will be able to join hands with little white boys and girls as brothers and sisters. . . .

I have a dream that one day every valley shall be exalted; every hill and mountain shall be made low, the rough places will be made plane, the crooked places will be made straight, and the glory of the Lord shall be revealed, and all flesh shall see it together. . . .[1]

Dedicatory Speeches.   A dedicatory speech is given when a building, monument, endowment, etc., is named or awarded in honor of a person, group, or institution. Dedicatory speeches marked the opening of such buildings as the Washington Monument, the JFK Library, and the Walter Reade Medical Hospital. One of the most famous dedicatory speeches is Abraham Lincoln's address at the dedication of the cemetery on the battlefield at Gettysburg, Pennsylvania in 1863:

Launching a new ship could require a dedicatory speech.

Fourscore and seven years ago, our fathers brought forth upon this continent a new nation, conceived in liberty, and dedicated to the proposition that all men are created equal. Now we are engaged in a civil war, testing whether that nation, or any nation so conceived and so dedicated, can long endure. We are met on a great battlefield of that war. We are met to dedicate a portion of it as the final resting place of those who here gave their lives that the nation might live. It is altogether fitting and proper that we should do this. But in a larger sense we cannot dedicate— we cannot consecrate—we cannot hallow this ground. The brave men, living and dead, who struggled here, have consecrated it far above our poor power to add or detract. The world will little note, nor long remember, what we say here, but it can never forget what they did here. It is for us, the living, rather to be dedicated here to the unfinished work that they have thus so nobly advanced. It is rather for us to be here dedicated to the great task remaining before us, that from these honored dead we take increased devotion to that cause for which they here gave the last full measure of devotion; that we here highly resolved that these dead shall not have died in vain; that this nation, under God, shall have a new birth of freedom, and that government of the people, by the people, for the people, shall not perish from the earth.

[1] From "I Have a Dream" by Martin Luther King, Jr. © 1963 by Martin Luther King, Jr. Reprinted by permission of Joan Daves.

ABRAHAM LINCOLN was born near Hodgenville, Kentucky, February 12, 1809. A lawyer and congressman, Lincoln ran unsuccessfully for the Senate in 1858, but his famous debates with Stephen Douglas over slavery brought him prominence. In 1860, he was nominated for president and narrowly elected. South Carolina then seceded and the Civil War broke out on April 12, 1861. In 1863, Lincoln delivered the Gettysburg Address, perhaps the most famous American speech. His speeches were characterized by eloquent compassion and simple, effective language. He was assassinated in 1865, shortly after his second inauguration.

Eulogies. A eulogy is delivered in honor of someone who has recently died. In most instances, a member of the clergy delivers the eulogy at the funeral, although a relative or close friend of the deceased may also speak.

Following are excerpts from a famous eulogy—Nehru's remarks upon the death of Gandhi:

> *Friends and comrades, the light has gone out of our lives and there is darkness everywhere. I do not know what to tell you and how to say it. Our beloved leader, Bapu as we called him, the father of the nation, is no more. Perhaps I am wrong to say that. Nevertheless, we will not see him again as we have seen him for these many years. We will not run to him for advice and seek solace from him, and that is a terrible blow, not to me only, but to millions and millions in this country, and it is a little difficult to soften the blow by any other advice that I or anyone else can give you.*
>
> *The light has gone out, I said, and yet I was wrong. For the light that shone in this country was no ordinary light. The light that has illumined this country for these many years will illumine this country for many more years, and a thousand years later that light will still be seen in this country and the world will see it and it will give solace to innumerable hearts. For that light represented the living truth . . . the eternal truths, reminding us of the right path, drawing us from error, taking this ancient country to freedom.*[2]

Nominating Speeches. Many nominating speeches are designed to inform voters of a candidate's strengths and to persuade them to vote for him or her. Most political nominations are clearly persuasive in

[2] Houston Peterson, ed. *A Treasury of the World's Great Speeches*, pp. 810–811.

intent. Others, however, are given primarily as a form of personal tribute. Speeches which nominate a person to an honorary position or to receive an award generally fall into this category. They are used to highlight a candidate's good qualities. Consider the following:

> *He has been tested and proven in our Democratic process of political campaign and election. He has had long and distinguished experience in public life as an executive and as a legislator. And every step has been marked by excellence and achievement.*
>
> *He knows the problems of all of our people in every part of our Nation. He knows the world and he knows its problems; and he has shown understanding and a deep concern for the strength of our country and for the peace of the world. He matches energy in the right with compassion for the needs of others. He matches strong convictions with understanding of the convictions of others.*
>
> *If you select him, you can proudly say to the American people, "This is not a sectional choice. This is not just merely the way to balance the ticket. This is simply the best man in America for this job. . . . I hope that you will choose as the next vice-president of the United States my close, my longtime, my trusted colleague, Senator Hubert Humphrey of Minnesota.*[3]

Guidelines for Organizing a Speech of Praise.

Know your subject.   If the person or institution being honored is not familiar to you, research the background. Try to look beyond the cold facts to understand the essence or spirit of the individual or organization. When praising a person, make your speech as personal as possible. Do not merely list his or her professional accomplishments. A list of achievements tells us little about the personality of a man or woman. The more human you can make your subject, the more an audience will understand why he or she is being honored. In praising an institution or organization, cite how it has affected the community and its citizens. List its achievements in a way the audience can understand and appreciate. You can only present a subject sympathetically if you know it well.

Don't lie.   If the subject being honored is well known as a loud-mouthed, strict disciplinarian, do not describe him or her as soft-spoken, and easygoing. There are tactful ways to tell the truth. More-

---

[3] Lyndon B. Johnson, August 26, 1964, as quoted in *History of American Presidential Elections,* Vol. IV, ed. by Arthur M. Schlesinger, Jr. (New York: Chelsea House, 1971), p. 3673.

over, certain points can be avoided altogether. It is possible to concentrate only on a person's good points. Remember no one is perfect. The main point is to make the subject as praiseworthy as possible while letting him or her be recognizably him- or herself.

Be appropriate. Ceremonies and official occasions require ceremonial and official presentations. Blue jeans and locker room slang are as inappropriate for a funeral as formal wear and an undertaker's demeanor would be for the annual awards ceremony of a bowling league. Audiences at ceremonial occasions expect something special, particularly at funerals, weddings, and graduations. This is not to suggest that all special occasion speeches must be serious in tone. On the contrary, award ceremonies, initiations, anniversaries, and weddings are happy, joyous events. Speeches given at them should reflect the levity, warmth, and good humor that they inspire. The good speaker knows when it is appropriate to be serious and dignified and when it is fitting to be lighthearted and gay.

Introductory Speeches

Have you ever heard an introductory speech that was twice as long as the speech that followed it? Or introductions that made you want *not* to listen to the speaker being introduced? Have you ever felt that an introductory speaker had no personal knowledge of the person he or she was supposed to be introducing? Introductory speeches are perhaps the most common special occasion speeches. Unfortunately, however, they are also generally poorly prepared and badly delivered.

There are several reasons why introductory speeches are so dismal, and all are the fault of the speaker.

Many occasions call for introductory speeches.

1. *Many speakers do not know the person they are introducing.* Instead of presenting someone to the audience, they content themselves with a dull listing of the person's professional accomplishments. Nothing is more boring than to hear an endless list of committees, occupations, and awards. Professional achievement should be mentioned, but it is more important to introduce the audience to a recognizable character.

2. *Many introductory speakers are too long winded.* They forget that their purpose is to introduce the main speaker. They themselves have only a supporting role. The introduction is given solely to focus the audience's attention on the principal speaker and his or her topic. Although an introductory speech should never last longer than three or four minutes, it can often be even much shorter than that. If the main speaker is already well known to the audience, a mere "Ladies

and Gentlemen, the president of the United States" is enough. On other occasions, speakers may require a lengthier—but still restricted—introduction:

> This gathering tonight is more than a meeting of Rotary Clubs of different cities. It is a meeting of fellow Rotarians of different nationalities and different languages. We here exemplify the true ideals of Rotary International.
>
> Our speaker tonight fits perfectly into this meeting. He is a Mexican, a fellow citizen of you who are members of the Mexican Club and who are our gracious hosts tonight.
>
> He acquired a good part of his formal education in the United States at Jefferson College in Louisiana. Moreover, in the good American tradition he worked in the United States to earn his way through that college. He returned to Mexico to complete his education at the University of Mexico, and in the years that have gone by has become one of the outstanding educators of Mexico. He was chosen by his government to become the Consul General of Mexico at Los Angeles, the most important consular post in the Mexican diplomatic service. Possessed of a keen insight into human nature, he has acquired an amazing understanding of the characteristics of the people in the United States. In addition, he is a fellow Rotarian, a member of the Rotary Club of Mexico City.
>
> No other man is better qualified to be the principal speaker at this meeting—a meeting of Mexicans and North Americans—a meeting of Rotarians, men brought together through the fellowship and ideals of Rotary.
>
> We in the United States have learned to admire and respect him as much as you admire and respect him. It is with a great deal of pleasure that I present to you, Doctor Francisco Villagran, Consul General of Mexico.[4]

3. *Many introductory speeches steal the main speaker's thunder.* Some try so hard to prepare the audience for the main speaker and his or her topic that they almost give the main speech themselves. To avoid this, remember your function: to introduce. Say the minimum necessary to fulfill that role and then sit down. Let the principal speaker give the principal speech.

4. *Many introductory speakers are artificial and forced.* They become intoxicated with their own hyperbole. They overpraise their subject. They fake interest for the speaker and his topic. They affect artificial enthusiasm. To avoid a speech overdecorated with artificial flowers, stick to the facts.

5. *Having made his or her remarks, an introductory speaker often*

[4] Herbert V. Prochnow, ed., *The Toastmaster's Handbook* (Englewood Cliffs, N.J.: Prentice-Hall, 1968), pp. 48–49.

behaves as though the job is done. But, in fact, their responsibility is twofold: (1) to introduce the speaker; and (2) to listen to what the main speaker has to say. An audience looks to the introductory speaker, seated at the head table, on the dais, or in the front row, to help prompt their behavior. If the introductory speaker fails to listen to the speaker who follows, the audience may also find it hard to pay attention. Introductory speakers help set the tone for the occasion. Once that tone is established, the introductory speaker must also help to maintain it.

Many occasions require speeches of introduction. The following two speeches are examples of the various types of introductory speech. The first is the kind of relaxed introduction that should be delivered at a business function. The second is a more formal speech delivered before a national audience.

> *First, may I present Miss Moore, that lovely and gracious lady who, at this very moment, is transcribing my poor words on the right here. Miss Moore is a skillful secretary, court reporter, stenotypist, and ticket seller. Verily, she is the quintessence of an amanuensis. And since you may not have the time to look up those words as I did, I would tell you that they simply mean, in the current slang of our children, that Miss Moore is on the beam, she's in the groove, and she's cooking with gas!*[5]

> *Mr. Shriver has served with great distinction in a number of high and difficult positions. President Kennedy chose him to organize and direct the Peace Corps, while under President Johnson he was the first director of the Office of Economic Opportunity. He later served as Ambassador to France under both President Johnson and President Nixon. A distinguished business leader, his life has been marked by a special dedication to the needs of the poor and to those who suffer from racial injustice.*[6]

Speeches of Presentation and Acceptance

Whenever people gather to honor someone by bestowing an award, two types of speeches are delivered. The person presenting the award talks about the recipient's accomplishments and explains why he or she deserves the honor. Later, the recipient replies with a speech of acceptance, thanking the donors of the award and explaining how much it means to him or her. In preparing to speak on these occasions, both presenter and recipient should remember that the pur-

[5] Herbert V. Prochnow, *The Toastmaster's Handbook*, pp. 50–51.
[6] George McGovern, "Recommendation for Vice President," *Vital Speeches of the Day*, August 15, 1972, p. 644.

Speeches of acceptance should avoid exaggeration and excessive emotion.

pose of these speeches is to communicate sincerely the honor, appreciation, and recognition felt both by those presenting the award and those receiving it. Moreover, the style of the speeches should correspond both to the honor bestowed and to the type of ceremony in which it is given.

When presenting an award, a speaker should be as factual as possible. The person is receiving the award because he or she deserves it. Let the accomplishments of the recipient speak for themselves. A speaker often has to state the criteria upon which the candidate has been judged and the goals and ideals for which the award stands. This is best done simply and honestly. Avoid exaggeration and excessive emotion. As in any public speaking situation, clarity, brevity, and appropriateness are virtues.

The same holds for the speaker accepting an award. Do not pretend that the award is less or more than it actually is. False modesty and artificial enthusiasm are always distasteful. Don't pretend that receiving a blue ribbon for the best cake at the country fair is as important as a Nobel Prize. If such a ribbon *is* more important, that's fine, say so. But don't lie about it.

The length and style of these speeches vary with the situation. When awards for the same accomplishment are being presented to several recipients, one presentation speech to include all the awardees may be most appropriate. This will still enable each of the recipients to accept the award and express his or her own thanks individually. The acceptance speech in this instance should be a brief "thank you." Only if the award is unique and the occasion special should the speech be a long one.

Speeches of Entertainment

There are many ceremonies, serious in nature, at which appreciation and honor are officially extended to worthy recipients. There are also, however, special occasions—equally ceremonial and official—which call for speeches of entertainment or good will. Friar's Club Roasts are a classic example of this type of special occasion, in which the guest of honor is praised with jokes and speeches of ironic humor. The most common form for a speech of entertainment is the after dinner speech. The following excerpt is from an after-dinner speech by James Russell Lowell, delivered while he was Ambassador to Britain:

> There is one virtue, I am sure, in after-dinner oratory, and that is brevity; and as to that I am reminded of a story. [Laughter.] The Lord Chief Justice has told you what are the ingredients of after-dinner oratory. They are the joke, the quotation, and the platitude; and the successful platitude, in my judgment, requires a very high order of genius. I believe that I have not given you a quotation, but I am reminded of something which I heard when very young—the story of a Methodist clergyman in America. He was preaching at a camp meeting, and he was preaching upon the miracle of Joshua, and he began his sermon with this sentence: "My hearers, there are three motions of the sun. The first is the straightforward or direct motion of the sun; the second is the retrograde or backward motion of the sun and the third is the motion mentioned in our text—'the sun stood still.' " [Laughter.]
>
> Now, gentlemen, I don't know whether you see the application of the story—I hope you do. The after-dinner orator at first begins and goes straightforward—that is the straightforward motion of the sun. Next he

Speeches of entertainment are often given to tease a guest of honor.

goes back and begins to repeat himself—that is the backward motion of the sun. At last he has the good sense to bring himself to the end, and that is the motion mentioned in our text, as the sun stood still. [Great laughter, in the midst of which Mr. Lowell resumed his seat.][7]

As with other types of special occasion speeches, there are guidelines to follow in preparing after-dinner speeches. First of all, the purpose of an after-dinner speech is usually to entertain. The occasion is a sociable one; the audience has just finished eating; they are relaxed and feeling good. Don't spoil the mood. Keep your remarks light and friendly. Now is not the time for complexity or heaviness. Above all, be brief. Your audience may already be relaxed, but a long speech will certainly bore them.

Four Principles of Speeches of Entertainment.

Be relevant.   If you are addressing an audience of business people, choose a topic to which they can relate—like sales or rising costs. When speaking to a group of librarians, talk about books or the interesting characters who frequent libraries. Since the purpose of the speech is to entertain and promote good will, slant the topic so it is lighthearted and funny rather than serious or controversial.

Keep a sense of humor.   Remember, after-dinner speeches are supposed to be fun. If you don't appear to be in a good mood and having a nice time, no one else will either. By keeping your speech pleasant and good-natured, you avoid offending your audience and turning the relaxed, friendly affair into an occasion for hurt feelings and distress.

Be adaptable.   Tailor your speech to appeal to the audience you are addressing. The speech you gave at the banquet for the Sisters of Mercy may not be as humorous when delivered to the United Auto Workers, and vice versa. Audiences must be treated individually. Although the essence of your speech may be unchanged, the examples and jokes you use to illustrate it should change to suit different audiences. The best way to accomplish this is to know your audience. Before you accept the invitation to speak, be sure that you understand the occasion and know who the audience will be, what purpose the event is to serve, and who and what else will be on the program. Thus informed, you can adapt yourself and your speech to fit the occasion.

[7] Lewis Copeland, ed., *The World's Great Speeches* (New York: Dover, 1958), pp. 659–661.

Be brief and to the point. This cannot be overemphasized or repeated too often: *The most effective after-dinner speeches are short and to the point.* Well-fed minds are sluggish. They cannot digest complex explanations and lengthy illustrations. Your audience will understand more and have a much better time if you illustrate one or two major points with simple, humorous examples.

A good tactic is to plan several cut-off points which you can use if you need to end your speech prematurely. If you see that your audience is nodding off or becoming restless, bring the speech to a logical close by stopping at the first available cut-off point.

Summary: Guidelines for Speeches for Special Occasions

As you may already have noted, there are similarities among the four major types of speeches for special occasions. The following guidelines apply to all four of these categories:

1. <u>Be informed</u>. When preparing your speech, find out all you can about the history of the event, the people involved, the audience you will be addressing, the purpose of the occasion, the other speakers and events on the program.

2. <u>Do your job</u>. If you are to introduce the program's main speaker, prepare a speech that conveys a sense of that person in a knowledgable and positive way. Remember, you are not the main speaker—you are only there to introduce. If you have to praise a person or institution, speak to make the audience appreciate him, her, or it. If you are to present an award, be certain you tell what the award stands for and why the recipient deserves it. When accepting an award, say what the honor means to you. If you are asked to deliver an after-dinner speech, your job is to entertain. People understand and appreciate what is familiar to them. For an after-dinner speech, pick a topic that relates to that audience and salt your speech with lighthearted illustrations that they will recognize and enjoy.

3. <u>Give the audience what it expects</u>. Meeting an audience's expectations means tailoring the style of your speech, not its contents. When you attend a funeral, you expect to hear a eulogy. When you attend a graduation ceremony, you expect a speech of congratulation. Life is filled with people's expectations. As a public speaker, it is your responsibility to be aware of what an audience expects on a special occasion and to fulfill it.

4. Treat the occasion with the proper respect. Fit your speech to the occasion. At most functions, the audience consists of people who are involved to a greater or lesser extent with the purpose of the occasion. As a speaker, you will lose the audience's attention, and quite possibly cause offense, if you fail to convey that you share or at least respect their feelings.

Exercises

1. Develop a three-minute speech of praise for your father or mother.
2. Introduce to the class your best friend. Make sure that your speech is factual and praiseworthy of the person being introduced.
3. Suppose you have just been given the "Best All-around Student" award by the local Rotary Club. Develop a three- or four-minute speech graciously accepting the award.
4. Develop a short humorous speech to your young cousin who is thinking of attending college. The topic is "What to Look for in College." Try your hand at being as funny as you can in reflecting on your college experiences.

By now, you may wonder how all of the material in the book ultimately fits together. For fifteen chapters we have discussed how to make good public speeches. The emphasis has been less on *using speech-making skills* than on *acquiring the skills themselves.* Public speaking skills are important because they can be used in a wide variety of contexts. And at this point, you should be able to deliver a coherent and effective public speech in any forum.

This chapter, however, will look at how to use these skills in the "real world." It has become a cliché in recent years that today's students are more "career conscious." They want their academic programs to relate to their careers after graduation. It may surprise you to learn that public speaking is a skill directly related to career success.

This chapter is intended to draw together all of the material on public speaking covered previously into a final framework involving careers and career organizations.

Our discussion will focus first on the nature and impact of careers. The emphasis will then shift to how specific aspects of public speaking can affect one's choice of and success in a career. Specifically, the chapter will cover: (1) how a job may involve public speaking; (2) the ways that people make speeches in organizations; and (3) how the skills discussed in this book can be used effectively in groups and organizations.

CAREERS AND CAREER DECISION MAKING

We spend more than forty years of our life working. All of us care about our present or future career. You are concerned, or you would not be in college. Yet, many students are still confused or uncertain about what they will do after graduation. Look at three typical students:

Doris: She wanted to be a teacher but found that she does not like to be in front of people. Doris's college puts student teachers in front of classes early in the program. When she had to be a student teacher in a sixth-grade class, she hated every minute of it. Now, she does not know what to do after college or even if she wants to finish.

Bill: In high school Bill was a star athlete. But in college he did not have much success against bigger and faster players. He had always wanted to be a professional athlete. This now looks impossible. Bill feels that he has no other abilities that will earn him success.

speaking and CAREERS

Tips for Speakers

1. All careers require at least some public speaking skills.
2. To be hired and promoted, one must think critically, listen well, and speak effectively.
3. Planning, selling, managing, reporting, and leading in any organization all depend on effective communication.
4. Formal group discussion is a distinct communication skill.
5. Formal groups require skills in organizing, analyzing, presenting, and summarizing.
6. Leadership within organizations requires public speaking and communication skills.

Many students have problems deciding what to do after graduation.

Gene: He attended college to please his parents. After four years of C's and a lot of fun, he is ready to graduate. But he has no idea what he wants to do. He has not given his career one thought in four years.

Some students are lucky. From the first day on campus, they know what career they want. Others have no idea. But most, like Doris and Bill, and perhaps like you, fall somewhere in between.

One of the best questions that a good consumer of higher education can ask of his or her college program is: *What will this help me do?* How will studying this subject make me a better person and/or professional? Public speaking should not be a subject that you eventually consider "irrelevant" to life. Instead, as you enter your career, you may remember your speech class as one of those that taught you skills that you can use everyday.

Current Trends in Career Decision Making

Before looking directly at public speaking skills, let us examine some of the current trends in career decision making. It is important to understand what a career is and how your career will influence your outlook and character.

Life-Career Path.   One's career is only a part of a person's entire life plan. People who study career planning recommend drawing up 1-, 5-, and 20-year life plans. Often people only plan their life from year to year. They refuse to take any long-term view. Let us suppose that your real goal in life is not to be president of a company but to retire at age 50 in a warm climate where you can swim and play golf all year. To reach that goal, you will need to take certain calculated steps at each stage of your life. If you do not have a long-term plan,

you will be unlikely to reach this ultimate goal. As you are challenged to think about your career in this chapter, consider developing a life-career plan based on long-term planning.

Today, people often change careers more than once in their lives.

Multiple Careers.   You will probably have several careers in your life rather than just one. In your classes you may already have seen signs of this. Housewives are starting a second career (as a student) as a step toward a third. In southern California in the late 1960s, a slowdown in the aerospace industry caused a number of engineers to change careers because there were no jobs in their field. We see people retiring earlier in their first career, so that they can start a second, or even a third. Remember, however, that all careers demand at least some skills. We must gain the right skills to prepare for the multiple careers that many of us will have.

You should also *expect* to make career changes throughout your work life. If you find yourself faced with a potential career change, relax; you will not be alone. In fact, it would be odd not to make some changes.

Work-Career-Earning: A Living Distinction.   The distinction between these three elements has not always been clear. At one time or another, all of us have to earn a living. We may or may not earn a living through our career. And, we may or may not "work" at our career. (Work may mean one thing to you and something entirely different to me.) One man, for example, drives a catering truck to earn a living. But his real work and career is as a minister to a small congregation in a fundamentalist church. Even though catering provides most of his income, he devotes most of his energies to the church. Many of us may find ourselves in a similar situation. We may become heavily involved in projects that do not help us earn a living. We should keep these distinctions in mind when we plan our own careers.

Midlife Career Change.   Another common trend is the midlife career change. For years, a man was a newspaper reporter. He was even promoted to assistant editor. But he became increasingly disenchanted with workaday journalism. He finally decided that he wanted to be a high school basketball coach. He went back to college and now coaches varsity basketball and teaches journalism at a small high school. With people living longer today and with the wider access to formal and informal education, we should see more midlife career changes.

COMMUNICATIONS AND CAREER DECISION MAKING

At some point all of us have to make a career decision. And one of the most critical factors to consider is whether you are skilled enough in public communication to do an effective job. For regardless of your present or future career, you will need the public-communication skills mentioned in this book. Communication, especially public communication, is required in almost every job.

Basic Public Communication Skills Requirements

Getting Hired. Students want their college education to help them get a job. College should increase one's *hirability*. Normally, to get a job, applicants have to show:

1. Appropriate technical competence
2. Willingness to work
3. Ability to relate experience
4. Appropriate educational background
5. Communication skills

Applicants are first required to submit a resumé of their experience and qualifications. Then, the appropriate candidates are called in for a job interview. This interview tests the applicant's ability to do the job. A potential job applicant is, in effect, making a persuasive speech with him or herself as the subject. You must persuade an interviewer that you can do the job better than the other applicants. To do this you must show that you are:

1. Able to get along with peers
2. Motivated to work
3. Able to understand what is required in the job
4. A good communicator
5. Potentially an asset to the organization

The person who does these things well in the interview will be much more likely to be offered the job than someone who does them poorly.

Talking to People. While every position does not involve giving formal speeches, almost every job does require good, well-organized speech. If you are a manager, you will have to talk with your subordinates often and with some sensitivity. If you become an architect you will be making presentations, sometimes very formal, to diverse groups. If you become a teacher, you will have to give lessons that your students can understand. Just about any career will require you to talk coherently. More will be said about this topic later in the chapter.

Listening Ability.   As we stated in Chapter 2, listening is a neglected skill. But while listening is important in all public speaking situations, it is critical on most jobs. Business executives complain constantly that their younger employees lack the ability to listen. Getting the point in a speech or a discussion may be difficult, but it *must* be done by a person on the job. Grasping the relevant information and applying it is what listening is all about. This requires the abilities to organize, interpret, and analyze—some of the important skills that have been covered in this book. Any organization that hires you will expect you to have good listening skills.

Thinking Critically.   Chapter 6 was devoted to critical thinking. Regardless of your field, you will need to:

1. Make decisions
2. Argue for your positions
3. Reach sound conclusions

These skills all involve critical thinking.

In a job you will find that many of the problems that arise do not have easy solutions. To solve them, the younger worker is often forced to go beyond his or her formal training. As one learns to develop a critical, searching attitude that comes with being a good consumer of public communication, the talent to think critically seems to develop naturally.

Promotability.   Once on the job, you must continue to "sell yourself" within the organization. When considering a particular job after college, students are often concerned about their potential to be promoted—to become a manager. In management, you direct the work of others. The manager must be able to handle both "people" and work, be it selling, nursing, or whatever. Candidates for promotion are often interviewed within the organization. Often one of the abilities that affects promotion is the candidate's public communication skills. Take the following situation:

Anne was hired out of college as an assistant branch manager at a bank. After five years, she applied to become a manager of another branch. To be promoted, Anne had to have interviews with the executive committee of the bank, a group of managers of other branches, and a committee of employees at the branch where the opening was. In each of these situations, she had to sell herself. She was asked to persuade the interviewers that she was qualified to be a branch manager.

People at the Top.   Some of you will probably move to the top of the corporate ladder. As one rises in management, more formal and informal public presentations are often required. Presidents of organizations give speeches to many audiences. The president speaks to people both inside and outside the organization. He or she represents the company in many formal and informal situations. Often the company's image is determined by the president's ability to speak in public.

WORK AND PUBLIC COMMUNICATION

Let us now look at the specific day-to-day activities that are important in any organization.

Planning

All organizations plan. There are long-term plans and short-term plans. When organizations make plans, they use three skills covered in this book: collecting data, organizing data, and presenting the plan.

Collecting Data.   To plan you need to collect data about the organization, its potential, its past performance, and its competition. This means deciding what information should be included and what should be excluded. It means separating what is relevant from what is unrelated to the organization.

Organizing the Data.   The data must next be organized to make a *projection*. Essentially, this projection is the plan. The information from the past and present is used to plan for the future. An organized plan has an introduction, a body, and a conclusion. The conclusion is based on the data gathered for the plan.

Presenting the Plan.   Eventually, the planner gives an informative speech about the plan. To give an effective speech, the planner must analyze the audience and tailor the presentation to that group. The planner normally develops visual aids and supporting material to make the presentation as clear as possible.

Professional planners are not the only ones who engage in this activity. Department heads developing their budgets, basketball coaches logging the work for the season, or the professional writer designing the format for an annual report, all have to plan. And, planning involves many public speaking skills.

Selling

Selling clearly involves public speaking. Again, it is not just salespersons who must sell. Many people within organizations are in "sales." Bus drivers, receptionists, repair personnel are all in effect salespeople, whatever they may be called. Most of us will be involved in some type of sales or public relations activities in our jobs.

When you sell, you seek to persuade by applying public speaking skills. The successful salesperson does three things:

1. Analyzes the audience
2. Determines which appeals will work best with that audience
3. Develops the right arguments

These were the essential tasks that were discussed in Chapters 13 and 14. When you are selling, you are simply practicing the principles of persuasion.

Managing

The manager uses public speaking in many ways. A *good* manager is expected to have *good* public speaking skills. Let us look at what a manager is expected to do and how public communication affects what he or she does.

Directs.   Directing others is a manager's basic task. As a supervisor, he or she is responsible for subordinates. Whether conducting a meeting, disciplining a worker, or running a department, a manager must have good speaking skills.

Motivates.   One of a manager's primary challenges is to keep his or her employees motivated. This involves mastering two types of speeches: (1) speeches of information designed to motivate employees by keeping them aware; (2) and speeches of persuasion—"pep talks"—to keep employees involved in their work. These informative and persuasive speeches will be given both to small groups of two or three or to much larger audiences. No matter what size the audience, however, if the manager is disorganized and unprepared, the chances are that his or her subordinates will not be motivated by the presentation.

Develops. A good manager will help his or her subordinates grow and develop. This means that he or she will try to show the employees how they can reach their own individual goals in the organization. Again, this will require speaking to persuade and inform.

Reporting

You have to speak persuasively to sell an idea.

Like sales, reporting is essentially speech communication. Most jobs require a person to report on the results of his or her work. Reporting usually involves speeches of information, but sometimes the reporter also needs to be persuasive in order to sell an idea or concept. Each time you make an oral report, you use a public speaking skill. Let us look at two examples of reporting in an organization:

1. The Product Development Department in the Townsend Corporation is responsible for the new designs and concepts that Townsend markets. Each member works on a design and develops a model. Then the designer of each model must report to the executive committee. The designers use their reports to inform the committee of what they have been working on and to persuade the committees that these designs are potential new products for Townsend.

2. Faculty members of a university's psychology department undergo a self-study every five years to determine whether the department is meeting the needs of its students. The faculty studies its curriculum, national trends in the field, where graduates have been placed, and what the students think about the program. After the self-study has been completed, the faculty members report the results to the dean. The results are then used to change the department's program.

Leading

All organizations need leaders. Leaders conduct meetings, train, instruct, and encourage workers to share in decision making. All of these activities involve speech communication. Let us look at two situations that call for a leader with public speaking skills:

1. Before Jon became the plant manager, the employees often complained about not knowing what was going on in the organization. Time and effort were wasted because people were not kept informed. Jon decided to hold a regular weekly meeting with all employees. He

limited the meeting to 15 minutes, but within that time he discussed what had happened during the week. In a short while, as the workers became more aware of what their company was doing, they also became more satisfied with it.

2. Rev. Doris Carlin decided that her parish council wasted too much time. Their meetings ran on because there was no agenda or schedule detailing which church business was to be discussed. The council now sets a precise agenda for each of the monthly meetings. The meetings last only two hours, and Doris sees that the meetings follow the agenda as closely as possible. This reform has kept the meetings on track.

ORGANIZATIONS, GROUPS, AND PUBLIC COMMUNICATION SKILLS

All groups need leaders.

All organizations bring people together to share common interests or goals. These can be as simple as a desire to play bridge every Wednesday night or as complex as a need to mobilize a community to fight the dangers of pollution. The structure of organizations may vary greatly; but their overall purpose is to set goals, to define the problems in reaching those goals, and to discuss how to solve those problems. Large organizations are often divided into smaller groups to facilitate discussion and decision making. For example, during the 1960s and 1970s, the United States government (truly a large organization) created a number of so-called *task forces* (the Warren Commission, the Kerner Commission, etc.) to study particular problems (the assassination of President Kennedy, racial unrest) and to recommend action. Indeed, it has become a cliché to greet each new problem with a new committee.

Nevertheless, although such groups are often an excuse to avoid facing a problem, group discussion is vital to any organization. And organizations have become increasingly important in modern American society—from citizen-action committees to self-help groups. Learning how to use public speaking skills in such groups is a vital part of the communication process.

Formal and Informal Groups

Groups within large organizations can be divided into formal and informal groups. When the president of a corporation calls in all the vice-presidents, that is a formal group. It is also called a *hierarchical* group. This means that a superior has called a meeting of subordinates. Another example is a staff meeting at a magazine in which an editor-in-chief summons the writers so that he can assign articles.

Not all formal groups are hierarchical, however. For instance, if the teachers of a high school meet to discuss the school's curriculum, this is a formal group but not a hierarchical one, since the teachers are equals.

Formal groups differ in many ways from informal groups; but the principal difference is that in a formal group, members reflect their positions in the organization. The same group of individuals may meet both formally and informally. When the sales manager of a department store meets with the sales staff to discuss the new spring line of clothes, that is a formal meeting. When the same group meet to go bowling, that is an informal meeting.

Although informal groups can be both useful and important, much of the important work of an organization is performed by its formal groups. The tasks performed by these groups depend on good communication and are governed by specific rules of conduct. Let us now discuss some of the forms these groups take.

Types of Formal Groups

As we have seen, formal groups may be task forces, committees, commissions, or any groups which are officially created to serve a particular purpose. Often, this purpose is to consider and formulate policy, and the discussions are conducted before an audience. These discussions usually take the form of a panel discussion, a symposium, or a debate.

Panel Discussion.   This is one of the best methods for conducting group discussion before an audience. It puts the informal give-and-take of discussion on a more formal basis. The panel usually consists of four to eight members who sit facing the audience in a semicircle around a table or on a raised platform. The panel leader opens the discussion and acts as chairman. He or she tells the audience what the panel will discuss, introduces the members, and directs questions to persons on the panel.

Panel members discuss the subject among themselves, questioning one another, or adding their own opinions to the statements of their colleagues. While the discussion resembles informal group conversation, it is in fact highly structured. Panel members are speaking for the benefit of an audience, not simply for themselves.

Symposium.   In a symposium, three to five persons deliver short speeches before an audience. Each speaker presents his or her views about the issue in question. The speakers do not—as in a panel discussion—talk directly to each other. Questions are generally reserved for a question-and-answer period after all of the speakers have presented their speeches.

A symposium is more formal than a panel discussion, but less so than a debate. Its purpose is to give an issue a thorough airing. In a symposium, the speakers have formed their conculsions before they speak. Their speeches present these conclusions to the audience.

The leader of a symposium is simply the chairperson. He or she introduces the speakers, makes a few opening remarks, and conducts the question-and-answer period.

Debate. Debate is, perhaps, the oldest form of discussing public policy. Unlike panel discussions and symposia, a debate is a form of advocacy. A debater is openly trying to persuade the audience of his or her point of view. A debater may critically discuss his or her opponents' presentations and rebut their arguments.

Usually, both sides in a debate speak from the same platform on the same occasion, and the rules are agreed upon in advance. Often, however, there are public debates in which the speakers never meet face to face. In a sense, a political campaign is a running debate that lasts several weeks or months (or even years). The candidates argue public issues, and pursue their interests in speech after speech, reply and counterreply, before audiences across a state or the country.

The Pattern of Group Discussion

Group discussion is an important facet of communication. Whatever your future career plans, you will inevitably be involved in some form of group discussion. Group discussion combines elements of public speaking and more casual interaction, but it is a distinct skill. Often, people who are excellent at public speaking are unsuccessful in group discussion because they are unable to perceive the difference between them. While a good public speaker must be able to lead his listeners through the topic of his speech, a member of a group discussion must follow the discussion, ask the right questions, and adhere to the group's overall plan.

Group Communication Skills. Group interaction is most successful when group members are aware of the skills needed for group communication. Let us consider six of the most important of these skills.

Organizing. Organizing skills include planning agendas and getting agreement on details of timing and arrangement. All groups need a framework within which to operate, and the framework should reflect the task to be accomplished. Arranging for the details of the meeting is often more important than proposing an idea for a solution. Regardless of the problem, meetings must be organized. This skill is often overlooked, but no group can function without at least one skilled organizer. This member is the one who reminds the others of their responsibilites and suggests how to fulfill them.

Analyzing. Groups need members who can dissect, focus, and direct an issue under consideration. These are analyzing skills. Analysis involves taking the ideas that others have contributed and refining them for use by the entire group. It entails making specific use of general information.

Presenting. Group members are often asked to report their findings or their decisions to other bodies or agencies. A group member must also be able to explain his or her position to the rest of the group. Both tasks require presenting skills. These skills are closely allied to the public speaking skills we have discussed throughout this book. They include concision, directness or purpose, effective use of language and figures of speech, and an ability to speak to the needs and interests of the audience.

Harmonizing. Certain members must be able to harmonize the group. That is, they must be able to work out compromises and promote cooperation. Often, interpersonal problems can destroy a group and frustrate decision making. Helping to overcome this kind of situation is vital to the group. Members who try to promote harmony must be able to remind arguers—without preaching to them—that solutions to problems should be based on what is best for the group as a whole, not for one or two members.

Coaching. Group members must sometimes coach or aid other members. This may include orienting another member of the group to what is happening; encouraging participation; coaxing another member toward the solution of a problem; developing and improving the climate of group cooperation; and helping to train group leaders. Ideally, several members of the group will coach. If only one member does, resentment toward him or her may develop. It is important to remember that coaching may be most effective when done "behind the scenes."

Summarizing. Whatever the group does, someone must be able to summarize group decisions. *Internal summaries* are made in groups to restate what has already been accomplished. Often, this is what sparks a group to go on to the next task. *Final Summaries* are made after all the group's discussions are completed. A final summary includes the major points covered, an elaboration of what the group is going to do next, and the group's most important findings and recommendations.

Leadership in Group Discussion

Styles of Leadership.   While all groups have much in common, their individual makeup can vary greatly. This is also true of styles of leadership. There are, in fact, as many styles of leadership as there are leaders. A style is often a highly personal matter, depending greatly on the attitude of each group member (including the leader) toward authority. In general, there are two broad styles of leadership—authoritarian and the participatory.

Authoritarian.   In this style, one or two members of the group do most of the influencing and are rarely influenced by others. The group is thus dominated by one or two members, often with the tacit approval of other members of the group. This is also called *autocratic* leadership.

Participatory.   In the participatory style of leadership, members themselves act as leaders. Most members exert some influence and are in turn influenced by one another. This is also known as *democratic* leadership and may involve a form of rotating leadership, in which members pick temporary leaders and change them on a prearranged basis.

In some situations, an authoritarian style of leadership is preferable.

While democratic leadership is generally favored in our society, at certain times an authoritarian style is preferable. Tasks which must be performed quickly, or under stress, are often best handled by an authoritarian leader. Sometimes, an overly participatory leadership in a group can open the way for an authoritarian leadership. If a group is unable to solve its problems because members spend too much time trying to influence one another, one member may try to impose his or her will on the group. This frequently happens in politics—for example, the recurring coups in Latin America and Africa. Such cases are not restricted to governments, however. It is helpful to remember that democratic leadership in a group depends on the good will of all the members and on their united efforts to move efficiently toward their goals.

Tasks of Leadership.   Although the tasks of a leader may depend on the nature of the group, there are certain general tasks that all leaders must perform. As stated earlier, they are to stimulate, guide, and unite the group. It is important to understand that in nearly all cases the best leader is the one who can make each member of the group give his or her greatest contribution. Leadership does not consist of performing all the tasks of the organization, but of persuading others to do their best. A leader need not be the "star" of a group. Indeeed, it is often better if the leader allows other members to "shine" in their own way.

Let us now consider more specifically some of the functions a leader must perform.

Creating.   This is the first job of any leader—to invent or discover new plans, programs, policies, or to encourage others to create them. Groups as a whole tend to be conservative in their attitude toward new ideas. Leaders must be open to and actively in favor of innovation.

Planning.   A leader must be able to help his or her organization plan for the future. Planning involves: (1) perceiving conditions in the organization's environment; (2) developing ideas that will let the group state its objectives; and (3) determining how to reach those objectives. A leader must be able to distinguish between short-range planning (the group's day-to-day operations) and long-range planning (the group's ultimate objectives).

Organizing.   This is one of the most important leadership skills. A leader may be effective at influencing a group, but unless he or she can organize the group's resources, all influence may be in vain. Organizing involves four separate duties: (1) assessing the task—understanding what is required; (2) assessing the people—determining group strengths and weaknesses; (3) assessing time—understanding how much time and effort will be required; and (4) matching task, people, and time—finding the best combination of group members and skills to do the task at hand.

Controlling.   Leaders should control both the human and material resources of their group. All organizations have control systems to affect the behavior of group members. In this context, *control system* should not be seen as a rigid means of organizing behavior. Rather, it means a combination of encouragement, persuasion, and established procedures by which all leaders achieve their goals. It is important to note that a leader is often most in control when he or she does not obviously control behavior. That is, when the leader exercises low-key rather than overbearing control.

Communication.   This is undoubtedly the most important aspect of any kind of leadership. A leader who cannot communicate—either with his or her superiors or his or her subordinates—is doomed to fail. Communication in leadership involves the attempt to establish open relationships with other group members. It obliges the leader to receive information as well as to transmit it, to listen to others as well as to make clear statements about intentions and objectives. Communication may vary more widely than the other skills mentioned here, because communication depends on the makeup of the group. But regardless of the personalities involved, without communication there can be no group effort, no leadership, and no achievement of goals.

Summary

Public speaking skills are useful for most careers because communication is required in all jobs. To be hired or promoted, we need to talk effectively, to listen well, and to think critically. On the job, certain skills such as planning, collecting and organizing data, and presenting materials are essential.

Moreover, most people work in or belong to organizations and groups in which they have to communicate effectively to succeed. Groups are either formal (official) or informal. Formal groups are more important in organizations because they exist to consider and make policy. Panel discussions, symposia, and debates are types of formal discussion groups. Panel discussions are structured conversations. Symposia involve three to five persons giving prepared speeches about a particular issue. In debates two sides argue opposing points of view before an audience.

Group discussion is a part of all careers and is a distinct communication skill used in most organizations. It involves six key abilities: organizing, analyzing, presenting, harmonizing, coaching, and summarizing. The most important element of a successful group, however, is leadership. Group leadership can be either authoritarian or participatory. To succeed, a group leader has to be skilled at creating, planning, organizing, reporting, controlling, and, especially, communicating.

Exercises

1. Find a person who is presently employed in a job that you would like to obtain after you graduate. Interview him or her about what it is like to hold the job. Make sure that you refer to the following in the interview:
   a. communication skills required
   b. public speaking skills required
   c. opportunities for advancement

2. Take stock of your talents and abilities. What type of job do you think you are most qualified for after graduation? Write a brief position paper as to why you think you would be good at that job.

3. Thinking about the various careers discussed in this chapter, which obvious public-speaking-oriented ones were not included? Develop a list of five additional careers along with the type of public speaking that the career is likely to use.

PART IV: SUGGESTIONS FOR FURTHER READING

Anderson, K. *Persuasion: Theory and Practice*, 2nd ed. Boston: Allyn and Bacon, 1978.

Bem, D. *Beliefs, Attitudes, and Human Affairs.* Belmont, Cal.: Wadsworth, 1970.

Bolles, R. *What Color Is Your Parachute?* Berkeley, Cal.: Ten Speed Press, 1980.

Cronkhite, G. *Persuasion, Speech, and Behavior Change.* New York: Bobbs-Merrill, 1969.

Eisenberg, A. *Understanding Communication in Business and the Professions.* New York: Macmillan, 1978.

Hunt, G. *Communication Skills in the Organization.* Englewood Cliffs, N.J.: Prentice-Hall, 1980.

Payne, R. *How to Get a Better Job Quicker.* New York: Taplinger Publishing Co., 1970.

St. John, M. "Do You Get Your Message Across?," *Nation's Business*, August 1972, 66–67.

Simons, H. *Persuasion: Understanding, Practice, and Analysis.* Reading, Mass.: Addison-Wesley, 1976.

Taylor, P. *How to Succeed in the Business of Finding a Job.* Chicago: Nelson-Hill, 1975.

Wilcox, R. *Oral Reporting in Business and Industry.* Englewood Cliffs, N.J.: Prentice-Hall, 1967.

Zimbardo, P., E. Ebbesen, and C. Maslach. *Influencing Attitudes and Changing Behavior*, 2nd ed. Reading, Mass: Addison-Wesley, 1977.

index

W. SUSSEX INSTITUTE
OF
HIGHER EDUCATION
LIBRARY